Appraising the Appraisal: The Art of Appraisal Review

Readers of this text may be interested in these related texts available from the Appraisal Institute:

- *The Appraisal of Real Estate,* eleventh edition
- *The Appraisal Writing Handbook* by Alan Blankenship, PhD
- *Appraising Residential Properties,* second edition
- *The Dictionary of Real Estate Appraisal,* third edition
- *Understanding Limited Appraisals and Appraisal Reporting Options* by Stephanie Coleman, MAI, SRA and Joseph L. Minnich III, SRPA, SRA
- The report writing guides in the *Communicating the Appraisal* series

THE ART OF APPRAISAL REVIEW

Richard C. Sorenson, MAI

The Definitive Guide for Reviewers

Reviewers: Frank E. Harrison, MAI, SRA
William H. Reeve, III, MAI, SRA
John A. Schwartz, MAI
Janice F. Young, MAI, RM

Vice President, Educational Programs and Publications: Sean Hutchinson
Director, Content Development and Quality Assurance: Margo Wright
Manager, Book Development: Stephanie Shea-Joyce
Manager, Design/Production: Julie B. Beich

For Educational Purposes Only

The material presented in this text has been reviewed by members of the Appraisal Institute, but the opinions and procedures set forth by the author are not necessarily endorsed as the only methodology consistent with proper appraisal practice. While a great deal of care has been taken to provide accurate and current information, neither the Appraisal Institute nor its editors and staff assume responsibility for the accuracy of the data contained herein. Further, the general principles and conclusions presented in this text are subject to local, state, and federal laws and regulations, court cases, and any revisions of the same. This publication is sold for educational purposes with the understanding that the publisher is not engaged in rendering legal, accounting, or other professional service.

Nondiscrimination Policy

The Appraisal Institute advocates equal opportunity and nondiscrimination in the appraisal profession and conducts its activities in accordance with applicable federal, state, and local laws.

Printed in the United States of America

Library of Congress Cataloging-in-Publication Data

Sorenson, Richard C.

Appraising the appraisal : the art of appraisal review : the definitive guide for reviewers / Richard C. Sorenson.

p. cm.

Includes bibliographical references and index.

ISBN 0-922154-50-3

1. Real property—Valuation—Handbooks, manuals, etc. 2. Real property—Valuation—Standards—Handbooks, manuals, etc. I. Title.

HD1387.S57 1998 98-16208

333.33'2—dc21 CIP

Table of Contents

I am grateful for the strength and support of the most important person in my life, my best friend, who just happens to be my wife, Ardie. Thank you for putting up with my idiosyncrasies through frustrations and setbacks and for providing a stable environment for my confidence to grow.

Acknowledgments

My thanks to my good friends who contributed "above and beyond" for the success of this project: Alan Hummel, SRA; Sam Hines, MAI; Harold Carlson; Jim Tellatin, MAI; and my former associates at First Chicago, Craig Slonkosky, MAI, and Rob Hanlon. My grateful thanks also to the authors of the articles listed in the bibliography for influencing me through the expression of their innovative thoughts and ideas in their writings.

Foreword

In the art and science of real estate appraisal, reviewing reports is an essential quality-control function. Unfortunately, misconceptions and miscommunication between appraisers and reviewers often make the process needlessly adversarial. Whether a review is conducted within the appraiser's own firm, by a business or banking client, by a professional association, or by a governmental entity, the goal is the same: to ensure that reliable, sound appraisals are communicated in logical, concise reports.

Appraising the Appraisal: The Art of Appraisal Review represents a real service to the profession, providing a wealth of practical information and fostering understanding between the writers and reviewers of appraisal reports. The author, himself a seasoned appraisal reviewer, enumerates the many potential pitfalls of the review process and suggests skillful ways for the participants to negotiate solutions. The text is refreshingly pragmatic, with anecdotes provided by a number of experienced review appraisers and humorous asides to help those on both sides of the review process see common ground.

In addition to the expected discussions of appraiser competency, reviewer guidelines, and common report deficiencies, the text provides a reviewer's perspective on appraisals of complex and special-purpose properties and the special problems associated with discounted cash flow computer programs. Also included are eight appendices with key definitions, units of comparison, reporting options, measurement techniques, and sample review forms and a bibliography of relevant appraisal literature.

In this era of heightened regulation and accountability, appraisal review has become increasingly important. This text provides an opportunity for appraisers to acquire the knowledge and skills they will need to successfully negotiate the challenges that lie ahead.

Joseph R. Stanfield, Jr., MAI, SRA
1998 President
Appraisal Institute

About the Author

Richard C. Sorenson was Vice President and Director of Appraisal Services for First Chicago Corporation (now First Chicago NBD) in Chicago, Illinois, until his retirement in 1996. At First Chicago he oversaw appraisal policy, quality control, and regulatory compliance and directed community banking appraisal services and in-house appraisal training. Sorenson had worked for First Chicago in a variety of real estate appraisal capacities, including chief appraiser, since 1958.

Mr. Sorenson served as the 1995 President of the Appraisal Institute, as a chair of Region III, and on the Appraisal Institute Board of Directors for six years. He has conducted seminars on a wide variety of real estate valuation topics including appraisal management, appraisal review, and FIRREA. Sorenson has also had several articles published in appraisal and banking journals and authored the chapter on appraisal review in the 10th edition of *The Appraisal of Real Estate*.

Purpose of Appraisal Review

Introduction

Most of an appraiser's work is directed toward deriving a supportable opinion of value. To complete the requirements of an appraisal assignment, however, the appraiser's investigation, analysis, and conclusions must be communicated to the client or reviewer in a convincing manner.

Why should appraisal reports be reviewed? Is it really necessary to spend time reviewing an appraisal report when the appraiser is known to be competent, knowledgeable, and experienced? Doesn't the professional designation and state regulation of appraisers, as well as the Uniform Standards of Professional Appraisal Practice, ensure that everything in an appraisal will be complete and accurate?

In virtually every trade and profession, certain persons review, criticize, critique, inspect, examine, cross-check, retest, question, judge, or comment on the work of others. The essence of appraisal review is to investigate, analyze, and verify the logic and procedures used in appraisal reports and to ensure the preparation of competent and thorough reports that result in sound value estimates. Ultimately, the purpose of an appraisal review is to reinforce the client's confidence in the reliability of the appraisal and the conclusions it presents.

Reviewers should understand the distinction between the valuation process and the appraisal report. The purpose of the valuation process is to solve a problem—that is, to estimate market value or some other value or to reach another conclusion concerning real estate. The appraisal report communicates the premises, data, reasoning, and opinions that are part of the valuation process. Reports do not appraise; appraisers appraise, and reports present their conclusions.

Why Review Appraisals?

If we lived in a perfect world, it would not be necessary to review the work of a qualified, competent appraiser. Unfortunately, we haven't yet found that utopia. Problems with appraisals arise for many reasons. Appraisers often work under the pressure of tight deadlines and may rush to get work delivered. Some appraisal firms may lack a meaningful quality-control process, but errors are possible even when strict quality-control and oversight procedures are followed. Competence can also be a problem, particularly when an inexperienced appraiser is given a complex appraisal assignment and does not receive appropriate guidance or training. Appraisal skill, judgment, and experience are the essential elements in creating a reliable appraisal.

A substandard work product resulting in an erroneous value conclusion can be produced by well-intentioned appraisers due to ignorance, error, or lack of effort. Faulty appraisals may result from the appraiser's lack of familiarity with certain aspects of financing, environmental regulations, or governmental policies and legislation. There is no excuse for ignorance about standards of professional practice or the proper application of techniques. Errors of technique or mathematics are caused by carelessness or inattention to detail.

Obviously, faulty appraisals due to a lack of effort are more likely when exceptional effort is required. First, the appraiser may not have obtained the best comparable data for all three approaches. Second, insufficient efforts may have been made to relate the data to the appraisal problem. Third, contradictions and inconsistencies may have been allowed to weaken the report content. Lazy people tend to be unsuccessful in the appraisal profession. The same may be said for appraisal reviewers.

The problem of maintaining consistent quality in an appraisal report stems from the nature of narrative writing and the complexity of the valuation process. Appraisers differ in their basic writing and organizational abilities. Even the most talented report writers make mistakes and may fail to catch errors and inconsistencies. A report is written at the end of the appraisal process, typically when the appraiser is tired and up against a delivery deadline. The appraiser may already be planning the next appraisal or, more likely, be involved in several other assignments. Errors will never be totally eliminated from appraisal reports. They can be avoided or minimized, however, if appraisers take active quality-control measures to identify and correct them before reports are submitted to the client.

Another source of potential problems was outlined in a recent workplace study. According to a 1996 survey by the Ethics Officer Association and the American Society of Chartered Life Underwriters and Chartered Financial Consultants, "Nearly half of workers engaged in unethical and/or illegal acts. . . . The pressure-cooker atmosphere at many workplaces may be to blame. Faced with the demands of overtime, balancing work and family, and downsizing, workers said they feel more stress than five years ago, as well as more pressure to act unethically." Their comments continue, "Daily pressures are extreme and it's those pressures that may be driving unethical practices." Cutting corners on quality was among the most common behaviors reported. This problem is not unique to the appraisal profession; it is common in many occupations.

Two hundred eighty appraisers responded to a 1996 study conducted by the Real Estate Research Institute at the University of Toledo, Ohio, on the subjective topic "appraiser feelings and attitudes at a time marked by unprecedented change."[1] The statement, "I know of a local appraiser who does sloppy, careless work." brought an affirmative response from nearly 80% of the respondents.

1. Gerald E. Smolen, PhD, and Donald Casey Hambleton, MAI, "Appraisal Company Status and Direction for Survival," *The Appraisal Journal* (April 1997).

Appraisal providers come in all shapes and sizes, from sole proprietorships to large national and international corporations, national alliances and consortiums of appraisal businesses, wholly owned subsidiaries of major financial institutions, and consulting arms of giant accounting firms. However, studies show that the typical appraisal firm has fewer than five employees. In most of these small offices, the owner-manager is also a producer.

The concern for and intensity of quality control varies considerably among firms within each category. The amount of personal attention and input that the firm's principal or managing appraiser devotes to the appraisal work product also varies. How assignments are meted out, who establishes time frames, and sometimes, unfortunately, who sets the fee can play a significant role in the way an assignment is conducted and the amount of quality control that is exercised.

Appraisal company managers suffer the same shortcomings and pressures as most small business managers. They too must deal with demanding bosses, unreasonable clients, uncooperative subordinates, poorly conceived company procedures, and unexpected delays, interruptions, and changes of plans. The appraisal profession is pursuing a course familiar to other professions that have faced rapid change: intense competition, continual technological advances, and an environment of increasing government regulation.

Real Estate Appraisal is a Unique Profession

The appraisal report is a specialized document. Like many technical specialties, real estate valuation has its own terminology, techniques, methods, and professional standards. Comprehending topics such as the elements of accrued depreciation, income capitalization (particularly yield capitalization), and highest and best use can be daunting, even for knowledgeable real estate professionals. Most individuals would not fully understand the many nuances of the appraisal process merely by reading a narrative or form report. Appraising is the least understood real estate discipline. It incorporates the elements of many professions and specialties: real estate law, engineering, contracting, cost estimating, real estate developing, real estate investing, statistics, mathematics, accounting, architecture, and the fundamentals of economics, certainly land economics, to name the most obvious.

In the art of appraisal, practitioners apply their judgment to the analysis and interpretation of data and present their conclusions in an appraisal report. To evaluate an appraisal, the reviewer must carefully read the report and follow the appraiser's reasoning. A good reviewer does not nitpick, arguing with everything in the report to justify his or her employment. The review should focus on the significant issues and factual information that have an impact on the appraiser's findings, the reliability of the report, and the value conclusion.

The problems reviewers find in appraisal reports usually involve issues of competence; inadequate data research, support, analysis, and reasoning; factual inconsistencies; ineffective quality control; misunderstanding the assignment; standards issues; vagueness; and the failure to check for reasonableness before making the appraisal final.

A satisfactory appraisal accomplishes three objectives:
✓ It adequately describes the property.
✓ It clearly reveals the appraisal valuation process.
✓ It supports the value conclusion in a reasonable manner.

Need for Appraisal Reviews

An appraisal review is a prudent business practice for any user of appraisal services. It should be part of the normal due diligence process and standard operating procedure for individual clients and companies of all sizes. Reviewing the appraisal demystifies the appraisal process and gives the client a better understanding of the valuation and greater confidence in the appraiser's conclusions. Each step in the valuation process must be tested for logic, consistency, and appropriateness.

The review function has become increasingly important as more government attention is focused on regulating financial institutions. *Quality control* and *compliance* are the watchwords for successful audits and examinations. Although they are not regulated to the same degree, the review functions of insurance companies, pension funds, and real estate investment trusts (REITs) have also intensified in recent years. The development of collateralized mortgage obligations (CMOs) as a major investment vehicle has made it necessary for investment bankers to conduct reviews, sampling a portion of the collateral appraisals of the real estate securities underlying those packaged portfolios.

The following list indicates why each appraisal report should be carefully reviewed:

- To provide a test of reasonableness for the user of the appraisal report. The user may have questions about the data, reasoning, analyses, and conclusions presented in the report as well as the reasonableness of the assumptions and limiting conditions.
- To test whether the methods and techniques employed in the appraisal are appropriate to the assignment. The reviewer also checks for consistency and mathematical accuracy. Because appraisal reports are not standardized products, reviewers must determine whether the data have been analyzed in a logical manner and whether the conclusions are consistent with the data presented. Inconsistencies arising from the use of nonstandardized reporting formats also require interpretation and verification.
- To bolster the client's confidence in the appraisal. The reviewer determines whether the appraiser has examined all relevant economic indicators, considered all elements of comparison, and applied all available techniques appropriate to the appraisal problem.
- To help lending institutions manage risk. The value conclusion and estimated cash flows reported can help establish an appropriate level of underwriting confidence in the loan-to-value (LTV) and debt service coverage (DSC) ratios and other real estate risk management criteria. The descriptive portions of the report should alert the lender to any special risks associated with the property. Because appraisals contribute to a business decision on the part of the client, a degree of due diligence is required.
- To support litigation and dispute resolution. In some cases, arbitrators may present appraisal reviews for consideration in lieu of formal litigation.

- To assess the work product of other appraisers for clients who do not have internal appraisal capabilities. These clients may need reviews for litigation support, peer review, lender due diligence, regulator audits, and client quality control.

CONCLUSION

Clearly, the review process is here to stay. It has already become an accepted part of the valuation process. The review occurs after the appraisal has been delivered to the client and, unfortunately, it sometimes consumes more time and energy than the original appraisal. At its worst, the review process can be slow, tedious, and difficult for both the reviewer and the field appraiser. At its best, an appraisal review can be a smooth, satisfying process that improves client satisfaction and confidence and establishes a mutually rewarding professional relationship between the client and the appraiser.

The appraisal review process can raise the level of professionalism among appraisers, encouraging them to produce uniform, high-quality reports. Many appraisers embrace the challenge of a thorough review because it gives them valuable input about how their work measures up to that of their peers. Good attitudes and cooperation between the reviewer and the appraiser will result in an improved report and a well-supported, more reliable value conclusion.

Review Procedures

Introduction

Before review procedures can be discussed, the attributes of the overall task must be considered. *First, reviewers need to digest a considerable amount of information.* An appraisal might be 200 or more pages long and contain thousands of individual pieces of data. Somehow a reviewer has to make sense out of all of this.

Second, all appraisers do not include the same information in their reports or use the same format. Although guidelines for appraisal reviews are presented in the Uniform Standards of Professional Appraisal Practice (USPAP), information can be presented in a variety of ways. It can be difficult to find information or to notice that essential information is missing. For example, the subject property's historical operating expenses might be listed under the heading "History of the Subject Property," included in the income capitalization approach section, simply mentioned in the reconciliation, or "hidden" in the addenda to the report.

Third, reviewing requires a substantial amount of expert judgment. Reviewers must be thoroughly knowledgeable about appraisal techniques and methods to conduct a complete review of an appraisal. Some parts of the review process require more expertise than others. For example, specific information in the appraisal can be found by clients or reviewers with relatively little experience if they have been trained to know what to look for. Evaluating this information, however, can be more difficult.

Types of Appraisal Reviews

Advisory Opinion 6 to the Uniform Standards of Professional Appraisal Practice distinguishes between two categories of appraisal reviews: technical reviews and administrative reviews. A technical review is performed by an appraiser in accordance with Standard 3 of the Uniform Standards to form an opinion as to whether the analyses, opinions, and conclusions in the report under review are appropriate and reasonable. An administrative review is performed by a client or user of appraisal services to exercise due diligence in making a business decision (e.g., underwriting, purchase, sale). On occasion an appraiser may perform an administrative review to assist a client with these functions. An appraiser or consultant may become a user of the appraisal, particularly when the report contains information that might not be available from other sources.

A technical review is

- Performed by an appraiser
- Performed in accordance with Standard 3 of USPAP

An administrative review is sometimes called a *compliance review.* Those who perform administrative reviews may find the outline provided by Standard 3 to be helpful, but they are not bound to observe the standard. Advisory Opinion 6 states,

> The administrative review is performed by a variety of individuals, including lawyers, accountants, loan underwriters, bank examiners, and corporate decision-makers. . . . The individual performing the administrative review may not necessarily have the competence or information sources to perform an appraisal. After completing the administrative review, this individual is in a position to understand the strengths and weaknesses of the information leading to the value estimate in the report under review. With this and related information, the individual would be in a position to make decisions on issues such as: whether or not to pursue litigation; what book value to establish for an asset; whether to apply conservative or aggressive underwriting guidelines; whether to make or accept an offer to purchase, etc.

An administrative review is

- Usually known as a compliance review
- Usually performed by a client or user
- May or may not be performed by an appraiser
- Not bound by Standard 3 of USPAP
- May be a preliminary review as part of the technical review process

Before an appraisal is submitted to a review appraiser for a technical review, another individual acting as an initial screener may conduct a compliance review to check the calculations and determine whether the appraisal meets basic content specifications. If any discrepancies in, or omissions of, items specified in the appraisal contract or engagement letter are found during the compliance review, the review appraiser should determine how significant the errors are and whether the omissions are justified. (Types of appraisal reviews are discussed in greater depth in Chapter 5.)

Review Procedures

Whether or not a compliance review is performed, the review appraiser who conducts a technical review renders a written opinion as to whether to accept, reject, or modify the conclusions contained in the report. In drafting this opinion, the review appraiser generally follows the procedures described below.

The review appraiser first checks the appraisal file on the subject property or project. The file will reveal the purpose of the appraisal and the scope of the assignment as well as the contractual obligations under which the appraisal was performed and the results of the appraisal analysis were presented in the appraisal report. Many review appraisers then do a preliminary reading of the entire appraisal report to get an overall impression. They take notes on the property description (overall square footage, special or outstanding features, physical characteristics), the units of comparison applied, and significant valuation issues.

The reviewer's initial perusal may suggest several intermediate courses of action. For example, the review appraiser may recommend that

- Additional market data be obtained
- Specific pages be corrected for the compliance review
- Interviews be scheduled with people familiar with the property (including the appraiser)
- Opinions be obtained from experts in related disciplines such as cost estimating, building demolition, property management, environmental hazards, and real estate law.

If the review appraiser has received more than one appraisal report on the same property, he or she may compare the reports at this point to uncover any inconsistencies. The review appraiser then analyzes the contents of the appraisal report, focusing on specific questions such as:

- Are the data compiled by the appraiser of adequate quality and quantity?
- Are the limiting conditions imposed by the appraiser both required and reasonable? (Too many limiting conditions may diminish the usefulness of a report.)
- If more than one appraiser has worked on the assignment, are their methods consistent?
- If the highest and best use of the property is rehabilitation, what level of rehabilitation has been suggested?
- If the purpose of the appraisal is to provide an estimate of value to determine the amount of the mortgage loan, does the report satisfy the requirements of the appropriate regulatory agency (e.g., OCC, HUD, FDIC, VA)?
- If the report is subject to litigation, is the supporting evidence admissible in court?

Field Reviews

When a field review is needed, the review appraiser conducts a thorough field inspection. In some offices most reports are subject to a desk review, and field inspections are performed only for a representative sampling. A field inspection is a quality-control procedure. A field review may be undertaken to augment the data reported by the appraiser or to resolve discrepancies between the facts or assumptions reported by two appraisers who have arrived at divergent market value estimates for the same property. Supplementary information can often be obtained or clarified by telephone or letter. Some offices do not routinely conduct field reviews, while others do field reviews of every appraisal report submitted. The extent of the review process should correspond to the relative importance of the purchase, sale, lending, or investment decision contemplated by the client and the level of risk considered acceptable. In any event, management should specify the situations and circumstances in which field reviews are required.

Responsibilities of the Appraisal Reviewer

The review appraiser must clearly distinguish between a difference of opinion with the appraiser who prepared the report and an objective review of the report itself. The review appraiser determines whether the data and analyses in the appraiser's report support the opinion reached. When a review appraiser makes a judgment or forms an opinion concerning the analysis or conclusions in the appraisal, his or her conduct is governed by Standard 3 of the Uniform Standards.

It is sometimes difficult to distinguish between a technical review and an administrative review. When an administrative review is performed by an appraiser, the appraiser's comments may be misconstrued as resulting from a technical review. This is especially likely when the review appraiser has strong or special appraisal qualifications. Therefore, the administrative reviewer should carefully explain that the scope of the work is not that of an exhaustive technical review. Moreover, the administrative reviewer should state any limitations that may apply to the review.

In addition to reviewing appraisal reports, review appraisers have other responsibilities. For example, they often clarify client guidelines for an appraisal, assess the qualifications of appraisers and decide which appraisers to retain, or serve as liaisons between clients and appraisers. Review appraisers may monitor the progress of appraisers on assignments to ensure that reports are submitted on time and comply with regulations.

One additional note of caution must be emphasized. The review should be conducted in the context of market conditions as of the effective date of the opinion in the report being reviewed. Information that could not have been available to the appraiser on the date of the report being reviewed should not be used by the review appraiser in the development of a review. If new information became available subsequent to the effective date of the appraisal and is introduced, it requires separate analyses and opinions by the review appraiser in a manner consistent with Standards Rule 3-1 (f) of USPAP.

Review Report Format

Minimum Requirements

Although there is no standard format for review reports, each review report should contain certain items, including

- ✓ Identification of the appraiser
- ✓ Specification of the property rights appraised
- ✓ The purpose and date of the appraisal along with the defined value
- ✓ Statement of the qualifying conditions and assumptions on which the appraisal is based
- ✓ The report conclusion(s)
- ✓ The opinions, conclusions, and recommendations of the review appraiser

Standards Rule 3-2 addresses the requirements to be met in reporting an appraisal review.

Standards Rule 3-2

In reporting the results of an appraisal review, an appraiser must:

(a) disclose the nature, extent, and detail of the review process undertaken;

(b) disclose the information that must be considered in Standards Rule 3-1 (a) and (b);

(c) set forth the opinions, reasons, and conclusions required in Standards Rule 3-1 (c), (d), (e), and (f);

(d) include all known pertinent information;

(e) include a signed certification similar in content to the following:

I certify that, to the best of my knowledge and belief:

- the facts and data reported by the review appraiser and used in the review process are true and correct.

- the analyses, opinions, and conclusions in this review report are limited only by the assumptions and limiting conditions stated in this review report, and are my personal, unbiased professional analyses, opinions and conclusions.
- I have no (or the specified) present or prospective interest in the property that is the subject of this report and I have no (or the specified) personal interest or bias with respect to the parties involved.
- my compensation is not contingent on an action or event resulting from the analyses, opinions, or conclusions in, or the use of, this review report.
- my analyses, opinions, and conclusions were developed and this review report was prepared in conformity with the Uniform Standards of Professional Appraisal Practice.
- I did not (did) personally inspect the subject property of the report under review.
- no one provided significant professional assistance to the person signing this review report. (If there are exceptions, the name of each individual providing significant professional assistance must be stated.)

Comment: Departure from binding requirements (a) through (e) above is not permitted.[1]

The review should be dated and signed. The review appraiser prepares an impartial review report and keeps the opinion of value and the judgment of the appraiser confidential from all but his or her client. It is important that the reviewer observe the rules of confidentiality in the interest of both the appraiser and the reviewer's client and to protect his or her own credibility and reputation. Review appraisers should always operate in accordance with the Uniform Standards of Professional Appraisal Practice as promulgated by The Appraisal Foundation.

Despite the importance of the appraisal review process, few tools are available to help reviewers. Most institutions have standardized review forms, which are developed to balance review completeness and efficiency. A form that is too complex will be costly to complete and difficult to use in decision making. A form that is too simple will not help reviewers identify problems in an appraisal report. Forms that provide a checklist but do not allow for expanded discussion of problem areas can mislead clients by giving them a false sense of security.

Review Form Examples

Appendix 7 contains examples of a Commercial Appraisal Review format, a Narrative Appraisal Review Checklist, and the Appraisal Institute's Checklist for Screening Residential Form Reports. Also included is an example of a Reviewer's Certification. Experience shows that one form does not fit all. Most financial institutions and independent reviewers prefer to customize the review format to fit their work patterns and staff requirements. The formats

1. The Appraisal Foundation, Uniform Standards of Professional Appraisal Practice (USPAP), 1998 ed.

presented in Appendix 8 are offered merely to illustrate what components a review may contain. The examples shown should not be copied and used verbatim but should be tailored by the individual reviewer to match his or her format preferences.

Residential Review Form

The Residential Appraisal Field Review Report form (Freddie Mac Form 1032/Fannie Mae Form 2000) is available through Freddie Mac and Fannie Mae and from various form supply companies. It can be used for reviews of single-family and small residential (two- to four-family) income property, an individual unit in a condominium or planned unit development (PUD) project, or a cooperative unit.

The Residential Appraisal Field Review Report divides the review process into the following steps:

1. Provide a history of sales and refinance activity for the subject property for the past three years.
2. through 4. Review the appraiser's overall description of the neighborhood, site, and improvements for completeness and accuracy.
5. Report on whether the design and appeal, quality of construction, and site of the subject property are similar to others in the area.
6. Verify that the comparable properties used were truly comparable to the subject property, representative of the subject market, and the best ones available as of the effective date of the appraisal.
7. Confirm the date of sale (contract date and/or closing or settlement date), sale price, and sales or financing concessions for comparables through the data sources that the appraiser has indicated. Also confirm that the comparables actually closed or were settled as of the effective date of the original appraisal.
8. Verify that the specific data for the comparables were accurate (time, location, design and appeal, quality of construction, age, condition, size, sales or financing concessions, etc.).
9. Comment on the reasonableness and support for the individual adjustments to the comparables (time, location, design and appeal, quality of construction, age, condition, size, sales or financing concessions, etc.).
10. If the subject property is a small residential income property (two to four units) or a single-family investment property, comment on the accuracy of and support for the comparable rental and expense data.
11. If the subject property is an individual unit in a condominium or PUD project, verify the accuracy and completeness of the project description.
12. Is the estimate of market value for the subject property reasonable as of the effective date of the appraisal? If not, provide an appropriate estimate of market value for the subject property and state the assumptions (exterior inspection only, property description and condition, etc.) that the opinion is subject to. (The reviewer is cautioned to comply with Standard 1 of USPAP if he or she provides an

alternative value estimate.)

13. Report any substantial change in the base economy in the area since the effective date of the appraisal.
14. If the subject property is a cooperative unit, review the completeness and accuracy of the original appraiser's description and analysis of the cooperative project. Specifically comment on the accuracy of:
    - the number of shares attributable to the unit
    - the prorated share of the blanket mortgage payments
    - the treatment of the monthly assessments of the comparable sales

In addition to filling out the form, the review appraiser should check the appraisal for factual and mathematical accuracy and completeness.

THE REVIEW APPRAISER'S FILE

The review appraiser's file on a completed assignment should contain

- A copy of the appraisal report
- A copy of any follow-up letters or memos from the appraiser in response to queries
- A copy of the review document
- The field notes and working papers of the review appraiser
- Copies of the final computer runs used to check calculations
- Names and phone numbers of all persons interviewed during the course of the review process—e.g., appraisers, brokers, investors

AN INDUSTRY-WIDE STANDARD REVIEW FORM

In his article, "The Reviewer is Always Right?" Lloyd Hanford recommends that a standardized review form would improve the review process (and help to eliminate adversarial results as well). He writes:

> Develop a standard review form, for industry-wide adoption, that avoids the use of ambiguous, compound questions a reviewer is expected to address with a "yes" or "no" answer. Some current institutional forms address more than one concern within a single item, often combining highly substantive questions with more minor questions of form. In one case, when asked if an appraisal met USPAP standards and the requirements of the client, a reviewer was forced to answer "no" because the appraisal omitted a very minor, non-substantive client requirement. Without further explanation of the "no" answer, it may look as if the appraisal did not meet USPAP standards—a potentially serious violation.
>
> To prevent such deceptive answers, a review form question that requires an answer of "yes," "no," or "not applicable" should be set forth in a crystal-clear, straightforward, and singular manner. The form should be standardized but

include room for any extra questions deemed necessary to comply with the additional requirements of the client.[2]

Limitations of Appraisal Reviews

The role of the review appraiser is not universally understood. An appraiser is sometimes asked to act as a review appraiser without clearly understanding what services he or she is expected to provide.

Understanding the distinction between an appraisal review and a second opinion of value is critical. An appraisal review does not lead to an alternative value conclusion. The review appraiser may disagree with the value estimate or the analytical process presented in the report, and he or she may even recommend that another appraisal be commissioned, but the review appraiser should not offer, nor be required to offer, a second opinion of value *while functioning as a reviewer.* The review appraiser must carefully differentiate between the review process and the appraisal process.

Once a review appraiser suggests an alternative opinion of value, he or she has assumed the role of an appraiser and is no longer acting as a review appraiser. He or she has changed hats and is assuming a new function for the client. Additionally, it is conceivable that the review appraiser may not be qualified (under competency or regulatory requirements) to develop an alternative valuation. To preclude any confusion concerning these different functions in the minds of market participants, appraisers who review appraisal reports should not sign the appraisal reports under review.

Review appraisers may have additional information available to them—either locally, regionally, or nationally—that was not available to the original appraiser. In such cases, it is certainly appropriate for the review appraiser to use this information in estimating value. Also, if the review appraiser finds an error due to omission or commission in the original appraisal report, a different opinion and conclusion may be expected.

The comment to USPAP Standards Rule 3-1 (f) establishes requirements for any review appraiser who develops an independent value opinion or conclusion different from that provided in the appraisal report under review. The comment states:

> An opinion of a different estimate of value from that in the report under review, or a statement that the value estimate in the report under review remains reasonable as of a more current effective date, may be expressed, provided the review appraiser:
>
> 1. satisfies the requirements of STANDARD 1;
> 2. identifies and sets forth any additional data relied upon and the reasoning and basis for the different estimate of value; and,
> 3. clearly identifies and discloses all assumptions and limitations connected with the different estimate of value to avoid confusion in the marketplace.

2. Lloyd D. Hanford, Jr., MAI, "The Reviewer Is Always Right?" *The Appraisal Journal* (July 1994).

The Statement on Appraisal Standards No. 1 (SMT-1) offers a clarification of S.R. 3-1 (f), explaining that the review appraiser can accept some portions of the appraisal report under review and not others. The review appraiser does not need to recreate the analyses presented in the portions of the report under review with which he or she agrees. Any items deemed to be not in compliance, however, "must be explained and handled in conformity with Standard 1" to produce a credible valuation estimate by the review appraiser. The review appraiser cannot simply state that he or she disagrees with the appraisal report under review. Substantive support must be provided for any conclusion that the appraisal report under review is not in compliance.

According to Statement on Appraisal Standards No. 1, a different opinion of value may be included in the appraisal review report and still conform with the requirements and specifications of S.R. 3-2, if the review appraisal report:

> . . . identifies and discloses all assumptions and limitations affecting both the development and reporting of the review appraiser's opinion of value with the information and data considered, the appraisal procedures followed, and the reasoning supporting the estimate of value.

Statement No. 1 also states:

> The report under review must be capable of standing alone as an independent document, whereas the review appraisal report is a supplementary critique intended for use in conjunction with the report under review.

Guidelines for Review Appraisers

Introduction

An important distinction must be made between the terms *appraisal review* and *review appraisal*. While a review appraisal produces an alternative value, an appraisal review does not. As noted previously, a review appraiser may disagree with the property valuation or the appraiser's analysis and may recommend that another appraisal be ordered, but he or she should not be required to render a second opinion of value. It is necessary to separate the review function from the appraisal or consulting process. Once a review appraiser develops an alternative value opinion, he or she has assumed the role of an appraiser. To avoid confusion, review appraisers should not sign the reports they review. There is a fine line between judging the reasoning and logic of another appraiser's work and substituting it with the review appraiser's own reasoning and value conclusion.

Reviewers should remember that appraisers may offer different opinions as to value of the same property, and reviewers may have different opinions regarding what constitutes an acceptable appraisal report.

The Review Process

Usually a review appraiser identifies and judges the reasoning and logic that underlies another appraiser's work in an impartial and objective manner but does not substitute his or her own judgment for the judgment of that appraiser. In some instances a review appraiser may be called upon to form an opinion of property value based on the information contained in the appraisal report. When this occurs, the review appraiser becomes an appraiser and is subject to all the requirements that apply to performing an appraisal. These can include the requirements of professional standards as well as those of state and federal regulatory agencies.

Although appraisal reviews are performed for a variety of reasons, many are routine assignments. Appraisal reviews are regularly conducted for government agencies involved in takings for public projects (condemnation) and for financial entities that use property as collateral for mortgage loans. Review assignments can have serious consequences, and appraisal reviews based on investigative work may have civil, or even criminal, implications.

In the past 65 years, real estate appraisal has evolved from an occupation of seasoned generalists into a highly technical discipline practiced by computer-literate specialists. In the past only the client reviewed an appraisal report, and because many clients were nonprofessionals, many appraisal reports were inadequately reviewed. Today appraisal reviews are increasingly necessary because the complexity of the appraisal process has increased; both the vocabulary and methodology of appraisal have become more technical. Greater specialization and accountability have resulted from the globalization of capital markets and the popularity of investment-grade real estate. Regulators scrutinize appraisal reports and carry out other audit functions designed to protect the public interest. These developments have created a need for qualified review appraisers, formal appraisal review procedures, and formal appraisal management policies.

The appraisal reports prepared by practitioners outside North America have historically been less comprehensive than those prepared by North American appraisers. As international standards take hold and the globalization of U.S. industries and corporations expands, the reports prepared by appraisers in other countries will likely become more comprehensive and the appraisal review function will likely expand as well.

STANDARDS RULE 3-1

Review appraisers should follow the guidelines in Standards Rule 3-1, which are paraphrased below:

- Identify the report under review, the real estate and real property rights being appraised, the effective date of the value opinion in the report, and the date of the review.
- Explain the extent of the review process that was conducted.
- Form an opinion as to the completeness of the report in light of standards requirements.
- Form an opinion as to the adequacy and relevance of the data and the appropriateness of any adjustments applied to the data. The review appraiser must determine whether the data support the appraiser's judgment.
- Form an opinion as to the appropriateness of the methods and techniques employed in the appraisal and, if they are considered inappropriate, explain why.
- Form an opinion as to the soundness and appropriateness of the analyses, opinions, and conclusions in the report under review and explain the reasons for any disagreement with these conclusions.

REVIEWER RESPONSIBILITIES AND ACCOUNTABILITY

Review appraisers should make themselves familiar with the primary market area in which they will be working. This familiarity should include not only an understanding of the demographics, growth trends, value trends, and economics involved, but a physical market area inspection as well. These data should be updated periodically to keep up with market shifts and changes. Current data will help the reviewer visualize the property in the context of its market environment. Even if the review is of a complete, self-contained report and does not require additional external support, the review appraiser will profit from a general knowledge of demographic and real estate market benchmarks and trends in the specific locale addressed in the report.

All reviewers should have a good working knowledge of the latest edition of USPAP. Usually this requires a subscription to the publications of The Appraisal Foundation and/or periodic attendance at a Standards of Professional Practice course or seminar. Such courses and seminars are offered by The Appraisal Foundation, the Appraisal Institute, other professional associations, state-approved education providers, and colleges.

Like field appraisers, review appraisers are accountable for their decisions and must not violate the rules of fairness and objectivity. A review should be a positive learning experience. Analytical ability and mature judgment are needed to conduct reviews effectively. The following practices constitute serious misrepresentations or deficiencies in an appraisal review:

- Analyzing only parts of an appraisal report and identifying this analysis as an appraisal review without reporting on the total work product.
- Refuting data in the original report without verifying that such data are inaccurate.
- Criticizing the methods applied in the appraisal without fully explaining why they are improper.
- Using an appraisal prepared at a different time as a benchmark in judging the appraisal report under review.
- Using hindsight in reviewing an appraisal. Reviews should be based on market activity and the perspectives of market participants at the time of the analysis. Subsequent events should not be used to refute the report unless, at the time of the appraisal, they seemed certain to occur.
- Ignoring or altering the definition of the appraisal problem stated in the report.
- Ignoring or altering any limiting conditions or special assumptions of the appraisal report without demonstrating why the conditions or assumptions are blatantly invalid.
- Overemphasizing the significance of minor errors in data, calculations, or word processing that the report may contain.
- Substituting the review appraiser's own judgment for that of the appraiser when the appraiser's original conclusion was a reasonable one.
- Submitting an unprofessional review, report, or other communication that contains subjective or pejorative comments.

Review appraisers violate rules of fairness and objectivity when they level undue criticism against an appraisal report. If an appraisal review contains factual errors or substitutes the review appraiser's judgment for that of the appraiser, it may constitute a breach of ethics regardless of the significance of the assignment. Ethics violations can cause serious harm to others.

At the outset of a review assignment, the review appraiser must understand the consequences of approving or rejecting the appraisal. Review appraisers are often required to examine the formats of appraisals as well as the valuation techniques and conclusions presented. The appraisal review document should clearly identify what has been reviewed and comment on all significant aspects of the appraisal that affect the value conclusion.

Review appraisers retained to perform technical reviews should be aware that their activities are subject to Standards Rule 3-1 of the Uniform Standards. After forming an opinion as to the adequacy and appropriateness of the report being reviewed, the review appraiser must prepare a separate report or memorandum setting forth the results of the review process and disclosing the precise nature of the work undertaken. In reporting the results of an appraisal review, review appraisers are subject to Standards Rule 3-2 of the Uniform Standards. This reporting requirement can be met in three different ways:

1. By preparing a separate report or letter.
2. By submitting a checklist form prepared and signed by the reviewer and attached to the report under review.
3. By providing a stamped imprint on the original appraisal report, signed by the review appraiser, which briefly indicates the extent of the review and references the file memorandum in which the review process is outlined. (This procedure separates the review function from the actual signing.)

Standards Rule 2-5 of the Uniform Standards states:

> An appraiser who signs a real property appraisal report prepared by another in any capacity accepts full responsibility for the appraisal and the contents of the appraisal report.

This rule is directed at the employer or supervisor who reviews and signs an appraisal report prepared by an employee or contractor. The employer or supervisor is just as liable for the content and conclusions in the report as the individual who prepared the appraisal report. Furthermore, insertion of a conditional clause next to the signature of the employer or supervisor does not exempt that individual from adherence to the standards.

What If the Reviewer Develops a Different Opinion of Value?

Under the terms of their job descriptions, some reviewers are expected to develop their own valuations if they experience problems with the original appraisal. Some may merely indicate that the appraised value appears "low" or "high," while others may be required to develop either a range of possible values or a point estimate of value. The reviewer may do this if he or she is qualified. However, if the reviewer develops a different value from the one reported in the appraisal, his or her actions are subject to Standards 1 and 2 of USPAP, which describe the requirements of developing and reporting an appraisal.

Statement on Appraisal Standards No. 1 (SMT-1) addresses situations in which the reviewer develops a different estimate of value and outlines how he or she may comply with Standards 1 and 2. SMT-1 states, in part:

- When review appraisers have additional information available to them, it is appropriate for them to use this information in estimating value.

- Those items deemed to be in compliance can be extended to the review appraiser's report.
- Those items not deemed to be in compliance must be explained and handled in conformity with Standard 1.
- If the review appraiser forms an opinion of value different from that in the report being reviewed, it is not necessary that the opinion be set forth in a separate appraisal report prepared in conformity with Standards Rule 2-2. The opinion of value may be set forth in the review appraisal report.

In other words, the reviewer does not need to create an entirely new appraisal report. Those portions of the original appraisal that are acceptable may be retained, and those portions that are not acceptable may be replaced by the additional information and the review appraiser's analysis and reasoning.

If the reviewer is merely correcting a mathematical calculation or another obvious error, and this correction results in a revised value indication, he or she is not required to comply with Standards 1 or 2. In such a case, the revised value would be part of the review report. It is usually a good business practice to point out the error to the appraiser and ask him or her to send a letter revising the value indication or to supply corrected replacement pages. Most often, the appraiser will request that the original reports be returned and the corrections made by him or her. This avoids a somewhat sticky situation in which multiple reports are circulated with different value conclusions. It is wise for the reviewer to maintain a copy of the original report reviewed in his or her file, if possible. This practice can prevent any disagreements about the changes made.

Presentation of a Review

A review should discuss the strengths and deficiencies of the appraisal and determine what effect any deficiencies noted have had on the appraised value. For example, if entrepreneurial profit was not included in the cost approach, this may not have had a material effect on the appraised value, especially if the appraisal placed only minimal emphasis on the cost approach. In such a case, the review should state that the problem found does not have a material effect on the value estimate in the report. This information will be helpful to readers of the review who are not knowledgeable about appraisal.

Often there are problems with a few major areas of the report that require additional input, reanalysis, or correction. There may also be numerous problems of less importance such as typos, language inconsistencies, rounding errors, and inconsequential mathematical mistakes. It is important to address the material issues that require attention while minimizing less notable errors. If an appraiser receives a letter indicating every typo and minor error along with the major problems, he or she may become frustrated and not bother to make any of the corrections. A review must be presented with some finesse, keeping in mind that the goal is to obtain a reasonable, reliable value estimate. The reviewer should ensure that the report reviewed conforms to the guidelines and specifications under which it was prepared and try to show the appraiser how he or she can prepare better appraisal reports in future assignments. The desired result is a higher-quality work product.

The review should contain significant discussion and analysis of all areas of concern. Reviewers often omit comments on the adequacy and reasonableness of the appraiser's conclusions. Simply reiterating the conclusions does not communicate the reviewer's opinion as to the relevance, reasonableness, or reliability of the conclusions to the reviewer's client, an examiner, or an auditor.

Tricks of the Trade

An underlying purpose of this publication is to present practical tips to make the reviewer's task as easy, effective, and productive as possible. Some suggestions are offered below.

A review should be worded professionally, not in a negative, condescending, or sarcastic manner. It may be the worst report ever written, but there are many ways to communicate that fact in a professional manner. One purpose of the review process is to provide quality feedback to appraisers.

When drawing conclusions about an appraisal report, the reviewer should remember that the appraiser is much more familiar with the property than he or she is. The appraiser should be given the benefit of the doubt when appropriate.

Because there are many different ways to analyze real estate, it is critical that the reviewer understand the particular appraiser's methods. If a reviewer encounters an unfamiliar type of analysis, it is the reviewer's responsibility to determine whether it is applied correctly. Review appraisers must be open to new techniques. If the appraiser's analysis differs from what the reviewer is accustomed to seeing, it is not necessarily incorrect. Exposure to many different report styles and techniques is a great learning opportunity for reviewers. They should regard it as such and keep an open mind.

Michael Arlen, a British novelist, described one of his character's mental expectations as follows: "She not only expects the worst, but makes the worst of it when it happens." This attitude characterizes many reviewers. Many problems in the review process are caused by reviewers who step over the line of professionalism and impose their own biases or opinions on the work products of others. The freedom that reviewers have to raise any and all issues can inadvertently lead to attempts to manipulate appraisers. In some cases, problems are caused by reviewers who do not have sufficient experience and knowledge of appraisal theory to understand fully the appraisals they review. Reviewers with limited experience tend to rely on strict, narrow interpretations of textbook ideas, falling back on dogma when presenting their critiques.

The review process can be a positive experience, providing fee appraisers with a better understanding of how the appraisals they prepare are being used in financial decision making. This understanding should, in turn, help appraisers focus their attention on issues of importance to clients.

Reviewing the Reviewer

If reviewers oversee the work product of appraisers, who reviews the work of reviewers and measures their performance? The reviewers' clients measure the job performance of reviewers using benchmark performance measures. Most often this is accomplished in a one-on-one meeting with the client or the principal appraiser or through a direct report to a corporation or financial institution. Beyond typical performance expectations, appraisal reviewers should be rated on their technical ability, the timing and quality of their work, reliability, and communication skills.

Technical ability is reflected in the individual's knowledge of USPAP, FIRREA (when applicable), and the client's specifications for appraisals and in the capacity to review a wide variety of complex appraisals competently.

Timing relates to turnaround time, meeting deadlines and performing in accordance with accepted benchmarks. The quality of work is a product of the reviewer's organizational skills, thoroughness, and ability to make well-informed, meaningful remarks on substantive issues. Reliability is demonstrated by a reviewer who accepts only sound valuations, is consistently accurate, and assists the client in making prudent business decisions with a high degree of confidence. In short, each reviewer should be rated on his or her ability to analyze, communicate, quantify, make decisions, and handle responsibilities.

Suggested Criteria to Measure Reviewer Performance

Technical ability

- Good knowledge of appraisal applications, techniques, and methods
- Working knowledge of USPAP
- Knowledge of regulatory requirements for appraisals, including FIRREA, if applicable
- Experience with a variety of property types
- Ability to deal with complex appraisals
- Good market insight
- Ability to analyze the input and output of analytical software programs, if appropriate

Timing (efficiency)

- Average turnaround time, compared with industry benchmarks
- Ability to perform at a faster pace to meet tight deadlines
- Matches intensity of review with client's associated risk

Quality of review

- Well-organized
- Makes informed, meaningful comments
- Thorough and focused
- Differentiates substantive issues from nonsubstantive issues
- Identifies risks, opportunities, and recommendations for client

Reliability (effectiveness)

- Is consistent
- Is accurate
- Communicates confidence to the client
- Final decision is reliable

Communication

- Effective oral communication and report writing skills
- Writes accurately, clearly, and concisely
- Good cognitive and interpersonal skills

REVIEWER-APPRAISER COMMUNICATION

The reviewer's ability to communicate with appraisers is a very important performance criteria. Of course, there is a natural tendency for reviewers and appraisers to conflict, as there is in any discipline in which professionals are critiqued by their peers. Some animosity undoubtedly results from reviewers abusing their role in the process and from appraisers' defensiveness and overreaction to criticism of their work product. Most problems, however, are the result of poor communication between the two parties. A good reviewer will exhibit discipline and "people" skills in handling sensitive issues. If handled wisely and fairly, a review can be a "win-win" learning experience for both parties and result in a better, more reliable valuation for the client.

> Direct and open communication is good "value-added" for success—in appraising and every other profession.

In his article "The Reviewer Is Always Right?" Lloyd Hanford cautions:

> The process inadvertently sets up an adversarial relationship between an appraiser and an institution (or reviewer). This problem results from two related causes. First, the reviewer probably has an agenda that goes beyond just opining on the adequacy of the report under review. A reviewer may wish to demonstrate his or her thoroughness and brilliance through a search for any item, important or otherwise, that could be criticized or questioned. As an employee or an independent contractor of the client, a reviewer's agenda is to sell himself or herself to a client through the review just as an appraiser's agenda is to sell himself or herself through the appraisal document. The future employment of each depends on the work product. Anyone who has been retained to review the work of others would, upon reflection, probably agree that this accurately reflects a reviewer's agenda.
>
> The second cause of the adversarial relationship between appraisers and reviewers stems from an institutional paranoia that is transferred to a reviewer. This paranoia appears to be induced by an overzealous regulatory environment. . . .
>
> This global problem places an independent fee appraiser in a very uncomfortable position. A reviewer has an unusual amount of power, to the degree that an appraiser's future employment with a particular firm may rest in the hands of that firm's reviewer.[1]

Hanford goes on to emphasize that the reviewers "should focus on questions of substance rather than questions of form."

1. Lloyd D. Hanford, Jr., MAI, "The Reviewer Is Always Right?" *The Appraisal Journal* (July 1994).

The keys to avoiding the problems cited by Hanford are attitude and the avoidance of a checklist mentality. The reviewer's attitude should be positive and encourage smooth communication. It is vital that the reviewer be fair and reasonable in dealing with appraisers. The reviewer must never coerce an appraiser into accepting his or her opinion, whether explicitly or implicitly. Objectivity and facts must rule. Professional reviewers must master communication skills. The adage "What goes around, comes around" is particularly true in the appraisal profession.

Many financial institutions rate the performance of their reviewers by sending feedback surveys to the appraisers who do work for them. The surveys generally are sent directly from the chief appraiser and the names of respondents are kept confidential. Key questions might be, "Was the reviewer: Cooperative? Friendly? Courteous? Knowledgeable? Prompt in responding to inquiries?" and "Was the review, given the complexity of the property: Fair and appropriately focused on value and regulatory issues? Overly simplistic? Overly detailed but generally focused on value issues? Overly detailed and focused on issues that did not affect value?"

Looking Back

It is always good policy, and good management, for reviewers and their clients (or direct supervisors) to allocate the necessary time and resources to research and reflect on past appraisal reviews, particularly if fundamental mistakes were made. Experience teaches worthwhile lessons, and it is sometimes beneficial to look through the rearview mirror to see where we've been. According to a Portuguese proverb, experience is the "fruit of the tree of errors," and, as George Santayana noted, "Those who will not remember the past are condemned to relive it." Many firms regularly conduct "lessons learned" sessions for their appraisers and reviewers.

One's value as a reviewer increases with experience. An experienced reviewer is usually able to penetrate the nuances of appraisal more deeply. Most appraisals are not excellent or awful; rather, they fall into that vast gray area in between. The astute reviewer will become a discerning judge of those various shades of gray. It is all too easy to be an ivory-tower critic, cut off from the real-world experiences and problems of the field appraiser. Reviewers must keep abreast of changes that affect the art and business of real estate appraisers by reading trade publications, attending seminars and conferences, updating course work, and talking to the movers and shakers in the real estate market. Keeping up to date is a serious responsibility, and it is absolutely necessary if the reviewer is to do his or her job well.

Types of Appraisal Reviews

Client Review Requirements

Appraisal review requirements vary depending on the client. The review requirements of lenders may be tailored to their specific policies and procedures, which include compliance with the requirements of federal agencies. Mortgage insurers have unique appraisal requirements, as do federal and quasi-federal agencies that conduct appraisal reviews as a normal part of their audit procedures. State and local governmental agencies such as highway departments conduct reviews in conjunction with the acquisition of rights-of-way. They have specific appraisal requirements for condemnation proceedings. Many corporations and private organizations such as relocation companies perform appraisal review services.

When an appraiser accepts an assignment to conduct a third-party review of an appraisal prepared by another appraiser, it would be wise for the review appraiser to inform the client of the different levels of appraisal reviews available and to recommend the type of review appropriate to the client's needs. The review appraiser should also clearly disclose the nature and extent of the review performed to preclude any misunderstanding or abuse of the review comments.

Administrative and Technical Reviews

In Advisory Opinion AO-6, the Appraisal Standards Board has identified only two types of reviews, administrative and technical.

Administrative review

Compliance review

- ✓ Usually performed by an administrative assistant
- ✓ Usually consists of an administrative checklist
- ✓ Assures that all blanks are filled in and arithmetic is correct
- ✓ Minimal judgment is needed

continued

Desk review

- ✓ Requires a trained, experienced reviewer; may or may not be an appraiser
- ✓ Usually consists of a detailed checklist or a formatted narrative review
- ✓ Normally does not perform independent investigation
- ✓ Requires judgment

Technical review

Desk review

- ✓ Requires a trained, experienced reviewer, who is usually an appraiser
- ✓ Usually consists of a detailed checklist or a formatted narrative review
- ✓ More thorough than an administrative desk review; includes research and investigation; more intense as a due diligence function
- ✓ Requires knowledge of USPAP and regulatory compliance
- ✓ Requires judgment

Field review

- ✓ Most intensive type of review
- ✓ Usually includes an inspection of at least the exterior of the subject and the comparable sales, some data verification, and all the elements of a desk review

The type of appraisal review performed varies with the scope or nature of the assignment, the requirements of the client, and the complexity of the property appraised. The distinction between a technical review and an administrative review involves the purpose of the review and the observance of Standard 3.

A review appraiser performing a technical review forms an opinion of the appropriateness and reasonableness of the appraisal and is governed by Standard 3. The technical review has these distinguishing characteristics:

- The reviewer's ability, set forth under Standards Rule 3-1 (f), to express a different estimate of value from that in the report under review
- Inclusion of the reviewer's certification as required by Standards Rule 3-2
- Performed by an appraiser

In the preparation of technical reviews, in-house reviewers are required to abide by USPAP in compliance with Standard 3 even if the review report will not leave his or her employer's place of business.

A reviewer performing an administrative review exercises due diligence in the context of a business decision and is not bound by the requirements of Standard 3. Administrative reviews are generally performed by clients and users of appraisal services. An administrative review is usually less detailed than a technical review, and the administrative reviewer does not render opinions under Standard 3.

An administrative review is usually not performed by an appraiser, but there is no prohibition against an appraiser performing such a review. The appraiser probably should make it clear in his or her report that this is an administrative review and has not been performed under USPAP since administrative reviews usually do not require the opinions identified in Standard 3. If the opinions identified in Standard 3 are required, the service should not be classified as an administrative review but as a technical review, and the report should be reviewed in compliance with Standard 3.

Types of Review Procedures

There are two basic types of review procedures: desk reviews and field reviews. Both represent acceptable procedures for checking the thoroughness and consistency of appraisals, but the desk review is more common.

A desk review is completed without a field inspection and is usually limited to the data presented in the report. The data in the appraisal report may or may not be independently confirmed, and additional market data are typically not researched. The review appraiser often uses a customized checklist. Mathematical calculations are checked; the appraiser's methodology is reviewed for appropriateness; and the appraisal is reviewed to ascertain that it was completed in accordance with the client's guidelines, appraisal policy requirements, regulatory requirements, and the Uniform Standards of Professional Appraisal Practice.

The thoroughness of desk reviews varies greatly. Seven levels of analysis can be identified:

1. The report is merely scanned.
2. The mathematical calculations are checked, and the data are examined for reasonableness.
3. Selected pertinent sections of the report are read.
4. The appraisal is checked to ascertain that the methodology is appropriate.
5. The entire report is read thoroughly.
6. Limited confirmation of market data is attempted.
7. Full confirmation of market data is attempted.

In addition to the tasks performed in a desk review, a field review may include

- Inspection of the exteriors of the comparable properties
- Limited verification of select market data
- Full verification of market data
- Independent research to gather additional market data
- Verification of electronic spreadsheet software, including the integrity of formulas and the accuracy of the data
- Verification of computer software and the data used in lease-by-lease analysis

Many variations exist in desk reviews, field reviews, and combinations of the two. Review policies should be flexible enough to allow review appraisers to exercise due diligence in each case. The extent of the review process will vary with the needs of the client and the client's level of confidence in the skill and expertise of the appraiser. The extent of the review is usually a function of the complexity of the property and the transaction value involved.

A special type of technical review is applied to the investment portfolios of lending institutions. This type of review may be undertaken to test the validity of previous appraisal reports. Usually an independent appraiser is retained as a consultant to review a sample of the appraisal reports pertaining to the investments in the portfolio. In these cases, certain issues must be determined at the outset: how the sampling criteria will be determined (i.e., properties with the highest dollar values, properties representing the most risk, or a purely random sampling), the intensity of the review (detailed, cursory, or something in between), and the size of the sample. In many sampling assignments, the sampling size and other procedures are spelled out by regulation.

Quality control checks may also be performed by the staff of a professional appraisal firm or lending institution to monitor the quality of appraisal reports. Overseeing the daily performance of staff appraisers may be done by independent appraisers as well. Finally, appraisers are sometimes called upon to review appraisals as independent, third-party arbitrators in dispute resolution cases involving questions of value.

A preliminary review addresses the thoroughness of the appraisal report and its adherence to performance requirements regarding format, methodology, consistency, and reasonableness. The review appraiser may use a checklist to help determine whether the appraisal report is complete and conforms to the criteria of the client.

Reviewer Checklists

Using a checklist helps the review appraiser systematize the review process, ensure that no section is inadvertently overlooked, and assess whether the appraisal report conforms to client requirements. The premises of the appraisal and other facts that the review appraiser notes on the checklist will help him or her evaluate the report's internal consistency. The list may also help the review appraiser relate the appraisal to market conditions and check its reasonableness in terms of externalities.

Strict adherence to a checklist can be overdone, however, and shortchange the qualitative aspects of the report. The checklist does not determine the acceptability of the appraisal report; it is merely a tool to help systematize the review process. Like appraisal formats, appraisal review checklists vary. No single review checklist is universally accepted. Most need to be tailored to the specific criteria of the institution, agency, or corporation that will use them.

The extent of the review depends on the quality and thoroughness of the appraisal. The review appraiser need not duplicate work that has been adequately performed in the appraisal. If the appraisal is well-researched and well-documented, little additional work may be required of the review appraiser. If additional data are required, the review appraiser's work may be almost as involved as a complete appraisal. When the review appraiser believes additional data or a different valuation technique is required, the matter should be discussed with the appraiser prior to completion of the review appraisal assignment.

Examples of an administrative review checklist and a summary of a technical review follow. More detailed sample checklists are presented in the appendices.

BRIEF ADMINISTRATIVE CHECKLIST

		Yes	No	Not Applicable
1.	The name and address of the subject property are consistent throughout the report.	❑	❑	❑
2.	The client is correctly identified and addressed in the letter of transmittal.	❑	❑	❑
3.	The information in the summary of important conclusions is consistent with the information in the body of the report.	❑	❑	❑
4.	The value conclusion and valuation date in the reconciliation are consistent with those in the letter of transmittal and summary of important conclusions.	❑	❑	❑
5.	The numerical conclusions of each valuation approach are consistent with those in the reconciliation and summary of important conclusions.	❑	❑	❑
6.	The letter of transmittal and the certification(s) have been signed by the appropriate persons.	❑	❑	❑
7.	Any certification statements or contingent and limiting conditions requiring inclusion/exclusion/modification have been so adjusted.	❑	❑	❑
8.	The "personal inspection" statement in the certification is accurate.	❑	❑	❑
9.	Any special limiting conditions set forth in the body of the report are included in the assumptions and limiting conditions section.	❑	❑	❑
10.	The definition of market value is appropriate to the assignment.	❑	❑	❑
11.	All exhibits and addenda referenced in the text are included in the report in proper sequence.	❑	❑	❑

SUMMARY OF TECHNICAL REVIEW

Scope of review: ____

____

____

Concluded value(s): ____

____

____

Property/locational data: ____

____

____

Significant assumptions: ____

____

____

Major valuation issues: ____

____

____

Risks: ____

____

____

Limiting conditions (reviewer): ____

____

____

Certification (reviewer): ____

____

____

Demystifying Appraisal

Introduction

Most reports are requested or initiated by clients. Reports prepared within business organizations provide information used in management decision making; scientific research reports disseminate knowledge in the fields of medicine or industry; and government reports inform the public or legislative bodies. Reports help those in authority to make decisions and set policy. They may present the findings of research, which can be used either to solve problems or to contribute to their solutions. Most reports are written after the researcher has

1. Defined the problem to be solved
2. Selected a method of research
3. Gathered and analyzed the findings of the research
4. Arrived at a conclusion or answer to the problem

These four steps reflect the skeletal organization of any report—problem, method, findings, and conclusion. An appraisal report is a business communication that familiarizes its readers with the problem-solving valuation process that precedes the preparation of the report.

It has been said that appraisal is an art, not a science, and the art of appraisal seems to be the least understood real estate activity. Contributing to the general public's ignorance of real estate appraising are the special words, phrases, definitions, and acronyms used to describe the valuation process and related regulations and technology. Unfortunately, this is not a unique situation. Most professions today have adopted changing technology and new ways to get things done that might seem strange to the uninitiated.

Participants in the real estate market commonly think of value in three ways:

1. The value indicated by recent sales of comparable properties in the market
2. The current cost of reproducing or replacing a building, minus an estimate for depreciation, plus the value of the land
3. The value that the property's net earning power will support

These are the important considerations in the valuation of real property that form the basis of the three approaches to value—the sales comparison, cost, and income capitalization approaches. One or more of these approaches may not be applicable to a given assignment or may be less significant because of the nature of the property, the decision to be made, or the data available.

The intended use of an appraisal report is to lead the reader from the definition of the appraisal problem through the analysis of relevant data to a specific conclusion. A well-organized and informative report must be carefully thought out by the appraiser.

Although the characteristics of properties differ widely, most appraisal problems can be solved through the systematic application of the valuation process. The process is described here for the benefit of appraisal reviewers who are not appraisers themselves.

THE VALUATION PROCESS

The appraiser's first step in the valuation process is to develop a concise statement of the appraisal problem. This sets the limits of the appraisal and eliminates any ambiguity about the nature of the assignment. The appraiser identifies

- the real estate to be appraised
- the property rights involved
- the use of the appraisal
- the definition of value
- the date of the value estimate
- the scope of the appraisal
- other limiting conditions

The second step is preliminary analysis and data selection and collection. In this step the appraiser plans for the collection and analysis of general, specific, and competitive supply and demand data.

General data consist of information on the social, economic, governmental, and environmental forces that affect property value. In analyzing general data related to property values in an area, appraisers study the interaction of these four forces. This interaction creates the economic climate in which property values at a specific time and in a specific place increase, decrease, or remain stable.

General data are essential in valuation because they

- Provide the background against which specific properties are appraised
- Supply information that can be used to infer possible trends affecting land values and to derive value estimates within the three approaches
- Form a basis for judgments about highest and best use, the reconciliation of value indications, and the final estimate of value

Specific data include details about the property being appraised (the subject property), comparable properties that have been sold or leased, and relevant characteristics of the local market. Specific data about the subject are provided in land and building descriptions. They help the appraiser select comparable sales and rentals and describe local market characteristics.

In the analysis of general data, national, regional, and local trends are emphasized; in the analysis of specific data, a set of properties similar to the subject property is studied. From these comparable properties an appraiser extracts specific sale prices, rental terms, incomes and expenses, rates of return on investments, construction costs, the expected economic lives of improvements, and rates of depreciation. The figures are then used in calculations to estimate the value of the subject property.

Competitive supply and demand data are needed to understand the competitive position of the property in its future market. Supply data include inventories of competitive properties (both existing and proposed), vacancy rates, and absorption rates. Demand data include population, income, employment, and survey data about potential property users. Vacancy rates and offering prices also indicate the strength or weakness of local demand. An estimate of the future demand for the present or prospective use(s) of property is developed from an analysis of these data.

Highest and Best Use

A crucial determinant of value in the market is the property's highest and best use. Highest and best use is considered both for the land as though vacant and for the property as it is improved. The conclusions must be consistent. To qualify as the highest and best use, a use must satisfy four criteria: it must be legally permissible, physically possible, financially feasible, and maximally profitable.

The highest and best uses of land and improved properties are selected from various alternative uses. An appraiser's conclusion about the highest and best use of a subject property forms the basis for the estimation of market value; the entire valuation process depends on the highest and best use conclusion.

Land Value Estimate

A land value estimate is derived in the valuation process through the application of one of six procedures, all of which are based to some extent on the three approaches to value. The most reliable procedure for arriving at a land value estimate is sales comparison. Sales of similar, vacant parcels are analyzed, compared, and related to the land being appraised. If sufficient sales are not available for comparison, or if the value estimate indicated by sales comparison needs substantiation, the appraiser may use other reliable land valuation procedures.

Site valuation procedures include

- ✓ Sales comparison
- ✓ Allocation
- ✓ Extraction
- ✓ Subdivision development analysis
- ✓ Land residual technique
- ✓ Ground rent capitalization

APPLICATION OF VALUATION APPROACHES

The appraiser estimates property value by means of one or more of the three valuation approaches. The approaches employed depend on the type of property, the use of the appraisal, and the quality and quantity of the data available for analysis.

The Three Approaches to Value

- Cost Approach
- Sales Comparison Approach
- Income Capitalization Approach

Cost Approach

In the cost approach an appraiser estimates the value of a property by adding the land value of the site to an estimate of the depreciated reproduction or replacement cost of the building and other improvements. Although cost and value are different concepts, the cost approach explores their interrelationship. For a new property developed to its highest and best use, the market generally presumes that the estimated reproduction or replacement cost of the improvements plus current land value should approximate market value, assuming no loss of value due to time. This concept recognizes that physical, functional, and external disadvantages will be recognized by the market and will result in lower sale prices. The cost approach specifically measures these disadvantages, and anything that diminishes value is termed *depreciation*.

There are three kinds of depreciation:

- Physical deterioration caused by the wearing out of the property improvements
- Functional obsolescence attributable to a layout, style, or design that is undesirable compared to that of a new property serving the same function
- External obsolescence, which is a loss in value from causes outside the property itself

One or more forms of depreciation may affect the value of a single property.

The 11 steps in the cost approach are described as follows:

1. Estimate the value of the land as though it were vacant and available to be developed to its highest and best use.
2. Estimate the reproduction or replacement cost of the principal improvements on the effective date of the appraisal.
3. Estimate other costs incurred after construction to bring the new, vacant building up to market condition and occupancy levels.
4. Estimate entrepreneurial profit from an analysis of the market.
5. Add estimated reproduction or replacement costs, other costs, and entrepreneurial profit to arrive at the total cost of the main structure. (Entrepreneurial profit is added to the total property value, including land, in the valuation of an existing property but not in the valuation of a new or proposed property.)

6. Estimate the amount of accrued depreciation in the structure due to physical deterioration and functional and external obsolescence.
7. Deduct the estimate of depreciation from the total reproduction or replacement cost of the building to derive an estimate of the structure's depreciated reproduction or replacement cost.
8. Estimate the reproduction or replacement cost and depreciation for any accessory buildings and site improvements and then deduct this estimated depreciation from the reproduction or replacement cost of these improvements.
9. Add the depreciated reproduction or replacement cost of the main structure, accessory buildings, and site improvements together to obtain the estimated total depreciated reproduction or replacement cost of all improvements.
10. Add the land value to the estimated total depreciated reproduction or replacement cost of all improvements to arrive at an indicated value for the fee simple interest in the property.
11. Adjust the indicated fee simple value, if appropriate, to arrive at an indicated value for the interest in the subject property being appraised.

Sales Comparison Approach

The sales comparison approach is a method of estimating value in which comparable properties that have been sold recently are compared with the subject property. Ideally, all the properties are located in the same geographic area. The sale prices of the comparables are adjusted to derive a value indication for the subject. The sales comparison approach presumes that the market will establish a price for the subject property in the same manner that the prices of comparable, competitive properties have been established.

The sale prices of the properties deemed most comparable to the subject property tend to establish a range within which the value of the subject property will fall. Through further analysis of the comparable data, the appraiser can derive a figure that represents the value of the appraised property as of the date of the appraisal, in keeping with the definition of value sought.

Essentially, the sales comparison approach is a systematic procedure for comparing properties. To apply the sales comparison approach, an appraiser

1. Researches the market to obtain information about transactions, listings, and other offerings of properties similar to the subject property
2. Verifies the information through a knowledgeable source, preferably one of the participants in the transaction, to determine whether the data obtained are factually accurate and the transactions reflect arm's-length market considerations
3. Identifies relevant units of comparison (e.g., dollars per square foot, income multiplier) and develops a comparative analysis for each unit
4. Compares the comparable sales to the subject property and adjusts the sale price of each comparable appropriately or eliminates the property from consideration

5. Reconciles the several value indications derived from the comparables into a single estimate of value

To determine the comparability of the properties, the appraiser considers the characteristics of properties and transactions that cause prices to vary. The elements of comparison considered include

- Real property rights conveyed
- Financing terms
- Conditions of sale
- Market conditions (time)
- Location
- Physical characteristics
- Economic characteristics (for income-producing properties)
- Use (zoning)
- Non-realty components of value.

Quantitative adjustments for these elements are made to the price of each comparable property as appropriate. Qualitative differences among the subject and comparable properties are also assessed to rank the properties according to their degree of comparability and to establish a bracket of value for the subject property. Quantitative and qualitative methodologies may often be applied together.

Income Capitalization Approach

The income capitalization approach to value is applied to properties for which a rental income can be identified. The appraiser applies a set of procedures to convert the anticipated benefits of an income-producing property into a property value indication. A single year's income expectancy or the annual average of several years' income expectancies can be converted into property value by applying a market-derived capitalization rate, which reflects a specified income pattern, return on investment, and change in the value of the investment. Alternatively, the projected annual cash flows over the anticipated holding period plus the reversionary value at the end of the period can be converted into a property value estimate by applying a market-derived discount rate. The capitalization methods, techniques, and procedures applied in a given analysis depend on various inherent assumptions concerning the quality, durability, and pattern of the projected income stream. The appraiser selects the capitalization method and procedures that best conform to the future income pattern of the subject property and the available data.

Capitalization is the conversion of earnings into an indication of value. Capitalization rates express the relationship between income and value. They may be applied to the total net operating income of real property or to various possible divisions of that income, such as the income to the land, the building, the mortgage interest, the equity interest, the leased fee estate, or the leasehold estate.

Capitalization begins with an estimate of net operating income (*NOI*). This estimate is basic to the income capitalization approach, and the value indication is only as reliable as the income projection from which it is derived.

Seven steps are followed to convert a projected income stream into an indication of value:

1. Estimate potential gross income.
2. Estimate and deduct a vacancy and collection loss allowance to derive effective gross income.
3. Estimate and deduct expenses of operation to derive net operating income.
4. Analyze the pattern and duration of the projected income stream.
5. Estimate the anticipated value of the property at resale or the reversionary benefit.
6. Develop the appropriate capitalization rate(s) or discounting factor(s).
7. Complete the capitalization process to derive estimated property value.

To apply the income capitalization approach, an appraiser must research market attitudes and perceptions and make critical judgments concerning projected income patterns and amounts, capitalization methods and procedures, and the selection of appropriate rates. Also to be considered are the physical, financial, and ownership components of property value—i.e., the land and the building(s), mortgage and equity interests, and leased fee and leasehold estates.

REAL ESTATE INTERESTS

The ownership of a real estate title in fee establishes the interest in property known as the *fee simple estate.* A lease typically divides this bundle of ownership rights into lease interests. The lessor and the lessee each obtain interests, which are stipulated in a contract and subject to contract law. The divided interests are the leased fee estate and the leasehold estate.

The leased fee estate is the lessor's, or landlord's, estate. Although the specific details of leases vary, a leased fee generally provides the lessor with rent to be paid by the lessee under stipulated terms; the right of repossession at the termination of the lease; default provisions; and the right of disposition, including the rights to sell, mortgage, or bequeath the property, subject to the lessee's rights. When a property is encumbered by a lease, the legal interest typically appraised is the leased fee.

The leasehold estate is the lessee's, or tenant's, estate. The tenant usually acquires the rights to possess the property for the lease period, to sublease the property (if allowed by the lease and desired by the tenant), and to improve the property under the restrictions specified in the lease. The tenant surrenders possession at the termination of the lease.

A property under a lease that specifies rent at market levels is appraised as a leased fee, not as a fee simple interest. Leases are classified as gross, modified gross, or net, depending on whether the landlord or tenant pays the operating expenses and taxes. The market value of a leased fee interest depends on how contract rent compares to market rent. A leasehold interest may acquire value if contract rent is below market levels, the lease allows for subletting, and the term is of a marketable duration.

Partial interests in property also include vertical interests, easements, transferable development rights (TDRs), and interests resulting from specialized fractional ownership. Vertical interests refer to subsurface rights (e.g., for mining or the construction of tunnels) and air rights for the use, control, and regulation of air space. Easements generally permit use of a portion of a property for access (e.g., for public utility lines, subways, or bridges). Preservation and conservation easements, which are granted by donors to nonprofit organizations or government agencies in return for tax considerations, prohibit certain physical changes to historic properties and natural resource lands.

Reconciliation of Value Indications and Final Value Estimate

Reconciliation is the step in the valuation process in which the appraiser analyzes alternative conclusions and selects a final value estimate from among the two or more indications of value derived. A thorough review of the entire valuation process may precede reconciliation.

In reconciliation appraisers draw upon their experience, expertise, and professional judgment to resolve differences among the value indications derived from application of the approaches. The appraiser weighs the relative significance, applicability, and defensibility of each value indication and relies most heavily on the one most appropriate to the purpose of the appraisal. The final conclusion depends on the appropriateness, accuracy, and quantity of evidence in the appraisal.

Once a final estimate of market value is reached, the immediate objective of the valuation process has been accomplished. However, an appraisal assignment is not completed until the conclusion has been stated in a formal report and presented to the client.

Appraisal Standards Reporting Requirements and Options

Each report or communication concerning the results of an appraisal must

1. Clearly and accurately set forth the appraisal in a manner that is not misleading
2. Contain sufficient information to enable the person(s) who will rely on the report to understand it properly
3. Clearly and accurately disclose any extraordinary assumption or limiting condition that directly affects the appraisal and indicate its impact on value

The Uniform Standards of Professional Appraisal Practice (USPAP) provide for two types of appraisals (limited appraisals performed under the Departure Provision and complete appraisals) and three reporting formats (restricted, summary, and self-contained). The type of report and the reporting format must always be identified. When a client requests a complete appraisal but specifies that the appraiser's opinion be communicated without detailed documentation (i.e., in a summary or restricted report), the appraiser must still undertake a complete analysis.

Regardless of how a report is conveyed, all data and notes as well as a summary of the analysis and conclusions should be kept in the appraiser's file.

A self-contained report generally has four parts plus addenda. The introduction contains a letter of transmittal, title page, table of contents, certification of value, and summary of important conclusions. The premises of the appraisal section identifies the type of appraisal, report format, assumptions and limiting conditions, the purpose and use, scope of the appraisal, and definition and date of value. The presentation of the data section includes the property's legal description, identification of personal or non-realty items, and data on the neighborhood, site, improvements, zoning, taxes, assessments, prior owners, and marketability. The fourth section, the analysis of data and conclusions, presents the highest and best use conclusion(s), land value, value indications derived from the approaches applied, a final reconciled value conclusion, the estimated marketing period, and the qualifications of the appraiser. The addenda may include legal documentation, statistical data, lease data or summaries, and other appropriate information.[1]

The typical format for a self-contained appraisal report is outlined as follows:

APPRAISAL REPORT FORMAT

Part One—Introduction

- Title page
- Letter of transmittal
- Table of contents
- Certification of value
- Summary of important conclusions

Part Two—Premises of the Appraisal

- Identification of type of appraisal and report format
- Assumptions and limiting conditions
- Purpose and use of the appraisal
- Definition of value and date of value estimate
- Property rights appraised
- Scope of the appraisal

Part Three—Presentation of Data

- Identification of the property, legal description
- Identification of any personal property or other items that are not real property
- Area, city, neighborhood, and location data
- Site data
- Description of improvements
- Zoning
- Taxes and assessment data
- History, including prior sales and current offers or listings
- Marketability study, if appropriate

Part Four—Analysis of Data and Conclusions

- Highest and best use of the land as though vacant
- Highest and best use of the property as improved

continued

1. Much of this material was adapted from the Appraisal Institute brochure, "Understanding the Appraisal."

- Site value
- Cost approach
- Sales comparison approach
- Income capitalization approach
- Reconciliation and final value estimate
- Estimate of marketing period
- Qualifications of the appraiser
- Addenda
- Detailed legal description, if not included in the presentation of data
- Detailed statistical data
- Leases or lease summaries
- Other appropriate information
- Secondary exhibits

Appraising the Appraisal

Introduction

The reviewer must carefully review the entire appraisal, making certain that the data presented, the underlying assumptions, the analytical techniques applied, and the appraiser's logic have led to consistent judgments. The data presented in the report must be reviewed to ensure they are authentic, pertinent, and sufficient. The value definition, the identified property rights, and the qualifying conditions imposed should be carefully considered by the reviewer to ascertain whether the appraiser's analysis specifically addresses each of these items. The reviewer should examine the differences in the conclusions derived from the various approaches, apply tests of reasonableness to these primary conclusions, and determine if the appraiser has satisfactorily resolved the differences among the various value indications.

All mathematical calculations should be checked; significant errors can lead to incorrect value indications, and even minor errors can diminish a user's confidence in the appraisal.

The logic employed throughout the valuation process should be scrutinized. Do the approaches and methods applied consider all the available data and systematically lead to a meaningful conclusion that relates directly to the intended use or uses of the appraisal? Does the appraisal provide the information required to help resolve the client's problem? For example, if the client wants to establish a depreciation basis to compute federal income tax, does the appraisal allocate separate values to the improvements and the land? A client who contemplates remodeling will want information on the costs and benefits of this plan. The client seeking insurance coverage needs a well-supported value estimate that is consistent with the carrier's definition of insurable value. If the client is considering whether to accept an offer to purchase, the appraiser must adequately analyze the terms of the proposed sales contract.

An appraisal client seeking a professional opinion will want to know the basis for that opinion. The final value estimate represents the application of the appraiser's judgment to mathematical results. The appraiser should employ the quantity of data that market participants would consider appropriate to solve the appraisal problem at hand. These data should be applied consistently in the specific approach or approaches applicable to the appraisal problem. The valuation process is a collection of available analytical tools from which an appraiser selects those appropriate to the assignment.

All estimates used in the approaches to value must be consistent with market perceptions. The appraisal conclusion should reflect market value and the data analyzed should support the appraiser's final value opinion, but data alone do not produce a value estimate. Through the intellectual process of combining data analysis with professional judgment, a sound value opinion is formed.

Sometimes an appraiser may offer substantive, albeit subjective, judgments when precise market information is not available. This most frequently occurs in the appraisal of special-purpose properties, for which transactional data are scarce, and properties in fully developed areas (e.g., older urban core areas) where land sales may not have occurred for several years. All too often, a lack of sales activity coupled with scarce net income information makes derivation of overall capitalization rates by direct sales comparison difficult, if not impossible. In these situations, substantive judgments by the appraiser are required.

Appropriateness, Accuracy, and Quantity of Evidence

Reviewing an appraisal helps establish its accuracy, its consistency, and the logic leading to the value conclusion. Appropriateness, accuracy, and quantity of evidence are the criteria an appraiser uses to form a meaningful, defensible final value estimate. These criteria are used to analyze multiple value indications within each approach and to reconcile the indications produced by the different approaches into a final estimate of defined value.

The criterion of appropriateness refers to how pertinent each approach is to the intended use of the appraisal. The appropriateness of an approach is usually directly related to property type and market viability. For example, an appraisal to estimate the market value of a 30-year-old community shopping center will ordinarily employ procedures associated with the income capitalization approach—i.e., the derivation of a gross rent multiplier, net income capitalization, or the discounting of cash flows. The cost approach might not be useful in valuing obsolete improvements, but it may be applied to estimate land value and determine, through an analysis of highest and best use, whether demolition of all or part of an improvement is appropriate. The sales comparison approach can be used to derive value indications through the analysis of physical units of comparison.

Although the final value estimate is based on the approach or approaches that are most applicable, the final value opinion need not be identical to the value produced by the most applicable approach. If two approaches are applicable, the final estimate of value may be closer to the value indication produced by one approach than the other. For example, the value indicated by application of the income capitalization approach may be lower than the value indicated by sales comparison. If market participants are primarily interested in income-earning potential, the final estimate may be closer to the conclusion produced from income capitalization than sales comparison. If the property is an owner-occupied dwelling, however, the sales comparison approach would likely be most relevant.

The criterion of appropriateness is also applied to judge the relevance of each comparable property and each significant adjustment made. The accuracy of an appraisal is measured by the appraiser's confidence in the correctness of the data and the adjustments made. The number of comparable properties, the number of adjustments, and the gross and net dollar amounts of adjustments may suggest the relative accuracy of a particular approach.

Even when they are supported with comparable data, adjustments reflect human judgment; small inaccuracies can be compounded when several adjustments are added or multiplied. For this reason, the precise arithmetic conclusion derived from adjusted data should support, but not control, the appraiser's judgment.

Appropriateness and accuracy affect the quality and relevance of the value indication derived from a comparable or an approach. Although these criteria are considered separately in the review process, both must be studied in relation to the quantity of evidence provided by a particular comparable or approach. Even data that meet the criteria of appropriateness and accuracy can be weakened by a scarcity of evidence.

Regardless of the quantity of evidence available, the responsibility of the appraiser goes beyond the manipulation of numbers. The appraiser has a duty to the client to provide a value estimate consistent with the definition of value specified in the assignment.

Common Reporting Deficiencies

An appraisal report should convey the appraiser's confidence in the solution being offered to the appraisal problem. A poorly written report will not be convincing to a client or reviewer. All the effort put into an appraisal assignment can be lost if the report lacks organization and is carelessly written. A clear and concisely written report not only facilitates comprehension, it also creates a favorable impression of the appraiser. If boilerplate is used in the report, it must be current and relevant to the specific valuation problem.

It is in the interest of all parties to get to the point early in the report. A 150-page report that does not describe the property until page 85 or does not address the derivation of market value until page 148 will only frustrate the reader. Critical issues should be highlighted, not buried in the report.

It is unnerving for a reviewer to read a report that contains tantalizing hints about potential investment risk but never addresses the problem head-on. A reviewer who is forced to read between the lines loses confidence in the value conclusion. Usually the reviewer orders another appraisal to confirm or refute his or her suspicions about the original report. Because appraising is problem solving, it is reasonable for a reviewer to expect a clear-cut solution.

Reviewers should be alert for incongruities. Is a claim made too often, too emphatically, or in too smooth a manner? Is an issue being avoided? Are there implicit rather than explicit references to a potential problem? Deception can take many forms. Inconsistencies within an appraisal—e.g., discrepancies between the data and analyses—detract from a report and erode confidence in its conclusions.

Some appraisers cloud otherwise straightforward appraisal issues with technical jargon or "appraisal-speak." An appraiser may resort to jargon in an effort to disguise his or her shortcomings, overwhelming the reader with unfamiliar verbiage to deflect attention away from an issue the appraiser does not understand. Excessive reliance on jargon can also create the false impression that the value indication derived in the appraisal process is both precise and scientific. Ultimately, jargon may prevent the client from understanding the appraiser's analysis and rationale.

The use of pretentious jargon has increased since the advent of the computer. Computer output appears authoritative and many people are duly impressed. The reviewer, however, must not be taken in by the attractiveness of desktop publishing page layouts or slick graphics.

As previously discussed, valuation is both an art and a science. Appraisers should never abdicate their responsibility and rely completely on technology. An appraiser's main task is to interpret the behavior of market participants—that is, the buyers, sellers, investors, landlords, and tenants who make up the market. No scientific process yet devised has the ability to measure or predict market behavior with total accuracy and replace the judgment of a trained valuation professional.

To provide a meaningful service, the appraiser must offer guidance in the decision-making process. Obvious problems should never be ignored. Too often a critical part of a report lacks essential analysis. For example, in valuing a property under an older, uneconomic use that is located in a growth area, the appraiser may fail to consider that the land might be worth more if developed to an alternative use. In this case, the analysis of the highest and best use of the land as though vacant did not receive sufficient emphasis.

The reasoning an appraiser uses to solve the appraisal problem should be straightforward and supportable. The analysis should be presented as simply as possible and lead to a logical conclusion. The rationale employed should reflect the way active market participants would approach the problem. In their quest to make the valuation process more scientific, some appraisers use esoteric techniques that would not be recognized or applied by market participants.

Real estate, particularly investment-grade property, involves potential risks, and appraisers must address all risk factors directly. The risk components in a real estate investment must be analyzed and weighed against the risks found in alternative investments.

Appraisers must also thoroughly investigate the motivation of market participants. Whether the appraisal concerns a single-family residence in suburbia or a trophy office building in the central core business district, an appraiser must ultimately know who the market participants are, what motivates them, and why. Without this knowledge, the analysis that underlies the value conclusion is totally meaningless.

Often appraisers do not have complete information about a sale or lease. They may not have asked the right questions or interviewed the right participants to a transaction. Some may proceed with an analysis based on partial data without alerting the client to the limitations of the data.

In the appraisal of a property that is being purchased, the appraiser should include the current transaction price. For a newly constructed property, the appraiser will need to provide a cost analysis. In both cases the rationale for variances between the market or cost data and the concluded value should be explained. When a transaction price differs from the concluded value, the variance may be explained by the poor negotiating skill of one party, duress, or the inordinate market influence wielded by a limited number of suppliers (oligopoly). A cost analysis at odds with the concluded value may suggest that the property is an overimprovement or an underimprovement.

Appraisal reports on existing, income-producing properties should clearly reconcile differences between the revenue and expense history of the subject property and the revenue and expense projections used in the appraisal analysis. The client should not have to surmise how the appraiser arrived at the revenue and expense projection for the subject or how it correlates with the past performance of the property. The report should present this information clearly, explaining where and why the projection differs from the property's recorded history. An appraiser may choose to synthesize much of the property's financial history in the text of the report, but it is good practice to include a complete copy of the historical data provided by the client in the report addenda.

The remainder of this chapter will follow the typical appraisal format, indicating what various sections should contain and pointing out common flaws and deficiencies noted by appraisal reviewers.

Part One—Introduction

Letter of Transmittal

The letter of transmittal is not a required element of the appraisal. The appraiser includes such a letter as a convenience to the client. All the information normally contained in the letter of transmittal can be found in various sections of the report. Most appraisers include the letter as an introduction to the appraisal itself. It formally presents the appraisal report to the client for whom the appraisal was prepared. The letter of transmittal should include the address and a brief description of the property, identify the property interest being appraised, and state the value estimate and the effective date of the appraisal.

Many appraisers prefer not to include the value conclusions in the transmittal letter to guard against the possibility that an unscrupulous user could detach these preliminary pages from the appraisal report and mislead others into believing that the letter constitutes a complete appraisal. If the client wants a report that contains a letter of transmittal, with or without the value conclusion, he or she should include that request as part of the letter of engagement.

The appraiser may take this opportunity to restate the essence of the engagement letter, highlighting any special agreements or understandings between the client and the appraiser. The letter of transmittal should state that the property inspection and all necessary investigations and analyses were made by the appraiser, identify the type of appraisal and the report format, and refer to the accompanying appraisal report. Any departures from Standard 1 of USPAP should also be described.

In regard to property inspection, the appraiser should indicate both who inspected the property and the extent of the inspection conducted (i.e., did the principal appraiser inspect the interior of the property, just the exterior, or neither?). Just who conducted the inspection could be an issue in the valuation of a complex property. Sometimes participation in the inspection by the principal appraiser is specified in the engagement letter. It is important that the name of the inspecting appraiser be stated. It is unacceptable merely to state that "at least one of the undersigned inspected the property." For further information on property inspection, the reviewer is advised to consult Advisory Opinion AO-2, issued by the Appraisal Standards Board of The Appraisal Foundation, which addresses the inspection of subject property real estate.

The letter of transmittal is the "most read" portion of the appraisal. Any extraordinary assumptions and limiting conditions of the report should be highlighted in the letter, and any special risks and underlying conditions should be fully disclosed. The appraiser must carefully explain in plain English any explicit or implicit situations that could mislead the client.

A prominent explanation is especially necessary when the appraiser has been requested to provide a new cover letter or transmittal letter for a lender to accompany an appraisal originally performed for another lender. The appraiser should be aware of the FIRREA rules that govern these situations. The ethics of the appraiser-client relationship require that the appraiser request and receive permission from the original lender-client before readdressing the appraisal report.

Common flaws in the letter of transmittal include

- No date on the letter
- Report issued without signature(s)
- Misspelling of the addressee's or the client's company name or misaddressing the appraisal
- Appraising the wrong property (e.g., valuing an undeveloped parcel at 1234 Peachtree Circle, instead of 1234 Peachtree Drive)
- Not highlighting special conditions of the appraisal

Certification of Value

The certification of value may be combined with the letter of transmittal, or it may be a separate page. This section normally contains a standard set of appraiser certifications, but the reviewer should be alert for any extraordinary certification statements. At a minimum, the appraiser's certification should include all of the statements specified in Standards Rule 2-3 of USPAP. The appraiser should warn the client of special restrictions by highlighting any unusual items. The effective valuation date should be stated. In conformity with USPAP, anyone who participated in the inspection or provided significant professional assistance in the valuation process should be identified. This information will be of considerable interest to the reviewer. Also, if the appraiser is a member of the Appraisal Institute, the report should include his or her continuing education status as well as a statement to the effect that "the use of this report is subject to the requirements of the Appraisal Institute relating to review by its duly authorized representatives."

Summary of Important Conclusions

Complex appraisals may be communicated in voluminous written reports, so a one- or two-page synopsis of significant data, observations, and conclusions is a courtesy and a convenience to the reader. Executive summaries are commonly found in business reports, and a summary can be a useful and valuable part of an appraisal report.

This section should contain

- Brief identification of the property
- Identification of the type of appraisal and the report format
- Statement of any special assumptions and conditions

- Determination of the highest and best use of the land as though vacant and the property as improved
- Stated age of improvements
- Estimate of site value
- Value indication from the cost approach
- Value indication from the sales comparison approach
- Value indication from the income capitalization approach
- Final estimate of defined value
- Allocation of value between the land and the improvements, between the leased fee and the leasehold estates, or between real and personal property

The items covered in a summary will vary with the complexity of the appraisal problem. If primary emphasis is placed on one value approach, the appraiser may want to provide additional information relating to this approach in the summary. For example, if the income capitalization approach is emphasized, the appraiser may indicate the gross market rent estimate; vacancy, expense, and net income estimates; and the capitalization method and rates applied.

Normally, this section should present only the facts most important to the reader. Sometimes the summary of important conclusions is omitted, particularly if the letter of transmittal briefly discusses the major conclusions of the appraisal report.

Part Two—Premises of the Appraisal

Identification of Type of Appraisal and Report Format

The appraiser should state the type of appraisal (i.e., limited or complete) and the report format (i.e., self-contained, summary, or restricted) in every appraisal report. The type of appraisal and the report format *must* be stated whenever the appraiser departs from the Uniform Standards and the Departure Provision is invoked. When departure is taken, the appraiser must explain how he or she departed from the standards. It is not necessary to state the number of the specific standard involved, although some clients and reviewers prefer it. The most important considerations are that the report not be misleading and that the departure and the appraiser's rationale be described clearly and concisely. In each case, the three conditions of departure must be met: the appraiser advises the client of the limitations and discloses them in the report, and the client agrees that the limited service is appropriate.

Assumptions and Limiting Conditions

Assumptions and limiting conditions are used to protect the appraiser and to inform and protect the client and other users of the report. Appropriate standard conditions are an important part of a report and should be stated clearly. Unusual items should be highlighted for the reader. The general assumptions typically found in an appraisal report relate to issues such as legal and title considerations, liens and encumbrances, property management, information furnished by others (e.g., engineering studies, surveys), concealment of hazardous substances on the property, and compliance with zoning regulations and local, state, and federal laws. In addition, any departure from the guidelines in Standard 1 must be clearly disclosed.

In recent years, the general public has become accustomed to disclaimers, disclosures, assumptions, and limiting conditions. In our litigious society, it is not just appraisers who are adding language of this nature—all professionals are doing so. As this practice becomes more accepted, disclaimers and disclosures can be more explicit without offending the public or casting doubt on the appraiser's professionalism. However, some limiting conditions may inadvertently render the appraisal report useless for the client's intended use. For this reason, the appraiser should submit a copy of his or her standard assumptions and limiting conditions as well as any special conditions at the time of engagement.

Improper or inappropriate practices include

- Imposition of limiting conditions or disclaimers designed to remove virtually all responsibility from the appraiser, thereby rendering the value conclusion useless to the client.
- Failure to emphasize any special, unusual, and unique value definitions, limiting conditions, and assumptions in this section, in the letter of transmittal, or in the value summary section of the appraisal.
- Failure to disclose whether or not the appraiser personally conducted an inspection of the property. Although not inspecting an appraised property does not violate any standards rules, it may violate the client's requirements and understanding.

Examples of assumptions and limiting condition statements that may be unacceptable to certain clients include the following statements excerpted from actual reports:

> The appraiser should be contacted with any questions before this report is relied on for decision making.
>
> This appraisal was prepared at the request of and for the exclusive use of the client to whom the appraisal is addressed. No third party shall have any right to use or rely upon this appraisal for any purpose." (Appraisers need to know that their reports sometimes travel widely in this global world. Real estate deals and loans, particularly those involving investment-grade properties, are commonly syndicated and involve the participation of investors and banking institutions worldwide.)
>
> It is our understanding that the function of this appraisal is for underwriting purposes by xxxxxxxxxx Bank, our client of record; its use for any other purpose or valuation date may invalidate the appraisal.
>
> Our report is to be used only for the purpose stated herein; any use or reliance for any other purpose, by you or third parties, is invalid. No reference to our name or our report, in whole or in part, in any document you prepare and/or distribute to third parties may be made without our written consent.

Purpose and Use of the Appraisal

The purpose of an appraisal report is the question for which the client seeks an answer. The intended use of the appraisal, which is established by the client, must also be stated. The intended use should be known by the appraiser before the assignment is accepted. For further clarification of *intended use,* the reader is advised to consult the Statement on Appraisal Standards No. 9 (SMT-9) of the Appraisal Standards Board of The Appraisal Foundation.

Definition of Value and Date of Value Estimate

The report should reflect the required definition of value or the definition specified in the engagement letter or contract. There are several acceptable definitions of value in addition to market value. Other types of value include liquidation value, insurable value, investment value, going-concern value, value in use, net realizable value, fair value (now outmoded), and others, such as public interest value. Different value definitions evolve in response to real-world valuation problems. Appraisals prepared for federally related financial institutions require use of the value definition specified in FIRREA with a source reference to the specific section or page within the client's appraisal policy.

Property Rights Appraised

The appraiser should define the rights or interests being valued. This is particularly important in appraisals of partial interests in property, limited rights such as surface or mineral rights, fee simple estates subject to long-term leases, and leasehold interests. Other encumbrances such as easements, mortgages, and special occupancy or use requirements should also be identified and explained in relation to the defined value to be estimated.

Scope of the Appraisal

This section should state

- What the appraisal was intended to do, which may or may not be to estimate market value
- How it was done, emphasizing any unusual methods necessitated by the nature of the property or the assignment
- Any reservations, cautions, or restrictions to which the report is subject

A clear and accurate description of the scope of the appraisal is desirable to protect third parties whose reliance on the appraisal may be affected. The term *scope of the appraisal* refers to the extent of the process of collecting, confirming, and reporting data. The standards clearly impose a responsibility on the appraiser to determine the extent of the work and the report required in relation to the significance of the appraisal problem. By describing the scope of the appraisal, the appraiser signifies his or her acceptance of this responsibility.

Additionally, it is very useful for the client to know the extent of the appraiser's inspection. Did the appraiser conduct a drive-by inspection of the subject and comparable properties, or did he or she physically walk through the properties? Exactly how many units of the apartment complex, the lodging facility, or the multitenant office warehouse were inspected? Most importantly, what was not inspected?

The purpose of the scope of appraisal section is often misunderstood by appraisers. Rather than describing the process of collecting, confirming, and reporting data, appraisers often cite the approaches to value or describe the steps of the valuation process. While this information may help the novice reviewer understand the appraisal, it does not provide sufficient detail to explain the extent of the appraiser's work. A reiteration of the appraisal process is typically included elsewhere in the appraisal report. A good scope of the appraisal section provides a succinct explanation of the research needed to assemble the data required to prepare a thorough appraisal.

If the appraisal analysis is limited in scope, the scope of the appraisal section should provide a detailed description of typical procedures that were omitted and why they were not considered appropriate. Although the scope of the appraisal section may seem trivial to many appraisers, it is important to reviewers and clients who rely on the data contained within the report.

Competency and the Use of Outside Experts

If an appraiser does not have the competence to handle a certain facet of an assignment, he or she should hire someone who does. This allows the appraiser to limit his or her exposure to interpretation of the results provided by the expert. This situation is analogous to a company or individual hiring an independent accountant and/or tax advisor for his or her specialized skills; the company or individual simply lacks the competency to do the job internally and is unwilling to accept the liability involved.

Hiring outside experts can benefit an appraiser in many ways. For example, if a property has problems related to wetlands and the appraiser does not hire an expert or recognize the degree to which the wetlands may affect the marketability and value of the parcel, the appraised value may be overstated. An appraiser who hires an expert learns more about the specialty area and becomes more knowledgeable in the process.

Some may argue that hiring experts from various fields is prohibitively expensive. An appraiser may be forced to either increase the fee to pay the expert or simply not do the report. These initial costs should not be an appraiser's primary concern, however; instead he or she should consider the potential liability of not securing expert opinions.

Part Three—Presentation of Data

Identification of the Property

The subject property is identified so that it cannot be confused with any other parcel of real estate. This can be achieved by including a full legal description of the property in the report. When a copy of the official plat or an assessment map is used, the appraiser may refer to it at this point and present it on a facing or following page. If the official plat is unavailable, the appraiser can describe the property by name, specifying the side of the street on which the property fronts, the street address, and the lot and block number. A photograph of the subject property on a facing page can enhance this section of the report. Personal property and other items that are not real property should also be identified.

Area, City, Neighborhood, and Location Data

All facts about a city and its surroundings that the appraiser considers pertinent to the appraisal problem should be included in the area data. The appraiser will weigh and consider all pertinent factors in data analysis, but the report should discuss only those data that were found to be significant to the problem at hand. Both positive and negative aspects of the area should be discussed. If the appraiser provides only positive or negative information, the report will be misleading.

If a considerable amount of supporting statistical data (e.g., population figures, cost-of-living indexes, family income figures) is needed, the appraiser may choose to incorporate that data into the body of the report or present them in tabular form on facing pages and reference them in the discussion. A separate section for area data is not always needed; in many reports area data are combined with neighborhood data.

Area data that may be significant to an appraisal report include

- Distance and direction from employment centers
- Types of employment and wage levels
- Adequacy of utilities and street improvements
- Proximity to schools, shopping, parks, and recreational areas
- Proximity to sources of nuisances
- Police and fire protection
- Rubbish collection
- Trends in the neighborhood or district
- Population trends
- Percentage of home ownership
- Conformity of development
- Vacancy and rent levels
- Restrictions and zoning
- New construction activity
- Percentage of vacant land
- Changing land use
- Level of taxes
- Adequacy of on- and off-street parking
- Type and amount of street traffic
- Road patterns, road layout, and street widths
- Type and amount of pedestrian traffic
- Proximity, cost, and frequency of public transportation
- Proximity to expressways, toll roads, and airports

- Rail connections and service for freight
- Concentration of advertising by retail merchants
- Other beneficial or detrimental influences

The primary purpose of the regional/city data and neighborhood sections of the appraisal report is to discuss the demand for and supply of uses that may be appropriate for the subject property. Without such a discussion, the estimate of value is based on the implicit assumption that the supply and demand for a particular use are in balance or have not changed since the comparable sales used in the report were transacted. Only by analyzing the factors that create a need for a particular use and the existing supply of competitive properties available for that use can one explicitly measure current and future demand. Such an analysis answers the often-asked question: Will this property sell for a price similar to competitive properties?[1]

The amount of neighborhood and location data required depends on the appraisal assignment and the intended user. When an appraisal is prepared for an out-of-town client who is unfamiliar with the property and the community, for example, it may be wise to

DILBERT reprinted by permission of United Feature Syndicate, Inc.

1. Charles W. Rex III, MAI, and Susan Motycka Rex, "Market Analysis in Appraisal Reports: Vitalizing Key Data Sections," *Valuation Insights & Perspectives* (Fall 1996).

include more community and neighborhood data than would be needed by a local client. If the appraisal concerns a major business property that derives its income from the purchasing power of the surrounding area, the appraiser should provide a detailed description of the neighborhood and discuss how the population and its purchasing power affect the value of the subject property.

To decide which items to include from the mass of information available about the market and the socioeconomic status of area residents, the appraiser must consider the property being appraised and its potential uses. The perceptive appraiser will only include data that are pertinent to the case. Too much data may be safer than too little, but clients often object to reports that are overloaded with irrelevant information.

The following outline might be used to structure the regional, city, and neighborhood data report section:[2]

I. Description and discussion of market area
   - A. Definitions and purpose of this section
   - B. Market area boundaries
   - C. Uses prevalent in the market area
   - D. Uses in the market area that are physically possible and legally permissible for the subject site
   - E. Demand and supply discussion of each use considered financially feasible in the highest and best use section
   - F. Conclusion

II. Neighborhood
   - A. Definitions and purpose of this section
   - B. Neighborhood boundaries
   - C. Uses in the neighborhood
   - D. Uses in the neighborhood that are physically possible and legally permissible for the subject site
   - E. Demand and supply discussions of each use considered financially feasible in the highest and best use section
   - F. Conclusion

The appraiser should also note the presence of special amenities or detrimental conditions in the neighborhood and provide reasons or data to support any conclusions about these factors. For example, if the appraiser states that the area is growing, actual growth figures or projections of construction starts should be included in the report. If the report states that the neighborhood is in decline due to abnormal deterioration or poor maintenance, the appraiser might refer to specific properties that exhibit these detrimental conditions or use photographs to support this conclusion.

2. Ibid.

Area and neighborhood data form the background against which a property is analyzed. The data are significant insofar as they reflect factors that influence property value. This section of the report is incomplete if the trends indicated by the data are not analyzed. The appraiser applies professional experience and judgment to interpret how relevant factors will affect the marketability of the subject property. Without interpretation, city and neighborhood data lose their significance.

In studying neighborhood trends, appraisers must abide by the provisions of fair lending laws and regulations. Analyses should never be based on assumptions or unsupported premises about neighborhood decline and a property's effective age or remaining useful life. Sales activity in the neighborhood already reflects market participants' economic perception of the area.

Examples of descriptive phrases that should be avoided follow:

- Poor neighborhood
- Low-income or high-income area
- Desirable or undesirable
- Transitional neighborhood
- Well-maintained or poorly maintained
- Pride of ownership
- Gang activity
- Crime-infested
- Exclusive neighborhood
- Ghetto-type neighborhood
- Curb appeal
- Riot area
- Graffiti
- Drug traffic evident or crack houses in neighborhood

The descriptions of the city and neighborhood should contain enough detail to show how well the property is suited to its use and how it relates to its surroundings, its competition, and its markets. An analysis of significant features and trends that influence marketability and value should be presented.

Common reviewer complaints about this section indicate "too much reliance on boilerplate" and "overuse of chamber of commerce-type material." Area descriptions should focus on factors that mean something to potential users and buyers of property. Appraisal reports that are padded with chamber of commerce statistics and do not provide adequate discussion of the local submarket and the immediate surroundings are of little use to clients. Also, appraisers who use boilerplate should remember the principle of change and update their city and neighborhood data before including them in an appraisal.

The following extract exemplifies a typical, ineffective neighborhood section of an appraisal report:

> In summary, although the Chicago multifamily residential market continues to show strong demand when compared to other markets in the U.S., the prices for multifamily residential properties are not expected to increase significantly in the near future. It is our opinion that property values will remain fairly stable given the age, marketability and overall condition of improvements in the subject neighborhood.

General statements such as these provide the client with little insight or analysis.

Site Data

Pertinent facts about the subject site may include descriptions of the property's frontage, depth, site area, and shape; soil and subsoil conditions; easements and restrictions; utilities; and any improvements that benefit or harm the site. The appraiser should offer a conclusion regarding the utility or adaptability of the site for existing or proposed improvements.

Appraisers who fail to note obvious, potential environmental or on-site housekeeping problems evident during the site inspection do not serve their clients' best interests. For example, the presence of stacks of chemical drums in the yard area of an industrial facility is worth noting in the appraisal report.

Sometimes troublesome easements are evident on the property. Easements in gross, which are typically granted to public utilities to extend service to the real estate, usually do not present a problem. Easements appurtenant can be created by agreement between neighbors or as a result of the subdivision of land. For instance, a lot might be subject to a driveway easement that allows a neighbor to reach his property from the street. If a parcel is landlocked, an easement appurtenant by necessity might be imposed on adjoining property. Prescriptive easements are created without the permission of the owner of the land affected, which is called the *servient estate.* Property owners may be unaware that a neighbor is acquiring an easement through open, notorious, continuous use of a portion of the land for a number of years.

Description of Improvements

In the description of the improvements, all building and improvement data relevant to the appraisal problem are presented and discussed. Although an appraiser considers and processes much data in the course of an appraisal, only significant property characteristics that influence the value conclusion are presented in the report. These characteristics may include

- Actual and effective building age and building size
- Number, size, and mix of units
- Structural and construction details
- Mechanical equipment
- Physical condition
- Functional utility or inutility

Property information may be supported and illustrated with drawings, photographs, floor plans, and elevations. If the description of structural details and mechanical equipment is long, an outline highlighting important components may be used in the body of the report.

The property description should tell the reviewer the basic facts he or she needs to know about the property: ownership, occupancy, leases, easements, zoning and other legal restrictions, size, age, condition, heating and cooling, market appeal, and, if necessary, column spacing, ventilation, or loading facilities. Again, items that affect utility and value are emphasized.

Although most appraisers state in their appraisal reports that they are "not specifically trained or qualified to detect environmental concerns," "no liability is assumed," and "an environmental professional should be retained," it is still helpful for the appraiser to indicate potential problems that were observed during the property inspection. Of specific environmental concern are industrial wastes, storage drums, stained soil, vent pipes, stained floor drains, and hazardous insulation materials. Most lenders routinely order Phase 1 environmental studies of commercial properties before committing to a new real estate loan, but the appraiser's casual observations can help make the client aware of a potentially risky situation. One note of caution is needed, however. Appraisers should be very careful about the wording of their statements to avoid giving the impression that they are acting as environmental professionals.

One common flaw in appraisals is the failure to consider and analyze the value-influencing forces affecting the subject building. What are the primary positive and negative value-influencing factors, and how do they relate to the market value of the property? Reports often contain a detailed description of the minute physical characteristics of the building improvements but little analysis of the positive and negative forces at work. The typical report user does not really think that describing the subflooring as "4-in. concrete slab with 6-in.-by-6-in., 10-gauge wire mesh over vapor barrier on compacted fill" is vital primary data.

Describing the functionality of an older structure can be very important. The layout of a residence, the bay sizes and clear ceiling height of an industrial building, and the vertical circulation of an office building can have a major impact on marketability and property value. Construction quality and current condition should be described in detail.

Consider a condition and functional utility statement such as "The subject was in average overall condition at the time of inspection. Sources of deferred maintenance include typical wear and tear for a facility of its age, use and construction. " This description is so generic that it could apply to any building anywhere. It tells the client nothing of value. Unfortunately, such statements are commonly found in substandard appraisal reports.

The Americans with Disabilities Act of 1990, which became effective as of January 26, 1992, addresses the removal of physical barriers in existing public accommodations. It applies to the alteration of existing public accommodations or commercial facilities as of the effective date and new construction of commercial facilities or places of public accommodation designed for first occupancy after January 26, 1993. Appraisals of existing places of public accommodation, alterations, or new construction conducted after these dates need to address whether or not the requirements of the act could affect the value estimate. The presence of architectural and communication barriers of a structural nature that would restrict access by disabled individuals may adversely affect the property's value, marketability, or utility For more information on this subject, the reviewer is advised to read Guide Note 9 to the Appraisal Institute's Standards of Professional Appraisal Practice.

Zoning

Zoning data can be included in the land description section of the appraisal report or presented in a separate section. Significant zoning and private restrictions should be discussed in detail. The appraiser should provide sufficient data to help the reviewer understand the limitations that zoning regulations place on the use or development of the site. If appropriate, the appraiser may explore the possibility of a zoning change. The reasonable probability of the zoning change is essential and should be thoroughly discussed by the appraiser. Assuming a zoning change without researching and verifying the reasonableness of that assumption is inappropriate.

All existing public and private restrictions such as floodplain regulations, scenic easements, and wetland restrictions should be discussed and their effect on the utility and value of the property should be described.

Taxes and Assessment Data

Current assessed values and ad valorem tax rates should be reported, and a calculation of the current annual tax load of the subject property should be included. Existing assessment trends or prospective changes in tax rates should be analyzed. It may be appropriate to discuss the tax assessment or tax load of the subject property in relation to the taxes on other properties, particularly if the difference is significant.

Clients need clear and concise information, preferably in chart form, regarding current assessed values and tax rates. Separate land and building assessments should be presented. When the appraiser presents the total assessed value, the reader does not always know the component assessments. If the difference between the appraised value and the assessed value is extreme, the appraiser should analyze and discuss the primary reasons for the difference. If the tax millage rate or the assessed values have changed dramatically in recent years, the situation should be discussed in the report along with projected future trends. If the property was recently reassessed, the probable impact of this change should also be discussed and reflected in the projected cash flows.

The tax and assessment presentation that follows omits a considerable amount of information that would be useful to the client.

ASSESSMENT AND REAL ESTATE TAXES

Permanent index numbers:		XXX-XXXXX-XX
		XXX-XXXXX-XX
Taxable value:		$473,270
1996 tax rate:		$7.9897 per $100
1996 real estate taxes:		$18,906.44
Payable in 1997:		
Gross taxes	$18,906.44	
State property tax credit	– 3,066.13	
Net taxes	$15,840.31	

This type of presentation leaves many questions unanswered: How do the taxes compare on a per-unit (square-foot) basis? How does the taxable value relate to the assessor's full 100% value? How is the state property tax credit calculated? Why is it applicable to this property, and will it eventually expire? When was the property last assessed? When will the property be reassessed? Is the assessment level considered fair in comparison to other, similar properties in the area? What trends in assessments and taxes have been observed in the area?

History

USPAP Standards Rules 1-5 (a) and (b) require an appraiser to consider and analyze (a) any current agreement of sale, option, or listing of the property being appraised, if such information is available to the appraiser in the normal course of business, and (b) any prior sales of the property being appraised that occurred within one year for a one- to four-family residential property or three years for all other property types. For income-producing properties, recent changes in the property's operating profile should be considered along with any offers to purchase. Historical property data may include information on

- ✓ Original assemblage
- ✓ Acquisition or construction costs
- ✓ Expenditures for capital additions or modernization
- ✓ Financial data or transfers of ownership
- ✓ Casualty loss experience
- ✓ History and type of occupancy
- ✓ Reputation and prestige or stigma attached to the property
- ✓ Other historical facts that may pertain to or affect the computations, estimates, or conclusions presented in the report

The appraiser should also investigate the previous ownership and use of the property to investigate for possible environmental problems.

It is not sufficient to merely state a transaction sale price. Rather, the report should analyze any prior sales of the subject property in the same way that comparable sales are analyzed in the sales comparison approach. The relationship between an historical sale price and the appraised value is also important, and any value difference between the prior sale and the appraised value should be explored. Advisory Opinion AO-1, issued by the Appraisal Standards Board, offers further clarification of the sales history section of an appraisal report.

Sometimes the history of the property section can "red flag" potential problems in the report. The following excerpt from a report on an apartment complex signaled a major problem in the appraisal:

> According to the public records, title to these two properties were [*sic*] transferred in October 1993 for $1,255,000. Included in this sale was the right to convert the complex into condominium buildings; however, the subject is currently operating as an apartment complex and no conversion is foreseeable in the near future. Therefore, it is the opinion of the appraisers

> that current ownership purchased these properties at a premium in anticipation of condo conversion.

The appraiser's logic was not based on any facts presented in the report. However, in the face of an appreciating market, it was the only plausible explanation for appraising the property for $825,000 two years after the purchase, *for tax appeal purposes.*

Other inconsistencies were found in the property history section that follows:

> The subject property has been under option since February, one year ago. A copy of the option agreement was not available. We understand that the property being acquired consists of the subject eight lots and the adjoining Lot 17 which has a three-story residential building. The reported option price is $950,000 and the purchaser plans to sell Lot 17 for $250,000.

The appraised value was $1,080,000. After determining that the net price for the optioned property was $700,000, it is incumbent on the appraiser to explain the apparent gap of some $380,000 between the option price and the estimated value. There could be very good reasons for the discrepancy: the optioned property was 83% occupied by a one-story, brick industrial building that had to be razed, and the property had to be rezoned by the optionee to develop the vacant site with 24 townhouse-style condominiums. Moreover, the developer was certainly entitled to some compensation for the risk inherent in the venture and the 24 months required from the time the option was negotiated until project completion. Providing a simple explanation can usually avoid unnecessary concern.

Appraisers sometimes overlook a current or pending sale of the subject property, which can often yield valuable market data. For example, if the property is leased, the estimated net operating income and sale price can provide an excellent indication of an overall capitalization rate. Perhaps even a yield rate or equity rate indication can be derived from the data. Many appraisers consult nationwide rate surveys to support their rate derivation, when one of the most reliable rates is the rate indicated by the sale of the subject property.

Marketability Study

In the appraisal of income-producing properties such as office buildings, shopping centers, and apartment buildings, a marketability study may be performed to find out how the subject property fits into the overall market in terms of rent levels and absorption rates. A marketability study is usually directly related to the conclusions presented in the appraisal report. Such a study may examine the specific real estate market or submarket, the supply of existing properties (e.g., inventory of space, construction trends, vacancy patterns, absorption rates), the demand forecast (e.g., projected expansion or shrinkage), the current balance of supply and demand, and competitive rent levels. For example, analysis of job creation and job growth is needed to estimate the demand for apartments.

Environmental Risk and Stigma

The environmental risks that impact real estate are varied and cover a range of substances, events, and land use activities. We may typically associate environmental risk with hazards such as groundwater or soil contamination, but environmental risk can be generated in many other ways as well. For example, property can be adversely affected by air pollution or airborne contaminants in the wind, by pollution of lakes or streams, by contamination of drinking water distribution systems, and even by the noise and vibrations emanating from a busy expressway or airport. An event such as a marine oil spill or the derailment of railroad tank cars carrying chemicals may create temporary environmental risks until cleanup is completed. Certain types of land uses, such as power plants, electrical transmission lines, landfills, waste incinerators, and chemical or radioactive material storage facilities, may be perceived as sources of environmental risk for adjacent and nearby real estate.

The stigma attached to real estate affected by environmental risk is generally defined as "an adverse public perception about a property that is intangible or not directly quantifiable." It is an additional impact on value, over and above the cost of cleanup or remediation. Stigma can affect sites that once contained contaminants and have since been cleaned up, sites undergoing cleanup, and sites that were never contaminated but are near to a property that contains or once contained contaminants.[3]

PART FOUR—ANALYSIS OF DATA AND CONCLUSIONS

Highest and Best Use Analysis

Highest and best use analysis is conducted to determine the subject property's most probable and profitable use. Typically, four criteria—physical possibility, legal permissibility, financial feasibility (market support), and maximum productivity—are discussed in this section. Land use patterns in the area, zoning regulations, and the profitability of existing or proposed improvements should also be discussed. Highest and best use is the fulcrum of the appraisal process since a property cannot be valued until a use is concluded.

In highest and best use analysis, the appraiser should bring together the subject property's physical, legal, and locational attributes (intrinsic analysis) and match them with property uses that create value within the market area (extrinsic analysis). Two separate determinations are made: highest and best use of the land as though vacant and highest and best use of the property as improved.

First, the appraiser considers the highest and best use of the land as though vacant and available for development to its highest and best use. The use on which the appraiser based the value estimate of the land as though vacant should be clearly stated in the report. The character and amount of data presented and analyzed in this section will be dictated by the purpose of the appraisal.

To determine the highest and best use of the property as improved, the appraiser discusses whether or not the removal and replacement of the existing improvements are economically warranted on the date of the appraisal. If the existing improvements are to be retained, the highest and best use determination is based on how the entire property should be used to maximize its benefits or the income it produces. An appraiser may suggest a possible course of action such as rehabilitation, improved maintenance, or better property management.

3. Appraisal Institute, Environmental Risk and the Real Estate Appraisal Process seminar workbook, Chapter 1 (Chicago: Appraisal Institute, 1994), 128.

It is imperative that the appraiser not violate the theory of consistent use and that the two kinds of highest and best use not be confused in an appraisal. According to the theory of consistent use, a site cannot be valued on the basis of one use while the improvements are valued on the basis of another. A site value estimate based on the site's highest and best use as though vacant may not be added to the value estimate of an improvement based on the highest and best use of the property as improved. The appraiser cannot choose the "best of both worlds" in arriving at a value indication.

There are two special situations in highest and best use analysis that commonly cause problems for appraisers—interim uses and legal nonconforming uses. The appraiser must recognize these situations and be prepared to deal with the special problems they create. An interim use is indicated when the highest and best use of the site as though vacant or of the property as improved for the near future differs from the highest and best use expected over a longer term. The short-term highest and best use is an interim use, which is warranted until the long-term highest and best use can be realized. The appraiser must analyze how long the interim use will last, what financial risks and rewards are associated with conversion to the long-term highest and best use, and what benefits or costs the interim use will contribute to the value of the site or improved property.

Legal nonconforming uses can also be problematic. These uses are usually created by the imposition of zoning or a change in zoning regulations after the original construction of the improvements. After a zoning change, a structure may be an underimprovement of the site. In this case, the nonconforming use would probably be maintained as an interim use until the existing improvement has depreciated enough to make conversion to the long-term highest and best use feasible. A zoning change can also transform a structure into an overimprovement of the site. In this case continuation of the existing use is permitted, but expansion or major alteration of the structure is not. Some municipalities also restrict the right to rebuild in the event of significant structural damage due to fire, storm, or natural disaster. In situations in which an overimprovement is created, an intangible bonus value attributable to the nonconforming use may be created.

Site Value

In the site value section of an appraisal report, market data are presented along with an analysis of the data and reasoning that lead to the land value estimate. The factors that influence land value should be presented in a clear and precise manner and the narrative should lead the reviewer to the land value estimate.

Approaches to Value

The appraiser develops the approaches applicable to the appraisal assignment and derives indications of value. For each approach applied, factual data and the analysis and reasoning leading to the value indication are presented.

Many intended users of appraisal reports are not familiar with the mechanics of the three approaches to value, so the appraiser briefly explains the procedures applied in each. The extent of explanation required depends on the circumstances. Simple statements that describe what is included in each of the three approaches can help the reviewer understand the report. It is important that the appraiser follow all of the procedural steps outlined for each approach. Reviewers and clients are often baffled when the methodology actually used in the appraisal does not follow the procedures described in the explanatory comments.

The three approaches are seldom completely independent of one another. An appraisal consists of a number of integrated, inseparable procedures with a common objective—a convincing, reliable estimate of value.

At a minimum, the following information should be contained in the valuation approaches:

- The cost approach should include an explanation of why and how the approach is applied with brief discussions of highest and best use, land value, the cost and depreciation concepts employed, and the basis of the appraiser's cost and depreciation estimates. If the cost approach is omitted, the appraiser should briefly explain why it is inapplicable.
- The presentation of the sales comparison approach should include current data, including offerings, in sufficient detail for the reviewer to judge the validity of the appraiser's ratings and comparisons. If necessary, the report should explain the insufficiency of the data or the inapplicability of the approach.
- The income capitalization approach should be explained in the simplest possible terms, with a description of data sources and methodology, a highlighted summary of the assumptions used with appropriate explanations, information supporting any estimates of current and future income and expenses, and evidence to support the capitalization and discount rates selected. If discounted cash flow analysis is used, printouts and a copy of the diskette should be provided.

The property's market position should also be discussed. The client deserves a careful analysis of the position of the property in its geographical and investment marketplaces. How desirable is it? How does it compare to the competition? Where is the property's natural market, and what is its condition? How easily can it be sold or leased, and how can it best be marketed? How well is the real estate doing in comparison with other investments? What will happen in years to come? Should anything be done to protect or enhance the property's value?

Data analysis should be presented in a logical order so that the reader can understand the reasoning that leads to the conclusion. Some reviewers refer to this as "leaving footprints." Clients may find the report unacceptable if the appraiser simply offers a mass of data and states that, based on an analysis of these data, a given value has been estimated for the subject property.

Deficiencies common to each approach are described in the following sections, which discuss the presentation of the approaches to value in an appraisal report.

The Cost Approach

The cost approach has severe limitations and is generally not used as a primary value indicator by market participants. It can be applied in estimating the market value of new or relatively new property if the site value is well-supported, the improvements suffer only minor accrued depreciation, and they represent a use that approximates the highest and best use of the site as though vacant. It also is useful in estimating the market value of proposed construction, special-purpose real estate, and other properties that are not frequently exchanged in the market. It is particularly useful in eminent domain cases that require estimates of direct damages as a result of partial takings.

The cost approach is emphasized when a lack of market activity limits the usefulness of the sales comparison approach and the subject property cannot be valued by the income capitalization approach. However, when improvements are older or do not represent the highest and best use of the site as though vacant, the cost approach has limited applicability. Value estimates derived by the cost approach that are not supported by market data must be regarded with caution.

Most real estate appraisers are not well versed in building techniques or particularly knowledgeable about different construction materials and their fluctuating costs. Most are not qualified to be quantity cost estimators. Therefore, appraisers consult construction cost service manuals for basic unit cost figures, which are then adjusted with a local cost modifier to reflect local building and labor costs. Use of such manuals can further complicate the cost approach and increase potential errors because the reproduction costs provided may not reflect the subject property. The unique features of many buildings and the general character of cost manuals make obtaining a true reproduction cost from such services extremely difficult. In addition, many appraisers fail to adjust the basic costs given for architectural and engineering fees, general and overhead costs, property taxes, marketing expenses, and mortgage loan interest during construction.

On the positive side, use of the cost approach often results in a more thorough inspection of the subject property by the appraiser. A thorough knowledge of the physical attributes of the subject property can help the appraiser make better comparisons in the sales comparison approach and assist in measuring income productivity and actual expenses in the income capitalization approach.

Some problems commonly associated with application of the cost approach are described below:

- Misapplication of the comparative-unit method. The apparent simplicity of the comparative-unit method can be misleading. To develop dependable unit cost figures, the appraiser must carefully compare the subject building with similar or standard structures for which actual costs are known. Errors may result if the appraiser selects a unit cost that is not appropriate to the building being appraised.
- "Doubling up" depreciation estimates. Regardless of the depreciation method applied, the appraiser must ensure that the final estimate of accrued depreciation reflects the loss in value from all causes and that no cause of depreciation has been considered more than once. Double charges for depreciation may produce value indications that are too low. Both the economic age-life method and the breakdown method provide estimates of the cost to cure curable items of depreciation, which should be recognized in the application of the other approaches. This is typically accomplished in the sales comparison and income capitalization approaches by deducting the cost to cure at the conclusion of the approach.
- Confusion or misunderstandings concerning entrepreneurial profit. Reproduction and replacement cost estimates each contain direct and indirect costs and entrepre-

neurial profit. Many appraisers confuse entrepreneurial profit with contractor's overhead and profit, which is considered a direct cost of building construction. Entrepreneurial incentive (also referred to as *developer's profit*) is the owner's expected reward for the time, energy, and effort expended to produce the property. It is the amount someone would pay over and above the value of the property to acquire it in a limited market. To the developer, entrepreneurial incentive is the expected profit over the cost of the improvements and the investment in the land. It can be measured in many ways, however, and the appraiser must be certain to measure it as it is measured in the subject property's market.

- Using a "back-door" approach in developing the cost approach analysis. An appraiser should not arrive at an estimate of total accrued depreciation by deducting the indication of property value (less land value) obtained in the sales comparison or income approach from the replacement or reproduction cost estimate. An independent cost approach analysis should be developed.
- Mistakenly using the terms *economic life* and *physical life* interchangeably. In the breakdown method of estimating depreciation, physical life must be used, not economic life. Economic life is used when the appraiser is able to measure all forms of depreciation—physical, functional, and external. The shorter economic life of the property should not be used in the physical deterioration step of the breakdown method.
- Use of physical age-life tables provided by cost services as part of the breakdown method. The tables measure the lives of buildings that are either torn down and replaced or are so substantially remodeled that they reflect the end of the economic life and not the end of the physical life of the building.
- Inappropriate treatment of superadequacies. To estimate the reproduction cost of a structure, an appraiser often has to consider the superadequacies that may exist in the building. Texts generally show a portion of the cost of the building's superadequacy taken out in physical curable and physical incurable deterioration, with the non-physically depreciated portion remaining. The cost of the superadequacy less the depreciation already charged must then be deducted under functional obsolescence. Instead, the superadequacy should be the first item subtracted from the reproduction cost of the building improvement. This procedure recognizes the additional cost in the building. The resulting figure is the replacement cost new, assuming the same footprint, from which the physical deterioration (curable and incurable), functional obsolescence (curable and incurable), and external obsolescence, if any, can be subtracted to produce a value indication. This process clearly shows the reviewer or user of the report what is superadequate or not accepted by the market, which should be explained in the highest and best use section of the report. In addition, this process lays out, line by line, the deductions from cost new made to derive value. The appraiser should also acknowledge superadequate items when deriving adjustments in the sales comparison approach and in the income capitalization approach.

Land comparable problems. Another problematic part of the cost approach is the selection of land sales used to estimate land value. The use of comparables that vary significantly in size may lead to an inaccurate valuation. A party interested in a particular land use generally does not consider parcels of different sizes as viable alternatives, even though they may be in the same vicinity and have the same zoning classification. For example, a service station site developer would not consider a 100-acre regional shopping center site an equivalent or comparable site. Of course, there is a range of site sizes within each of the various land submarkets, and buyers and sellers would view parcels of slightly different sizes as reasonable substitutes. Parcels that fall outside of these size ranges, however, would not be considered comparable by investors and should not be considered by real estate appraisers.

In his studies of size comparability, James Boykin states:

> Generally, the use of larger-size comparables understates the value of a smaller subject property. Smaller-size comparables, on the other hand, tend to overstate the value of a larger appraised property. Moreover, the amount of size adjustment between markedly different-size parcels becomes problematic, and the reliability of such adjustments is also questionable.[4]

More accurate valuations may be expected when the appraiser uses comparable land sales that are approximately the same size as the subject property.

Another crucial determinant of whether or not a particular land sale is, in fact, a comparable is whether it has the same highest and best use as the appraised parcel. If not, then it is probably not a valid comparable sale. A parcel may be nearby and have similar zoning, terrain, and access features, but because of a difference in size, it may have a different highest and best use and unit value.

The economic conditions in place at the time of sale is another element of comparability. All too often an appraiser will state that the highest and best use as though vacant is to hold the property for three to five years before developing it and then use sales that were transacted in good economic times as comparables. Because these sales reflect a land value today that the potential buyer will not realize for three to five years, discounting must be considered.

The Sales Comparison Approach

The sales comparison approach is a powerful tool that appraisers apply in many situations with a variety of qualitative and quantitative techniques. The approach derives its usefulness and analytic power from several factors. It is a direct application of the principle of substitution. It is simple, makes use of observable market data, and has wide applicability; clients find the approach persuasive because the reasoning is easy to follow. The sales comparison approach does, however, have some important limitations. A conclusion derived from comparable sales is only as reliable as the data that support it. If the only recent sales are of properties that differ substantially from the subject, the prices of these comparables will be subject to major adjustments and the reliability of the conclusion may be questionable. When the

4. James H. Boykin, MAI, SRA, PhD, "Impropriety of Using Dissimilar-Size Comparable Land Sales," *The Appraisal Journal* (July 1996).

approach is applied in markets with few recent sales, the appraiser must proceed with extreme caution and pay careful attention to all factors that could affect current market conditions.

Some common problems found in the sales comparison approach are described below:

- Failure to use the unit of comparison that the market uses. The market unit of comparison can be described as the market's basis for purchase and sale decisions, the object the market uses to make mental comparisons, and the unit that produces the most consistent pattern of value in the analysis. A property type may have more than one market unit of comparison. In such cases, it is best to make comparisons and adjustments for each unit and reconcile them within the approach.
- Not bracketing a value range for the subject property through the use of comparables. Ideally, the approach should include meaningful comparable sales that are obviously inferior to the subject as well as sales that are obviously superior. If sufficient sales cannot be found, it may be necessary to expand the geographic and temporal limits of the search for sales. Listings and contract offers can also provide insight and bracketing benchmarks.
- Use of comparable sales and rentals that are old, incompletely reported, poorly analyzed, inaccurately summarized, or not truly comparable. A sale with a highest and best use different from the subject's does not meet the basic definition of a comparable sale, which is a property that the market would view as competitive with the subject. No adjustment or narrative explanation can reconcile two properties that have different highest and best uses.
- Use of properties that have dramatically different tenancy profiles as comparables. For example, a multitenant, 100,000-sq.-ft. warehouse would not be a suitable comparable in the appraisal of a single-tenant, 100,000-sq.-ft. warehouse. Properties of different sizes appeal to different buyer-seller profiles, so 20,000- to 40,000-sq.-ft. industrial buildings are not comparable to a 150,000-sq.-ft. facility.
- Merely stating comparable sale prices with no additional facts or analysis. Inclusion of the date of sale, the grantor, the grantee, the transaction sale price, the cash equivalent sale price, the terms of sale, the conditions of sale, the units of comparison, and the occupancy at the time of sale is critical to the analysis. Of course, all these data should be confirmed.
- Lumping value-influencing differences together. When adjustments are made in a comparative analysis, they should not be aggregated. Doing so prevents the reviewer or user of the report from checking the comparative analyses for consistency or contradiction, thus rendering all the adjustments suspect. A major error often encountered is lumping together several inequalities into a single dollar or percentage adjustment. When inequalities are considered offsetting, they must not be lumped together in a manner that hides the relative importance of each item. The reviewer must be able to assess the relative significance of each difference that influences value in the market.
- Contradictions in the comparative analysis. Most of the errors in reasoning that reviewers and clients find in appraisals are contradictions. Contradictions are

usually omissions, such as failing to adjust a sale for the same difference by the same amount or in the same direction as another sale. Contradictions can also appear in narrative sections. For example, an appraiser may describe a difference as important and then downplay or even omit its value impact in the correlation or value indication.

- Failure to clarify which adjustments are "supported" and which are "unsupported." "Supported" adjustments are derived using classical methods such as consultation with a professional, use of a published source, application of the matched pairs technique, capitalization of rent differences, or direct comparison. "Unsupported" adjustments based on the appraiser's judgment are certainly allowable as long as they are consistent and small in size and number. Unsupported adjustments are usually preceded by the phrase, "in my opinion," and offer the appraiser's rationale. Professional opinion can be a very appropriate part of comparative analysis.

If the subject property is being sold or a sale is pending, it is incumbent upon the appraiser to investigate all terms and conditions of the sale, just as he or she would research the terms and conditions of other comparable market data. Sometimes appraisers overlook these data and fail to ask the client or the seller or broker key questions concerning the transaction. As mentioned previously, arm's-length transactions concerning the subject property can often provide the most valuable and reliable market indications available to the appraiser.

The sales comparison approach can produce the most persuasive indication of value, but the approach can also be manipulated in a most insidious manner. The source of errors is usually the selection of comparable sales. At the heart of the direct sales comparison technique is the requirement that the physical features of comparable sales and the appraised property be similar. By isolating dissimilarities in size, location, quality, physical condition, occupancy (multitenant versus single-tenant, owner-user versus tenant occupancy-investor owned), and motivation (sweat-equity versus pure investment-grade), the appraiser can bracket the likely value. The appraiser's experience and knowledge are of great value in the comparison process. However, the process of estimating value by comparison can also be "steered" by an unethical appraiser.

For example, the following comparable sales were analyzed in the appraisal of a one-story supermarket building of 15,500 square feet built in 1955 on a 50,000-sq.-ft. site:

- Sale 1 – a 16,000-sq.-ft., 10-tenant retail center built in 1965.
- Sale 2 – a 7,900-sq.-ft. store building built in 1949, which has been extensively renovated into a medical office facility.
- Sale 3 – a 6,500-sq.-ft. store building built in 1958. This sale was dissimilar, and the appraiser provided the following sale information, which cast further doubt on use of the sale as a comparable: "Reportedly, the sale price was established in 1992 (five years prior to the appraisal) by a purchase option included in a lease. The property is now bank-owned, after being deeded to the lender in lieu of foreclosure. The lender/owner then agreed to abide by the purchase option contained within the original lease agreement. The sale took several years to close due to an environmental clean-up, which was paid for by the seller."

- Sale 4 – a 15,300-sq.-ft., single-tenant store building built in 1976.
- Sale 5 – a 23,000-sq.-ft., single-tenant store building built in 1966, which was sold three years prior to the appraisal date.
- Sale 6 – a 9,000-sq.-ft., single-tenant store building built in 1953 on an 18,000-sq.-ft. site. This three-year-old sale was seller-financed.
- Sale 7 – a 20,000-sq.-ft. commercial building built in 1972 as a furniture store and subsequently renovated into multitenant office use.

After analyzing the above sales, the reviewer would be hard-pressed to agree with the value indication derived by direct sales comparison. This is a not an example of an appraiser doing an unethical job, although some might argue that point; rather, the appraiser has performed incompetently and done a disservice to his or her client.

Even when bona fide comparable sales do exist and are used, appraisers who seek to "steer" values can adjust them to achieve a desired result. Adjustments for time or market conditions can be exaggerated and quality adjustments can be manipulated. Location is a prime target for erroneous adjustments. The reviewer must recognize what are reasonable adjustments for specific property types. This knowledge is developed through experience and a conscientious effort to read each appraisal as thoroughly as possible. Good reviewers take the time to contemplate the logic and reasoning presented in an appraisal report.

Income Capitalization Approach

Every appraiser is taught early in his or her career that a value estimate represents the present worth of the future benefits a buyer anticipates receiving from the ownership of real estate. The idea that a purchaser's pricing decision is based on perceptions of the future is so important that it is embodied in the principle of anticipation, which is one of the central tenets of valuation practice.

Appraisers must be able to prove their rates of conversion, whether they are capitalization rates or yield rates, and should know the many ways to prove or disprove a rate selection. All too often appraisers are comfortable using only one method to create or prove a capitalization rate in their appraisal assignments; many do not know how to check or prove the rate with other methods. It is imperative that the appraiser look at all the ways an overall capitalization rate can be developed and use all the data available in the market to develop and test overall rates for every income valuation problem.

When the appraiser relies on a band-of-investment technique using mortgage and equity components to "prove" a rate, the lender-client should carefully scrutinize the mortgage terms independently to determine if they are reasonable in light of current mortgage market conditions. Often the rates used to build up capitalization rates are dated and do not reflect current terms and conditions. Additionally, the reviewer should ask: Does the equity return appear reasonable in comparison to the returns available from other investment opportunities in current equity markets? Too often, this section is used repeatedly without conscientious updating by the appraiser.

Another pertinent question to ask is: Which income capitalization technique is most appropriate, direct or yield capitalization? There are many commercial properties that should be valued by direct capitalization. Discounted cash flow (DCF) analysis may be the only way to value investment-grade real estate, but for the bulk of smaller, noninvestment-grade real estate, direct capitalization simulates the decision-making process of buyers and sellers in the market.

Some common problems in the application of the income capitalization approach are

- Oversimplification of the methodology used. The valuation of income property is a difficult and complex undertaking, and there is no easy and consistently accurate way to do it. A choice has to be made. Selecting a valuation method simply because it is easy to apply is a common mistake. Oversimplification is an easy trap to fall into because simple methods seem to require fewer assumptions and users reason that the results produced must be correct because the data required are available in the market. These appraisers are unaware that simple valuation methods are based on as many assumptions as more complex methods. Users of simple methods forget that these methods involve many hidden assumptions. Hidden assumptions are easily overlooked because there seems to be no need to address them directly.

  Some appraisers mistakenly believe that a gross rent multiplier (*GRM*) developed from one type of property can be universally applied to all properties. Multipliers developed from one market may not be applicable to similar properties in a different location. Serious errors can result when data derived from a simple method are indiscriminately applied to a broad range of valuation problems. The direct capitalization method is often selected because it seems to obviate forecasting property income and expenses over an extended period. Because it is much easier to establish the market rent for a property today, the resulting value estimate is presumed to be more accurate than one based on the property's future cash flows. Users of direct capitalization often forget that the technique is simply a shortcut for discounted cash flow analysis. Although the method does not require a forecast of future income and expenses, the overall rate includes assumptions about how a property's income is expected to change over time. This fact is effectively hidden with a capitalization rate that is a single number. Direct capitalization appears to be a simplistic approach because the complicated mathematics underlying the overall rate can be easily disguised.

- Abuse of statistical techniques. Some appraisers overwhelm the client with technical jargon in describing statistical distributions (e.g., linearity, nonlinearity, multicollinearity, heteroskedasticity) and variance (e.g., ordinary least squares fit, standard error, statistical coefficients). Reliance on statistics is often inappropriate. Rarely do the comparable data lend themselves to meaningful statistical analysis. The most common misuse of statistics is developing a multiple regression analysis without a statistically significant sampling.

- Use of complex mathematical calculations such as iterative models, circular reference valuations, and simultaneous valuations, which are not widely understood and cannot be recalculated by the typical client or reviewer. Complex methods and techniques should not be used unless they can be explained in elementary terms and used in conjunction with traditional valuation models. More importantly, they should not be used unless they simulate the thinking of market participants.

Appraisers can avoid erroneous results by recognizing that the sophistication of the technique applied does not necessarily improve the accuracy of the answer. Complex formulations have their weaknesses and disadvantages. Formulas have weak points where errors originate because they call for data inputs that are difficult to support or relationships that are poorly understood. For this reason the sensitivity of a forecast to minor changes in assumptions should always be scrutinized. Complicated methods can obscure the fact that a cash flow forecast does not match the most likely pattern of income and expenses.

- Misuse of gross rent multipliers (*GRMs*). Gross rent multipliers are often used by appraisers because of their simplicity. Most comparable sales reflect effective gross income multipliers (*EGIMs*)—i.e., the gross income amount net of projected losses from vacancy and collections—not potential gross income multipliers (*PGIMs*), which represent 100% of potential gross income. Rent multipliers are easy to derive and apply in an appraisal and require very little data. The appraiser need only find a few sales for which sale prices and gross rental information are known. When using *GRMs*, it is vital that the appraiser derive them from properties that are physically comparable and economically competitive with the property being appraised. The importance of these selection criteria often escapes an inexperienced analyst. When selected data have no relevance to the problem at hand, the result is often a serious valuation error.
- Developing a net income multiplier. This all-too-common practice is misleading and redundant. Applying a net income multiplier is simply the inverse of direct capitalization. It is highly suspicious when the appraiser uses a "smoke and mirrors" effect, showing two methods (which are actually the same) to prove an argument.
- Confusion over the distinction between overall capitalization rates and yield or discount rates. A discount rate is used to convert a specified future income stream for a given period, plus terminal or reversionary value, into present value. It is equivalent to a yield rate or internal rate of return. An overall capitalization rate, on the other hand, is computed by dividing the net operating income of a recently sold comparable by its sale price. Although the terms are not synonymous, a definite relationship exists between the overall capitalization rate, the discount rate, and the compound change in value and/or income over the projected holding period of the investment. Simply put, the discount rate is the sum of the overall capitalization rate and the compound rate of change in value during the holding period. If there is no change in property value over the holding period, the yield rate equals the overall capitalization rate. Therefore, once the compound rate of change in value has been measured, any change in the yield (discount) rate must also be reflected in the overall capitalization rate. ($Y_O = R_O + CR$—exponential rate change formula)
- Misleading rate derivation from non-real estate sources. One or more factors are often overlooked by analysts when they extract yield rates from non-real estate sources for use in real estate valuation. These factors include risk differences among yield sources, the impact of taxes, and the recovery of capital. When capitalization

rates are extracted directly from real estate market data, the rates represent investor expectations concerning risk, income growth, and income change and are therefore valid predictors of investor price behavior.

- Failure to analyze the relative "risk rating" of the subject property. As with all financial investments, an investment risk is associated with buying real estate. Each property generally has a different risk level based on its physical characteristics, location, lease structure, and other factors. Estimating the investment risk in real estate can be difficult. Appraisal reports on investment-grade properties typically identify, analyze, and summarize the yields on alternative investments such as money market and capital market instruments before the selection of the capitalization rate for the subject property is presented. The user of the appraisal needs to know the primary investment risks associated with purchasing the subject property and how risky this purchase is in relation to the purchase of competitive properties.
- Ignoring the actual condition of relevant mortgage and credit markets. Too many appraisers assume the availability of mortgage funds and rely on outdated interest and discount rate reports quoted in quarterly publications. Appraisers should keep abreast of current trends by networking with informed market participants and reading daily newspapers.
- Assuming the soundness of property leases and the likelihood that they will be honored. When tenants go broke due to bad times or bad markets, they seek to renegotiate the terms of their leases or find ways to terminate them. Brokers and leasing agents who represent tenants exclusively have created a new market niche. Appraisal reports that fail to discuss the possibility of leasing problems are seriously incomplete.
- Erroneously assuming that a cycle or trend will persist indefinitely. Such assumptions can bias a forecast, and the problem will be magnified if the real cause of the cycle or trend is not properly understood.
- Absence of a professionally prepared rent roll summary in chart form as well as a separate, titled section for the analysis of rents. The characteristics of the rent roll should be analyzed and discussed to answer relevant questions such as: What is the average rent per square foot? What is the typical lease term? How are expenses to be divided? What rental rate per square foot is indicated by the most recent leases? Is there any rental discount for large-space users? How will lease rollovers affect the valuation? How does the subject rent roll relate to the rental characteristics of competitive properties? Are rent concessions granted? What is the nature of the tenant's business? What is the tenant profile for the subject property? Most importantly, the appraiser must assess the quantity, quality, and durability of the income stream and discuss how these characteristics relate to the capitalization rate selected. Like the rent roll analysis, the expense and vacancy analysis should be detailed and thorough.
- Unexplained inconsistencies between a property's historical or actual operating income and expenses and those projected by the appraiser in the report. There can

be legitimate reasons for differences between actual and projected figures (e.g., change in management or ownership, rehabilitation, systemization), but the rationale must be explained in the report.

- Inadequate analysis of existing leases or too much reliance on externally prepared abstracts of leases. An appraiser may fail to read a representative sampling of primary leases or fail to exercise due diligence in considering lease terms. Within the scope of the appraisal section, the appraiser may want to describe the exact number of leases read in detail and the amount of reliance placed on lease briefs or abstracts prepared by others. If actual leases are not made available to the appraiser, he or she should insist on receiving a rent roll that is signed and certified to be accurate by the building manager.
- Failure to consider the quantity, quality, and durability of the economic benefits created by the leases. Readers of the report may ask: What is the term of the lease? What is the likelihood that the tenant will be able to meet all the rental payments on time? Are rents to be paid in a form other than cash—e.g., in the form of services to be provided by the tenant? Are the various stipulations in the lease typical of the market, or do they create special advantages or disadvantages for one of the parties? Is the leased fee interest or the leasehold interest transferable, or does the lease prohibit transfer? Is the lease written in a manner that will accommodate reasonable change over time, or may it eventually become cumbersome to the parties involved? What obligations are specified in the lease for the owner of the leased fee?
- An assumption that each of the estates created by a lease has a market value.
- Errors in the data input into computer software—e.g., electronic spreadsheets and programs for lease-by-lease analysis. Keystroke errors and incorrect formulas can distort value conclusions.
- Unrealistic cash flow projections in the operating statement. It is unrealistic to base cash flows on perfectly regular growth in rental income over the projection term, a declining expense ratio that runs contrary to actual experience, or an assumption that expenses can be fully recovered from the tenants with no operating costs paid by the owner. It is also improper to omit line items such as capital expenses or replacement reserves and to fail to recognize local variations in revenues and expenses.
- Failure to indicate whether gross rents or net rents were derived from the analysis of comparable rental properties.
- Using property data from ground-leased property and investment property owned in fee simple interchangeably. The data are not comparable because ground-leased property landlords have no management responsibility, no maintenance costs, and no market risk, given a typical long-term, triple-net ground lease. In terms of risk, a ground lease is often much like a bank certificate of deposit or a corporate bond.
- Failure to read ground leases thoroughly. The appraiser must know about any inflation-adjustment clauses, reappraisal clauses (which bring the ground rent back

to market levels), subordination clauses (which make it easier for a lessee to finance a project on the ground-leased parcel), and the lease term (generally a longer term is more favorable to the lessee).

- Assuming the rentability or re-rentability of tenant space in a deteriorating local economy. How long it takes to rent a vacant space can be vitally important to the economics of a property. Is the space rentable at all? If so, for how much and on what terms? What will happen when existing leases expire or the tenants vacate?
- Failure to justify the use of a particular overall capitalization rate or discount rate. It is extremely difficult to obtain a discount rate, or any other return rate such as an overall capitalization rate or equity yield rate, from most investors. Relatively few investors actually know the return rates on their real estate investments. Even if they do, their quoted rates are only estimates until the properties have actually been sold. Overall capitalization rates are generally easier to estimate than yield rates. Appraisers typically arrive at a capitalization rate extracted from market sales and supplemented by current financial market information. The discount rate can be approximated as the sum of the estimated capitalization rate plus the annual compound growth in value. It is all too common to come across projections in which the appraiser claims to have observed market capitalization rates of 10% and growth rates of 3.5% per annum and then blithely discounts the cash flow to present value at 11%. This combination will produce a significantly overstated estimate of value.

DILBERT reprinted by permission of United Feature Syndicate, Inc.

- Inconsistencies in calculating net operating income (*NOI*) and overall capitalization rate (*OAR*). John Francis points out that *NOI* and the *OAR* do not have precise, universal meanings among real estate professionals, not even among appraisers. Therefore, great care must be taken to ensure that these terms are used consistently. Francis explains that for every way of calculating *NOI*, there is a corollary and related way of developing the *OAR*.[5] Reviewers must also be careful to ensure that there is consistency between the development of *NOI* for an appraised property and the development of the *OAR* at which it was capitalized. He describes three methods:

5. John M. Francis, MAI, "The Elusive Definitions of *NOI* and *OAR*," *The Appraisal Journal* (January 1998): 56-61.

Method 1: *NOI* after capital replacement reserve deduction but before tenant improvements (TIs) and leasing commissions. (The tenant improvements made to a property in preparation for a new tenant are also known as *buildout and fit-up*.)

Method 2: *NOI* before capital replacement reserve deduction, TIs, and leasing commissions.

Method 3: Cash flow after capital replacement reserve deduction, TIs, and leasing commissions.

For example, the representative income and expenses for a suburban office building are shown as follows:

Potential rent		$21.00
Vacancy allowance ($21.00 x 8%)		– 1.68
Stabilized rent		$19.32
Total operating expenses	$6.56	
Fixed expenses	+ 2.51	
Total operating and fixed expenses		– 9.07
NOI (Method 2)		$10.25
Reserve for replacements		– 0.25
NOI (Method 1)		$10.00
Leasing costs		– 2.12
NOI (Method 3)		$ 7.88

If this building sold for $95.00 per rentable square foot, the capitalization rates derived using Method 1 would be 10.53%; using Method 2, 10.79%; and using Method 3, 8.29%.

An appraiser can get back to the actual selling price ($95.00 per square foot) by dividing any of the three *NOI*s by its related cap rate (e.g., using Method 2 figures, $10.25/10.79%). But it is not possible to get the same result by dividing the *NOI* found using Method 1 by the cap rate derived using Method 2. Similarly, in actual practice an appraiser will not arrive at a meaningful appraised value if an income figure derived using Method 3 is capitalized by a cap rate derived using Method 2. Consistency of definitions between *NOI* and the cap rate is crucial.

- Using a terminal capitalization rate that is lower or equal to the "going-in" capitalization rate. Most investors project a slightly higher terminal capitalization rate for resale value estimation. The theory behind this decision is that, all else being equal, an investor will pay less for an older building with a shorter remaining economic life than for a new building. In addition, the increment of risk associated with the uncertainty of future market conditions is reflected in a higher terminal capitalization rate. Furthermore, investors usually deduct costs associated with a sale at the end of the holding period to estimate net reversion. There is some justification for projecting a lower terminal rate: contract lease terms may be favorable to the lessor's interest, or extraordinarily strong market trends may indicate significant future value appreciation for the property. In these cases, providing the appraiser's rationale and justification in the report is an absolute necessity.

- Failure to cross-check a value indication obtained through computer analysis with an indication obtained directly from the cost or sales comparison approach. Tests of reasonableness must continually be applied to detect errors in the data input as well as errors lurking in the program. Mathematical solutions to problems take on a special legitimacy when they have been derived by a computer. A computer's unerring ability to manipulate numbers is widely respected, and a mathematical solution to a problem is often perceived as preferable to one derived by nonquantitative means. The use of mathematical formulas adds to the confidence placed in a solution; answers based on judgment, unfortunately, are not accorded the same respect.
- Inconsistencies in the reported data and inconsistencies between the analyses and conclusions. The appraiser must recognize the interdependency of the three approaches. The appraisal process comprises a variety of interrelated and inseparable procedures directed at a common objective—a reliable and convincing value estimate.
- Failure to keep current with changing market conditions, transaction data, and market behavior.
- Reluctance to make forecasts. Some appraisers believe that because the future is unpredictable, only historical data should be used to develop a value estimate. It is their position that the use of forecasts results in speculative value estimates and that value estimates should be based only on an analysis of recent sales, recent costs, and current income. One of the most pervasive fears among appraisers is that they might be held accountable if their forecasts turn out to be wrong. As comforting as historical data may be, experience has shown that its use does not eliminate valuation errors. Rents may fall when they were originally expected to rise or tax laws may change overnight. Reliance on historical data does little to mitigate the effects of unanticipated events. Rather, appraisers should seek to minimize forecasting errors to improve the accuracy of their appraisals. This goal is achievable if appraisers accept the fact that unexplained events are best understood if they are studied using a rigorous, systematic approach. Valuation errors can be minimized by identifying and quantifying potential sources of forecasting errors and by limiting the duration of a forecast to the shortest possible period.
- Inadequate analysis of the profile of potential tenants or buyers. Such analysis is particularly important in the appraisal of complex projects and projects proposed for construction or rehabilitation.
- Failure to estimate the available supply (i.e., the total amount of unoccupied square footage in the specific property market), which provides the basis for forecasting market absorption. The subject space should be included in the analysis of market share.
- Not recognizing the availability or lack of willing sellers and actual buyers with access to funds. Many reports make the tacit assumption that the local market is alive even when it is clearly dead, or that an unsalable property will somehow find a

buyer. During the early 1990s, the market showed a standoff between sellers unwilling to accept deep discounts and buyers unable to finance their purchases on acceptable terms. Older sales that reflected more favorable market conditions were irrelevant.

- The use of obsolete valuation techniques, which are probably unknown to the market participants whose actions they purportedly simulate. Valuation methods that do not accurately match the behavior of market participants will not produce acceptable results even if accurate market data are used. Misuse of the Ellwood technique is a common example.

Discounted cash flow (DCF) analysis is often the analytical technique of choice when investment-grade, income-producing properties are appraised. Many appraisers, however, are using a "generic" analytical process in terms of the length of projection periods, the reversion calculations, and their approach to discounting in general. Data collection is only part of the analysis. Also to be considered are the projection period, the selection of an appropriate capitalization rate for the reversion, the application of appropriate methods for rate selection, and the recognition of risk as it applies to the discount rate as opposed to the capitalization rate.

Common flaws in DCF analysis include

- Arbitrary choice of a 10-year projection period without considering the property type, the phase in the property's economic life, or market factors. Other important considerations in selecting a projection period are the expiration dates of significant leases, significant step-ups or step-downs in lease rates, and other tenant options.
- Use of a monthly discount rate. This practice is erroneous and misleading because it results in an artificially high value indication. The discount rate chosen from the market must be applied to cash flows in the same manner as it was extracted. A discount rate reported by market participants as annual must be applied to annual cash flows.
- Not employing the same forecasting procedures applied by investors who use DCF analysis in their decision making.

Reconciliation of Value Indications

The reconciliation of value indications should lead the reader logically to the final estimate of value. During the reconciliation process the appraiser examines the differences in the analyses and conclusions derived in the various approaches and resolves any inconsistencies. Also, the logic employed throughout the valuation process is scrutinized. The appraiser should employ the amount of data that market participants would consider appropriate to solve the appraisal problem. The data should be applied consistently in each approach that is relevant to the problem. When precise market information is not available, the appraiser must support conclusions with an explanation of the reasoning and judgment applied to derive them.

Reviewers note that the most common deficiency in the reconciliation section is the use of meaningless boilerplate, but no real rationale for reconciling—i.e., explaining the differences for and reliance on the value indications from each approach in arriving at the final value conclusion. The conclusion should repeat the purpose of the appraisal and the condi-

DILBERT reprinted by permission of United Feature Syndicate, Inc.

tions and assumptions to which it is subject, spell out the definition of value used, and explain in sufficient detail how the findings were reached.

Another common problem is inconsistency within the value approaches utilized. For example, if the subject property, which is an 80,000-sq.-ft. industrial property, needs a new roof costing $200,000, did the appraiser apply an adjustment for that exceptional item of deferred maintenance in deriving each indication of value? Frequently, the appraiser will perform an adjustment in the cost approach but will ignore it in the sales comparison and income capitalization approaches.

Appraisal reviewer Ralph Emerson III states that a narrative reconciliation should contain the following information:[6]

- Statement of the appraisal's purpose
- Restatement of the value definition
- Critical elements typical in most appraisals
- Critical elements of each approach applied in the particular appraisal

6. Ralph H. Emerson III, MAI, "Proper Reconciliation in Narrative Reports Favors Substance Over Form," *The Appraisal Journal* (January 1998): 94–95.

- Explanation as to whether these critical elements support one another or create conflicts
- List of these consistencies or conflicts
- Statement as to whether these consistencies or inconsistencies are linked to the market or have been created by the appraiser
- Description of how these inconsistencies are resolved
- Justification that the value conclusion reflects existing market conditions or that the analysis anticipates certain events that will affect property value in the near future

Estimate of Marketing Time

The discussion of marketing time in appraisal reports is optional. However, many clients, including most financial institutions, require that appraisals consider the "reasonable marketing period" for the property at the concluded value. Advisory Opinion 7 of USPAP states,

> Since marketing time occurs after the effective date of the market value estimate and the marketing time estimate is related to, yet apart from the appraisal process, it is appropriate for the section of the appraisal report that discusses this issue and its implications to appear toward the end of the report after the market value conclusion. The request to estimate a reasonable marketing time exceeds the normal information required for the conduct of the appraisal process, and should be treated separately from that process.

A reasonable marketing period is generally considered the time (e.g., number of months) from the date the property is listed to the date a contract for purchase and sale is executed. The estimated market value and the estimated reasonable marketing period are interrelated. It is not possible to present a market value estimate without a reasonable marketing period estimate. In valuing a property, many appraisers mistakenly assume that the marketing period has already expired, which essentially makes the valuation useless.

Reasonable exposure time is a requirement in appraisals concluding with a defined market value and is inherent to the market value definition. Reasonable exposure time is always presumed to precede the effective date of the appraisal. Exposure time is different for various types of real estate and under different market conditions. The estimated time period for reasonable exposure is not intended to be a prediction of a date of sale or a single statement. Instead, it is an integral part of the analyses conducted in the appraisal assignment. The estimate may be expressed as a range and can be based on one or more of the following:

- Statistical information concerning days on the market
- Information gathered through sales verification
- Interviews with market participants

PART FIVE—ADDENDA

Narrative appraisal reports are often lengthy and warrant the inclusion of graphics to aid communication. Tables, graphs, maps, and pictures should be included when they complement the written narrative.

Appraisers differ in the amount of data and the number of items they include in the body of the report and those they place in the addenda. Depending on the size and complexity of the appraisal assignment, some information that would interrupt the narrative portions of the report may be presented in the addenda.

Some appraisers prefer to keep the body of the report relatively uncluttered to maintain continuity and make the report more readable. They feel that photographs, maps, and exhibits should only be included in the body of the report if they are essential to support the appraiser's analysis; all others graphics are placed in the addenda and referred to in the text. Other appraisers make the body of their reports complete in all aspects and leave little for the addenda. Their reports may not be easy to read, but they avoid the problem of citing references.

In either case, the appraiser should refer to meaningful exhibits as frequently as necessary. The quantity of data included in most appraisal reports lends itself to tables and graphics, which can contribute to readers' understanding.

The following items might be included in the addenda, if they are not incorporated into the body of the report:

- Plot plan
- Plans and elevations of buildings
- Photographs of properties referred to in the report
- City, neighborhood, and other maps
- Charts and graphs
- Historical income and expense data
- Building specifications
- Detailed estimates of the reproduction or replacement costs of buildings
- Sales and listing data
- Leases and lease abstracts
- Market analysis data (e.g., information on construction trends, vacancy trends, and competitive rent levels)

Common flaws in the addenda section include

- Lack of illustrations or graphics, inadequate graphics, or inadequately labeled graphics
- Including too many irrelevant photographs
- Failure to read the legal description and ascertain that the property appraised was the property described in the legal description

- Filling the addenda with irrelevant, redundant material that adds weight, but not substance, to the report
- Including graphics or maps that cover such a wide area that their relevance to the subject property is unclear or completely lost

Location of Subject Property

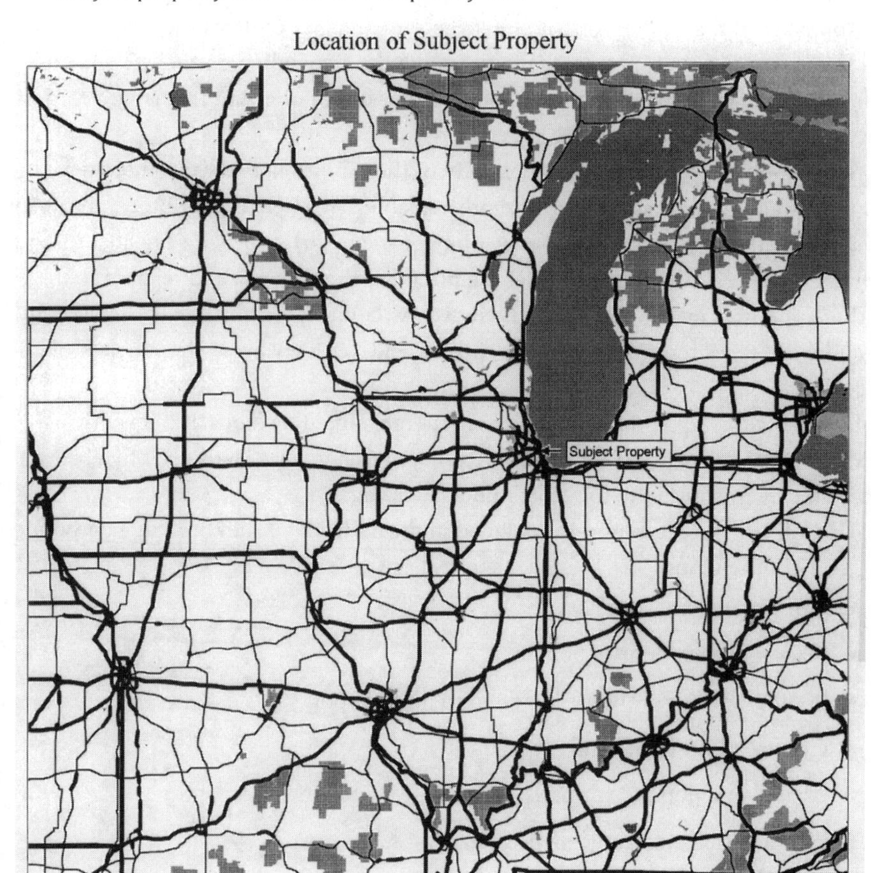

Common Deficiencies in Appraisals

INTRODUCTION

Users of appraisal services uncover certain shortcomings in appraisals on a regular basis. This chapter presents some of their observations. The topics discussed include

- A survey of chief appraisers
- Report deficiencies by category
- Use of new techniques
- Objectivity
- State Appraisal Board observations
- Appraiser liability insurance issues
- Writing: language and syntax

CHIEF APPRAISERS SURVEY

Based on a survey of institutional chief appraisers conducted by the author in January 1997, the most frequent appraisal problems and abuses are

- Ignoring the assignment specifications stated in the engagement letter, including the promised delivery date.
- Misleading language. As the old saying goes, "The large print giveth and the small (or hidden) print taketh away!" This is true of legal documents and also appraisals. Reviewers look for unusual limiting conditions and conditional value statements that, in effect, nullify the value and/or relieve the appraiser of all liability and responsibility for the contents of the appraisal. Clients may discover that they do not have a reliable value conclusion and solid collateral base as indicated on the first page of the appraisal. So-called "weasel words" can have the same effect on the reliability of the report.

DILBERT reprinted by permission of United Feature Syndicate, Inc.

- Failure to identify the competition for the property being appraised or its specific market. Sometimes the appraiser explores the macromarket with macrostatistics but fails to discuss the all-important micromarket. How will the subject property fare in the market considering its location and physical characteristics?
- Lack of meaningful or thoughtful analysis and reasoning. Many reports merely offer a cursory explanation of the valuation process, a large amount of quantitative information, and very little discussion to support the appraiser's judgment.
- Not relating the appraised property to the market. Some appraisals lack pertinent market data and market substantiation.
- Failure to identify the typical buyer and/or tenant for the appraised property.
- Too much "canned" information in reports. Many reports contain excessive boilerplate, "off-the-shelf" material often prepared for a previous appraisal of a similar property. Lenders are simply not willing to pay for chamber of commerce information presented without analysis or any tie-in to the subject property and its estimated value.

- Inclusion of unedited "transplants" taken from other reports. These passages can be hilarious for reviewers, particularly when the subject property is dramatically different than the one described in the original report. Reading the downtown San Francisco office market statistics in an appraisal of a suburban Detroit office building is guaranteed to amuse the reviewer.
- Omission of sources of data and supporting verification. The report should state who was contacted—i.e., brokers, developers, other appraisers, investors, tenants, sellers, etc.
- Inconsistencies within the report with regard to sizes, zoning, property type, physical details, etc.
- Omission of basic information such as floor or land dimensions, property ages, and market conditions. Aspects of depreciation should be described before the amount to be charged is estimated. In short, the report should contain no surprises, no conclusions for which the reviewer has not been prepared.
- Lack of understanding and/or proper development of the sales comparison approach.
- Unsupported assumptions in a discounted cash flow analysis. The appraiser's assumptions should be cross-checked for reasonableness with investor surveys. (Appendix II lists sources of investor surveys and other references.)
- Problems with software modeling. Reviewers should scrutinize appraiser's self-created, lease-by-lease analyses prepared with Lotus, Excel, and other electronic spreadsheet programs. These analyses can be fraught with serious errors.
- Use of outdated information. Reports may make use of comparables that are not similar because they are dated and occurred under completely different economic and market conditions.
- Lack of substantiation. Reviewers complain of reports written in a "trust me" tone, which require the reader to make leaps of faith to understand the derivation and selection of key assumptions used in the analysis.
- Mathematical errors.
- Poor writing with too much appraisal jargon. References to "the Inwood coefficient," "the J factor," and "the coefficient of skewness" may impress other appraisers, but they do not help communicate the appraisal to the client. If a technical term must be used, it should be clearly defined in simple language. Other detractions include garbled sentences and the pointless repetition of words, phrases, and definitions.
- Verbose writing. Reports may be too long relative to the significance and/or complexity of the valuation problem (often a clear signal of uncertainty or incompetence). The perceptive appraiser will only use data that are pertinent to the case. Too much data may be safer than too little, but clients may object to reports that are overloaded with irrelevant information.
- Failure to structure reports deductively, to take the reader from the general to the specific.

- No analysis of current occupancy, operating data, or lease situations. Some appraisers assume that the market is forever in balance and supply and demand will take care of themselves—the "field of dreams" approach.
- Overlooking possible value-influencing factors (e.g., pending street widening or change to one-way traffic, a nonassumable mortgage).
- Use of inexperienced staff on complex assignments and inadequate quality-control procedures.
- Reference to material that is not in the addenda of the report. Reports may announce or introduce material or discussions that are later inadvertently omitted.
- Ignoring the client's needs in terms of the report type, specifications, etc.
- Failure to cross-check the value indications derived in the three approaches. The indications should be reconciled and the appraiser's rationale provided. If the value indications vary considerably without any reasonable explanation, the reviewer will sense a problem.
- Obvious lack of independent verification evidenced by use of the owner's or developer's operating statements, line item by line item.
- Lack of balanced analysis. In some reports, all projections are overly optimistic. The appraiser reports no problems or deficiencies with the property and anticipates no leveling off of activity within the market.
- Failure to comply with regulations or standards (e.g., FIRREA, USPAP).
- Fails the acid test by not concluding with a reasonable analysis or valuation based on the facts presented in the report.

In a speech to a national conference of institutional chief appraisers, one banker stated:

> It's important that the appraisal report focus on the pertinent valuation issues. Sometimes, when appraisers write a report, they throw in every bit of rosy, chamber of commerce gobbledygook they can find. This detracts from the important points being made in the report. We're simply not willing to pay for an appraisal that includes all of those frills. We just want solid data and analysis that address the key issues impacting value.
>
> Appraisers sometimes want to address all the valuation issues and resolve all the questions relating to the property when they perform an appraisal. While a high level of due diligence is oftentimes commendable, appraisers who serve lenders need to understand that sometimes, based on risk parameters, that degree of scrutiny is not necessary. I think that it is important for appraisers to understand the lender's needs.

Report Deficiencies by Category

Most of the problems that reviewers find in appraisal reports may be attributed to deficiencies in one or more of the following general categories:

Analysis and Reasoning

- Inadequate analysis and reasoning, reliance on stale market data, and discrepancies between the data presented in the report and key assumptions deemed essential to the final value conclusion. An appraiser may fail to strike a balance between aggressive, upside assumptions and conservative, downside assumptions.
- Inadequate highest and best use analysis when the highest and best use determination is critical to the value conclusion.
- Failure to present both the negative and positive attributes of the subject property, which can influence property value and marketability. If an appraiser soft-pedals negative features and overstates positive features, the reviewer is forced to "read between the lines" looking for clues about the actual situation. Stressing the negative and downplaying the positive can also be a disservice and create hardship for the client. The appraiser should try to achieve a balanced presentation.
- Overemphasis of historical trends rather than current conditions, which may be significantly different. For example, rental data over the past 10 years may show an overall, annual increase of 8%, while rates for the past three years show an actual decline of 2% per year. The more recent figure would be considered a better indicator of future trends.
- Inadequate explanation of a wide discrepancy between a current or recent transaction price and the appraiser's value conclusion.
- Misinterpretation of data.
- Failure to ask the right questions and necessary follow-up questions of market participants and sources when confirming or verifying data.
- Misrepresentation of conditions or circumstances, which can render the appraisal hypothetical. For example, an appraisal may state, "Assuming the zoning change is approved, the highest and best use of the property will be a high-rise office building." The valuation is conditioned on a change in zoning, but the reasonable probability of a zoning change has not been established. The resulting valuation is purely hypothetical and could be misleading even though the report contains an appropriate limiting condition.

Data Collection and Investigation

- Inadequate research or documentation.
- Overreliance on data provided by the owner or developer of a proposed project without cross-checking the data against independent data sources or undertaking an independent investigation.
- Failure to question an assumption about the likelihood of a zoning change or to provide appropriate verification of the reasonableness of such an assumption.
- Reliance on insufficient transaction data. If the market is characterized by a lack of sales activity, the appraiser should describe the market conditions and explain the

reasons for the scarcity of data. There are usually significant economic reasons for a dearth of real estate sales in a particular area. Rather than dealing with the symptoms (i.e., lack of sales, rentals, etc.) and lamenting the lack of current data, the appraiser should analyze the cause of the situation. This analysis will be far more valuable to the client than an analysis of stale comparable sales.

- Failure to confirm a sales transaction with at least one of the parties involved. Confirming a sale can not only verify transaction data but also provide information on the purchaser's motivation and possibly on the reuse or redevelopment of the property purchased. It is important that the appraiser communicate with one of the principals involved in the transaction and ask follow-up questions to ferret out the facts and establish who, what, where, when, why, and how the transaction occurred.
- Not using common sense in deciding which items to include from the mass of information available about the market and the socioeconomic status of market participants. The appraiser must choose data that are relevant to the property being appraised and its potential uses.

Appraisal Management and Quality Control

- Errors resulting from carelessness, lack of attention to detail, and poor quality control. Typos, grammatical errors, mathematical mistakes, and inappropriate exhibits are detrimental to the credibility of an appraisal report.
- Inconsistencies such as stating different value conclusions in the letter of transmittal and summary at the front of the report and the reconciliation section at the end of the report.
- Overreliance on boilerplate to document an appraisal and overuse of promotional reports published by the local chamber of commerce.
- Problems resulting from the delegation of complex assignments to inexperienced staff.
- Submission of a form report for a complex valuation that warrants a more comprehensive narrative report. For example, a URAR form report without supporting addenda and exhibits should not be used to communicate the valuation of a complex, multimillion-dollar mansion.
- Confusion over the effective date of the value conclusion. An "as is" date of value that falls before or on the completion date for the project does not make logical sense. An "as is" date is typically assumed to be synonymous with the date of the appraiser's inspection. On the other hand, an "as of " future date assumes that the proposed project is already completed and perhaps operating at stabilized occupancy.
- Ineffective quality control procedures.
- Submission of the appraisal report after the contracted date of delivery.
- "Cloning" the substance of another report, comps and all, for a current appraisal assignment.

Appraiser-Client Communication

- Misunderstanding the scope of the assignment.
- Failure to complete the report in accordance with the client's guidelines or disregarding the client's specific instructions. Communication problems between the appraiser and the client can be avoided by using engagement letters, which ensure a meeting of the minds at the inception of the assignment and fewer disputes when the report is delivered. Of course, the client's instructions should not prevent an appraiser from exercising his or her professional judgment.
- Failure to comply with the regulatory requirements of the Financial Institutions Reform, Recovery and Enforcement Act (FIRREA) and other federal or state regulations and with those requirements specific to the client.
- Failure to segregate, when appropriate, the value of non-realty items such as the business or going-concern, personalty, furniture, trade fixtures, and equipment, as required under USPAP and FIRREA.
- Preparing an appraisal based on specific financing assumptions or after-tax considerations, which potentially limit the concluded value to a narrow range of circumstances that are extremely unlikely to occur.
- Failure to highlight critical problems in the appraisal. Open dialogue with the client throughout the appraisal process should be encouraged.
- Failure to inform the client in advance that major, unforeseen problems in the assignment will require an extension of the due date or an adjustment to, or renegotiation of, the fee originally agreed upon.

Standards Issues

- Failure to meet the minimum requirements of the Uniform Standards of Professional Appraisal Practice.
- Failure to identify the type of appraisal and the report format.
- Failure to meet the requirements of the report type. Self-contained and summary reports must contain certain elements that define these types of reports.
- Not clearly identifying the property rights being appraised.
- Failure to distinguish between the value of a property at sellout and its wholesale or bulk sale value, particularly in the appraisal of subdivision developments and condominium projects. Moreover, the aggregate retail value of the individual components must be distinguished from the market value of the whole property.
- Failure to estimate the future value of phased developments properly in terms of the present value to a potential purchaser.
- In appraisals of the "as is" value of a project being built or rehabilitated, intentionally vague discussion of what work has been done and what work remains to be completed.

- Submission of misleading or biased appraisal reports.
- Submission of an incompetent work product. Usually incompetent appraisals result because appraisers accept assignments on complex or special-purpose properties (e.g., lodging or health care facilities) that require specialized knowledge or experience that they lack. They may unrealistically overestimate their own professional capabilities or underestimate the nuances and complexity of the assignment. In either case, the appraiser may violate the Competency Provision of USPAP if he or she does not retain the services of someone with the required expertise or make efforts to attain the necessary skills.

Vocabulary and Syntax

- Lack of clarity and conciseness. Reports may be adversely affected by the excessive use of legalese, appraisal-speak, or other jargon; hackneyed or arcane vocabulary; and reliance on the passive voice.
- A writing style that is verbose, vague, or redundant. For example, defining *market value* several times in the report serves no useful purpose.
- Overuse of hedge words such as *appear, seem, likely,* and *probably,* which leave the reviewer in doubt as to the true meaning of an otherwise decisive statement.
- Unnecessarily complicated language. Reports should be written in plain English. It all boils down to two words: good editing. *If* is preferable to *in the event of* and *to* is more concise than *in order to.* Using plain English will make it easier for the client and reviewer to identify and understand the appraiser's analysis and reasoning.

Use of New Techniques

Over the years, new techniques are developed and added to the archives of appraisal theory and methodology. Some reviewers might question the validity of appraisal techniques that are considered outdated or unpopular, but appraisers will find that using different techniques sometimes helps to explain market behavior. The appropriateness of a particular method of analysis should not be dismissed merely because it is not currently in the forefront of appraisal theory.

When new methods or techniques are used, the appraiser should not only explain the unusual technique but also discuss why the usual methods are not appropriate.

Objectivity

Maintaining objectivity is more difficult than most people imagine. Investigators often find that eyewitness accounts of an event vary widely. Even reliable witnesses may differ markedly in describing what they thought they saw. Although appraisers are paid by their clients to be objective, they cannot escape the human tendency to interpret information before it can be processed. Objectivity can be lost when information is evaluated from a biased perspective.

In evaluating a proposed venture, an appraiser may be tempted to justify a loss of objectivity with the knowledge that the future is uncertain. It is easy to argue that a venture has just as much chance of success as failure. Because neither position can be supported with absolute certainty, the easiest course may be to take the path of least resistance. If the venture does fail, it can be argued that there is no accurate way of forecasting the future. Personal beliefs or a socially desirable objective can also cloud an appraiser's judgment. While the pressure to arrive at a popular and enthusiastically supported conclusion cannot be completely eliminated, the appraiser must endeavor to do so.

A loss of objectivity is not always the result of a conscious desire to deceive. Objectivity can be lost when the analytical process is begun after a conclusion has been formed. Testing a conclusion to determine whether sufficient evidence exists to support it is a method that scientists frequently use. However, the conclusion reached may be based on circular reasoning because the data search was limited to data that support the particular conclusion. Information that might have resulted in a different conclusion may have been overlooked.

> Exasperated reviewer to appraiser: "If you're not going to tell the truth, could you at least make it sound more interesting?"

Shortcut research methods can result in erroneous forecasts because all relevant information is not examined. To avoid losing objectivity, an appraiser should be wary of adopting a conclusion early in the valuation process. A desirable or appealing conclusion can blind the appraiser to a different way of thinking or understanding. The appraiser should always examine such a conclusion against one that appears to be supported by the available data. The best appraisers know that the accuracy of value conclusions depends on careful research. They form opinions only after completing their analysis.

Appraisal Institute members participating in the peer review process report that the most common complaints involve misleading and biased appraisal reports.

State Appraisal Board Observations

In his work as an investigator for several state appraisal boards, Alan Hummel, SRA, has observed the following deficiencies in appraisal reports. Items 1 through 3 are listed in the order of frequency, while Items 4 through 10 occur with equal frequency.

1. Insufficient information given in the report to allow the reader to understand how the appraiser reached his or her conclusions
2. Improper or absent labeling of report type and confusion in stating appraisal type (complete or limited)
3. Using "standard" adjustments rather than investigating market reactions
4. Improper use of, or disclosure of, departure when performing a limited appraisal
5. Improper use of a restricted report and failure to meet all the reporting requirements under S.R. 2-2 (c)
6. Failure to consider and analyze current agreements of sale or lease and prior sales within the last one to three years (depending on property type)
7. Failure to separate real estate from personal property, FF&E, going-concern, and business values

8. Relying on published data without verifying its accuracy or reliability
9. Failure to determine the users' needs adequately and perform the appraisal to meet the relevant supplemental standards (e.g., eminent domain, Fannie Mae lending, relocation, assessment protest)
10. Outright incompetence in performing the appraisal assignment, evidenced in both methodology and reporting

Appraiser Liability Insurer

What kinds of things do appraisers get sued for? In his seminar, "Loss Prevention Program for Real Estate Appraisers," Robert C. Wiley, president of Liability Insurance Administrators, presents the following outline describing the most common causes of negligence-based lawsuits against appraisers:

1. Failure to discover and disclose defects in the property. Such claims typically arise after the buyers discover defects in the property that weren't noted in the appraisal report. (The best way to limit exposure is for the appraiser to specify the scope of his or her duties and qualifications in a disclaimer.)
2. Failure to disclose conditions surrounding or affecting the property. Some clients argue that an appraiser also has a responsibility to investigate the surrounding area to detect conditions that may affect the value.
3. Errors in the computation of square footage. This type of claim is one of the most frequently reported. An accurate measurement of a property's square footage can be difficult to achieve. Recently, the American National Standards Institute (ANSI) approved a national standard of measurement, but previously there was no universal standard. Should rooms below grade, partly finished rooms, or garages be included in the gross living area? Although many appraisers rely on standards set by Freddie Mac or Fannie Mae, there still is a lot of gray area. In fact, it is highly unlikely that any two appraisers will arrive at the same figure. Many appraisers simply rely on other sources for necessary square footage figures and do very little verification, not realizing the risk they take. When a gray area of interpretation is involved, the appraiser should document and explain the reasoning for whatever methods he or she used to calculate the square footage.
4. Appraising the wrong property. This generally happens when the appraiser is valuing vacant land. Appraisers can avoid this error by verifying the parcel location with the client.

Conclusion

Appraisal review is the quality-control function of the appraisal profession. Review appraisers test the reasonableness of the logic, assumptions, and value conclusion presented in a report and ensure that the appraiser has complied with professional standards, the client's criteria, and appraisal regulatory requirements.

Most problems with appraisal reports are the result of incompetence, inadequate data research, inadequate support, poor analysis and reasoning, inconsistencies, ineffective quality control, misunderstanding the assignment, lack of adherence to standards, vagueness, and the failure to check for reasonableness before finalizing the appraisal.

The art of reviewing changes constantly, just as the technology and methods applied in the appraisal profession change to reflect the activities of real estate markets. The ultimate goal of a review appraiser is to accept an appraisal report in which the data and reasoning presented have led to a valid conclusion. A good report reflects the skill and judgment of its author, who has communicated the complicated valuation process in a meaningful, interesting, clear, and logical manner.

Single-Family Residential Reviewer Guidelines

Use of Form Reports

Many lending institutions and certain government agencies require that a form report be used rather than a narrative report, particularly for single-family residential appraisals. The printed appraisal form has boxes to be checked and blanks to be filled in by the appraiser with figures, words, and comments.

Form reports are efficient because the review appraiser can quickly find all essential elements of the appraisal. However, many appraisals require special analyses or discussions, in which case the form must be supplemented with attachments that are cross-referenced to specific sections of the form.

Unacceptable Practices

The following list specifies practices that are considered unacceptable by Fannie Mae, the Federal National Mortgage Association, which is the world's largest financial services company:[1]

- Inclusion of inaccurate data about the subject neighborhood, site, improvements, or comparable sales;
- Failure to comment on negative factors with respect to the subject neighborhood, subject property, or proximity of the subject property to adverse influences;
- Use of comparables in the valuation process even though the appraiser has not personally inspected the exterior of the comparables by, at least, driving by them;
- Selection and use of inappropriate comparable sales or the failure to use comparables that are locationally and physically the most similar to the subject property;

1. Fannie Mae, *Property and Appraisal Analysis,* Chapter 1, "Appraiser Qualifications," Section 102, Unacceptable Appraisal Practices, 1994.

- Use of data—particularly comparable sales data—that were provided by parties who have a financial interest in the sale or financing of the subject property without the appraiser's verification of the information from a disinterested source. For example, it would be inappropriate for an appraiser to use comparable sales data provided by the real estate broker who is handling the sale of the subject property, unless the appraiser verifies the accuracy of the data with another source and makes an independent investigation to determine that the comparables provided were the best ones available;
- Use of adjustments to the comparable sales that do not reflect the market's reaction to the differences between the subject property and the comparables, or the failure to make adjustments when they are clearly indicated;
- Development of a value conclusion that is based—either partially or completely—on the sex, race, color, religion, handicap, national origin, or familial status of either the prospective owners or occupants of the subject property or of the present owners or occupants of properties in the vicinity of the subject property; and
- Development of a value conclusion that is not supported by available market data.

Common Errors in Form Reports

A major, national, first mortgage originator reports that the most common errors discovered in the review of thousands of form reports include the following:

- Errors in mathematical calculations.
- Inadequate explanation of atypical factors, adjustments, or analyses.
- Failure (or reluctance) to ask sensitive questions during the property inspection concerning the need for major repairs or replacements.
- Incorrect identification of the type of property under appraisal—e.g., single-family detached or attached, condominium, planned unit development (PUD).
- Lines left blank on the completed form. Lines should be marked "N/A" to indicate that data are not available or that the entry does not apply to the subject property. An empty line creates the impression that the item was inadvertently overlooked.
- Inconsistencies involving trend indicators, adjustments for market conditions, or estimates of marketing time.
- Discrepancies between the photographs of the subject property and the physical description provided on the form.
- Photo of subject property showing "For Sale" sign on the front lawn without any mention in the report of offers or the asking or selling price.
- Failure to report a one-year sales history of the subject property.
- Meaningless statements in the "comments" sections of the form.
- No explanation as to why large gross or net adjustments were made to the comparables and inconsistencies among the adjustments applied.

- Incorrect calculation of gross living area.
- Inconsistencies in the application of the gross living area adjustment per square foot in the sales comparison analysis grid.
- Failure to provide adequate support or justification for large dollar or percentage adjustments.
- No reasonable reconciliation of the wide range of values indicated by the adjusted sale prices of the comparables or the values derived in the various approaches employed.
- Discrepancies between the factual data provided on the front of the form and the valuation analysis described on the back.
- Selection of dated or distant comparables or comparable sales that do not bracket the subject's value. Comparables should reflect a sampling of representative sales that are priced both higher and lower than the subject. The rationale for the selection of comparables must be explained, especially the appraiser's reasons for using any comparable sales from outside the subject neighborhood.
- Failure to recognize and adjust for functional problems evident in the floor plan sketch of the subject.
- Inconsistencies between the information reported by the appraiser (e.g., reproduction or replacement costs, land values, sales data, comparable adjustments) and similar information reported by other appraisers for similar properties in similar neighborhoods.
- Failure to make an adjustment for personal property that was included in a comparable sale. Also, mistakenly including personal property in the appraised value.
- Failure to report items observed on the property that are in violation of the current zoning regulations, such as boarders or business and office uses that are not permitted under the zoning code. For example, "in-law" apartments and additions to single-family residences are often in violation of residential zoning ordinances.
- Including the value of the land in the appraised value when the property is on leased land.

DID THE REPORT ANSWER THESE QUESTIONS?

1. Is the location of the property perceived by the general public to be an area of increasing property values? Surrounding areas should be investigated to avoid "surprises" that could detract from the property value. For example, the appraiser should make sure that a garbage dump, industrial park, or other unwelcome facility is not planned for a nearby parcel of undeveloped land.
2. Do adjacent homes add to or detract from the value of the subject property?
3. Is the subject property equal to or lower in value than surrounding homes?
4. Does the floor plan have any major functional problems?

5. Does the house (particularly the kitchen and bathrooms) require major remodeling to make it comparable with similar homes in the same price range?
6. Is the number of bedrooms and baths in the home comparable to similar homes in the same price range?

Reviewers may also ask: Did the appraiser perform an adequate inspection? Did he or she spend enough time at the property to observe potential problems? For example, new basement paint could hide persistent flooding. Heavy carpeting may mask a rotting floor and that attractive wainscot may be home to thousands of wood-eating insects.

Other Common Deficiencies in Residential Reports

When reading the real estate section of a local newspaper, one often comes across a question-and-answer exchange that reads something like this:

Q: We made an offer to purchase a house, which was accepted a few weeks ago. The appraiser came out one week ago, but the bank has now notified us that the loan was declined because the appraisal report said the house was worth $9,000 less than we agreed to pay. We got a copy of the report and found that the appraiser said the house has only three bedrooms and two bathrooms, even though it has four bedrooms and 2-1/2 bathrooms. What should we do now?

A: It sounds as if the appraiser did a sloppy job. Contact the appraiser to point out the errors and then ask that he or she issue a new report. If the appraiser won't correct the mistakes, call the lender and explain your problem. You have the right to request a reappraisal of the home and to submit any evidence (photographs, floor plans, etc.) to substantiate your claim that the property is larger and worth more than the first appraiser's estimate. Since the original appraiser goofed, you should also ask the lender to pay for the second appraisal or to reimburse the cost of the first one.

A situation like this can be embarrassing, and sometimes costly, to all parties concerned. This is not to say that the buyers are always right and the appraisers are always wrong. Eager buyers, particularly new home owners, often overpay and may count rooms incorrectly. If, however, the appraiser did miscount the rooms and baths, the mistake can cause considerable inconvenience to all concerned. The repercussions will be felt throughout the sale transaction process.

It is the appraiser's responsibility to estimate value objectively using the best data available. If the appraised value varies from the proposed purchase price, so be it. However, the value must be based on reliable data and a conscientious inspection of the residence, the comparables, and the market area. Unfortunately, letters describing deficiencies in appraisal reports and carelessness on the part of the appraiser appear all too frequently in the press.

Other common deficiencies in single-family residential appraisal reports include

- Use of sales that are not arm's-length transactions
- Misuse of proper sequence of adjustments in sales comparison
- Misuse of adjustments to comparable sales

- Disregarding special financing and cash equivalency
- Miscalculating gross living area
- Overlooking functional obsolescence in property floor plans
- Use of dissimilar comparables in deriving gross rent multipliers (*GRMs*)
- Ignoring Equal Credit Opportunity Act (ECOA) and Fair Housing Act considerations
- Misuse of cost services

These topics are covered in detail in the following sections.

Use of Sales That Are Not Arm's-Length

Sales that are not arm's-length transactions should be eliminated from consideration as comparable sales. This is not to say that if a sale is an arm's-length transaction, no adjustment for motivation is necessary. Some arm's-length sales may reflect atypical motivations or sale conditions such as unusual investment or tax considerations, sale at legal auction, or eminent domain proceedings. If these sales are used in the sales comparison approach, an appropriate adjustment must be made for motivation or sale conditions.

Misuse of Proper Sequence of Adjustments

In recording sales adjustments on their market grids, appraisers must adjust for the following elements of comparison in sequence: property rights conveyed, financing terms, conditions of sale, market conditions (changes over time), location, and physical characteristics. If an adjustment is required for the property rights conveyed, this adjustment is made first and an adjusted sale price is calculated. Making the financing adjustment next removes any premiums paid for favorable financing. The conditions of sale adjustment is made next and results in a cash equivalent sale price consistent with transactions reflecting typical buyer and seller motivations. The adjustment for market conditions is then made to the price adjusted for financing and conditions of sale to bring the adjusted price in line with the date of the value estimate.

Misuse of Adjustments to Comparable Sales

All adjustments should be explained in the addenda to the report. Market condition (time) adjustments should be examined closely by the reviewer. If the comparable sold four months prior to the effective date of the appraisal, is a 4% adjustment justified? In a very active market, the 4% adjustment may be correct, but in a "normal" market such an adjustment would be extraordinary.

The comparables used should bracket the market value conclusion. Some will be inferior, some superior, and others very similar to the subject property. For atypical properties, more than the required three comparables should be used to prove the value.

Appraisers commonly use an across-the-board adjustment for an element of comparison, using the same rate regardless of the age or quality of the residences they are appraising. For example, many appraisals show adjustments of $500 per bathroom, regardless of the price and age of the residence. This may be the only adjustment used by some appraisers, even though the ages of the subject houses range from new to 90 years old and the quality ranges from low-end tract housing to expensive custom homes. Obviously the fixtures in a inexpensive home are not worth the same amount as those in a luxury residence, and the adjustment per bath for an older home should not be the same as for a new home. The same holds true for adjustments made for differences in the physical characteristics of properties.

Disregarding Special Financing and Cash Equivalency

Appraisers must understand how changes in the availability of mortgage funds and the terms obtainable affect the pattern of market activity and, ultimately, the market value. If a property sells with nonmarket financing, the special financing must be considered an inducement separate from the value of the real estate. To use such a property as a comparable in estimating market value, the appraiser must calculate the value of the inducement and adjust the sale price accordingly. Cash equivalency calculations are commonly used to adjust sales in which the seller pays points or finances the loan. Adjustments for atypical financing may be derived either by analyzing paired data sets or by discounting the cash flows created by nontraditional mortgage contracts at market interest rates.

A common error in adjusting for seller-paid points is to calculate the percentage adjustment using the total selling price rather than the mortgage amount to derive the cash equivalent dollar amount.

Although cash equivalency can be calculated mathematically, the financing adjustments derived must be rigorously tested against market conditions and perceptions. As always, adjustments must be market-derived to be legitimate.

Miscalculating Gross Living Area

Robert C. Wiley, president of Liability Insurance Underwriters, states that, "the most frequently reported errors and omissions claim is that involving an error in the calculation of square footage. Too many appraisers simply rely on other sources for necessary square footage figures and do very little verification." As mentioned in Chapter 8, there is a new ANSI-approved national standard for the measurement of square footage. It is strongly recommended that the appraiser follow whatever guideline is applicable to the assignment—e.g., Freddie Mac, Fannie Mae. To avoid misleading the client, the appraiser should state the calculation method used and provide the reasoning for including or excluding certain rooms or areas of the house that might fall into a "gray area" where measurement is concerned.

Gross living area is defined as "the total area of finished and above-grade residential space." It is the standard unit of measurement for residential property and is recognized by federal agencies involved with lending, including Fannie Mae, Freddie Mac, the FHA, and the VA. Gross living area is calculated as follows:

1. Measure the length of all first-floor walls.
2. Determine the size of each above-grade floor for homes with more than one level.
3. Exclude the basement area, even if it is finished and heated. A finished basement should be considered either finished, below-grade space or finished basement area, not gross living area.

4. Exclude any garage, shed, carport, or other outbuilding that is not heated and fully finished.

5. Exclude all open and enclosed porches that are not finished and heated.

6. Exclude balconies and decks.

7. If the attic is finished, heated, and has at least a five-foot clear ceiling height, its area should be included. Any part of the attic that does not meet these criteria should not be included.

Sometimes appraisers have a difficult time calculating gross living area. Bi-level homes (also known as *raised ranches*) and split levels present problems when the lower level is heated and finished in a manner similar to the rest of the home. Partial upper stories and significant roof slopes will affect interior gross living area.

Overlooking Floor Plan Functional Obsolescence

The functionality of floor plans is often overlooked. Functional obsolescence or inutility refers to an impairment of the functional capacity or efficiency of the residence. Some floor plans are functionally obsolete in theory but are accepted by most buyers; others are glaringly obsolete. For instance, a two-bedroom home is functionally obsolete in many markets, and mortgage underwriters will only accept the appraisal if the comparable sales contain two bedrooms. Three-bedroom homes are not considered comparable.

Appraisers should understand the market in question, recognize if a floor plan has items of functional obsolescence, and assess the impact of the obsolescence on the marketability and/or value of the home. Most floor plans reflecting functional obsolescence fall into a few, general categories. Common items of obsolescence in floor plans are listed below.

Front door and entrance	Front door leads to another door, creating an enclosed foyer; access to key areas such as the kitchen, bathrooms, or bedrooms is less convenient as a result.
	Front door leads directly into the living room.
	No coat closet near door.
Bathrooms	An insufficient number of full bathrooms in relation to the number of bedrooms or inconveniently located bathrooms. In most markets, there should be at least one bathroom in a three-bedroom home and two in a home with four or more bedrooms.
	Bathrooms too small to be functional.
	Bedrooms are upstairs and the bath is downstairs.
Living room	Bedrooms or bathrooms are visible from the living room.
	Traffic flows through conversation circle.
	Front door opens directly into living room.
	Arrangement of doors, walls, entrances, and passageways does not accommodate functional placement of furniture.

Dining room	Traffic flows through dining area. Insufficient clearance for furniture placement. No screening of kitchen view from dining room.
Kitchen (the room most likely to experience functional inutility)	No door to outside from the kitchen or pantry. (This is not regarded as functionally obsolete in all markets.) No windows in kitchen. Location and type of appliances do not meet market tastes. Ideally the sink, stove, and refrigerator should be positioned to form a triangle. This is the most efficient layout for food preparation. Kitchen eating area is too small. Insufficient amount of counters or cabinets. Poor access to dining areas. Bathroom is located directly off the kitchen. Kitchen is located in the front of the house. (Not regarded as functionally obsolete in all markets.)
Bedrooms	Absence of a window or closet. Insufficient room for furniture placement. Not convenient to hallway or bathroom. Bedroom serves as passageway to another area of the house.
Stairways	Stairway is accessible through a bedroom, not a hallway.
Extensions/recreation room	Extensions do not connect with the kitchen or pantry.
Basements	No door to the outside. No powder room in a finished basement; occupants must walk up to the first floor to use a restroom.
Closets	Insufficient number or size of doors.
Ceiling height	Ceilings are too low or too high.

Appraisers must keep in mind that the market is the final arbiter of functional obsolescence or inutility. Functional inutility must be judged in light of market standards of acceptability, specifically the standards of buyers who make up the market for a particular type of residence. Additionally, the appraiser should not penalize the subject residence if all competitive properties have the same deficiency or inutility.

Overlooking Problems Commonly Found in Older Homes

Many older homes are built better than modern houses, but they may have pre-existing conditions that the appraiser should be familiar with and the reviewer should be alert for. These conditions can include outdated materials and construction methods that no longer meet building codes, foundation problems, insulating materials that are inadequate or no longer allowed, and windows and frames that need upgrading.

Some common problems found in older homes are described as follows:

- Asbestos-containing insulation around heating pipes, which constitutes a health hazard if it is flaking or damaged.
- Insulation of hazardous urea-formaldehyde foam (usually installed after construction).
- Inadequate wiring, often less than the minimum 100 amps; 120-240 volt electrical service is currently recommended.
- Windows that are difficult to repair. The window trim often must be removed to repair sash cords.
- Plaster walls and ceilings that sag due to loosened plaster or sagging wood lath.
- Porous old stone or brick foundations. As the mortar deteriorates, water is allowed to penetrate.
- Low water pressure and volume in hot water heating systems.
- Brass or galvanized water piping that has corroded, causing low water pressure and deterioration.
- Slate or tile roofs, which are long-lasting but require routine maintenance and repair. Such roofs are more costly to replace than wood or asphalt shingle roofs.
- Lack of solid roof sheathing, which is needed for proper backing and nailing if asphalt shingles are to be added after the original slate, tile, or wood roof is removed or surfaced over.
- Deterioration of chimney masonry. Many older houses have brick chimneys without flue liners, which can deteriorate.

Use of Dissimilar Comparables in Deriving GRMs

Gross rent multipliers must be extracted from active, current market data. Rent estimates must be derived from actual rents, and properties used as comparable sales must have rented at or near market levels as of the date of sale. The appraiser can misapply the approach if he or she does not consider differences between the subject and comparable properties in matters such as the furnishing of space (Is it rented furnished or unfurnished?) and the allocation of responsibility for utilities payments (Which utilities are paid by the tenant and which are paid by the owner?).

Ignoring ECOA and the Fair Housing Act Considerations

Appraisers must be extremely careful to ensure that their words and phrases do not exert undue influence on lenders. Appraisal reports communicate opinions, and communication is a two-way street. If the readers of appraisal reports are making decisions that are discriminatory, appraisers may bear some responsibility for those decisions and consider changing the way they report their opinions. As noted in Chapter 7, certain words and phrases should be avoided in appraisal reports.

✓ Church	✓ Exclusive or prestigious neighborhood
✓ Graffiti	✓ Executive homes
✓ Crime-infested	✓ Pride of ownership
✓ Gang activity	✓ Desirable/undesirable
✓ Riot area	✓ Well-maintained or not well-maintained
✓ Curb appeal	✓ Wrecked or abandoned cars
✓ Poor neighborhood	✓ Family room
✓ Low-income area or high-income area	✓ Transitional neighborhood

In addition, appraisers must be careful about the photographs they include in reports. Photos showing people, broken-down cars, or graffiti should not be used because they may influence a lender in an unfair manner. On the other hand, appraisers should note all pertinent factors influencing value in the appraisal. Properties in neighborhoods with "wrecked cars and graffiti" are not to be undervalued nor should appraisers inflate values in certain neighborhoods.

If crime statistics are used to illustrate the dangers of a neighborhood factually, the appraiser is cautioned to present similar crime statistics for each neighborhood in which he or she appraises. Criminal activity should not be highlighted only in "certain" neighborhoods.

For further clarification of fair housing laws and how they affect the content of appraisal reports, the reader is advised to consult Advisory Opinion 16 (AO-16) of the Appraisal Standards Board of The Appraisal Foundation.

Misuse of Cost Services

Appraisers misuse cost services when they do not know which construction items and costs are and are not included in the various basic unit costs used by the cost service. For example, in the Marshall Valuation Service calculator section, the actual costs used are final costs to the owner and include average architect's and engineer's fees; in the segregated cost section and most unit-in-place cost sections, however, the architects' fees are omitted. The costs of buying or assembling land, which may include the cost of escrow fees, legal fees, property taxes, rights-of-way, demolition, storm drains, rough grading, pilings, and hillside foundations, are not included.

Comparing Two or More Appraisals of the Same Property

Reviewers often receive assignments from their clients or employers to compare two or more appraisals of the same property to determine which is the most reliable. This service may be required in lending, divorce, litigation, dispute resolution, arbitration, employee relocation, and other situations. A convenient method is to set up a comparison chart highlighting the significant line items of the appraisals. Once the highlights of each appraisal are compared side by side, it usually becomes apparent which appraisal is more reliable. Such a comparison chart is illustrated below.

RESIDENTIAL APPRAISAL COMPARISON

	Appraisal 1	Appraisal 2	Appraisal 3
Date of appraisal	Current	Current	Current
Gross living area	2,359 sq. ft.	2,291 sq. ft.	2,312 sq. ft.
Total basement area	1,002 sq. ft.	1,058 sq. ft.	901 sq. ft.
Finished basement area	100%	81%	89%
Neighborhood	Adequate	Adequate	Adequate
Property condition	Fair decor Large adj.	Very fair decor No adj.	Good decor No adj.
Sales & listing area	2.5 miles	2.5 miles	2.0 miles
Listings with pools (special feature)	0	1	1
Listings with same architectural style	0	3	1
Listings in same subdivision	0	1	2
Sales with pools (or special feature)	3	2	1
Sales with same architectural style	2	1	1
Sales in same subdivision	1	2	0
Comparability of sales	Fair	Good	Poor (out of neighborhood)
Adjusted sales range	\$200,000 to \$225,000	\$210,200 to \$250,900	\$291,028 to \$298,678
Total net adjustment range	\$-23,000 to \$-111,200	\$-10,100 to \$-12,800	+\$3,678 to \$-22,919
Average net adjustment	-24.90%	5%	0.60%
Average gross adjustment	33.70%	20.10%	11%
Appraised value	\$205,000	\$230,000	\$297,000
No. of sales adjustments (per comparable)	Avg. 10	Avg. 7.7	Avg. 7
Major problems	No listings Subjective comments about décor. Questionable comps with very large adjustments on average. Comps 2 & 3 were not comparable due to location and excessively large adjustments.	Listings superior Very subjective comments about décor; otherwise appears to have the most reasonable conclusion.	Listing far superior None of the three sales used were comparable. All three were taken from a superior neighborhood.

A comparison chart like the one shown can help the reviewer sort out the positive and negative features of each appraisal. In the above example, Appraisal 2 appears to be the most reliable. Additional analysis would be needed to check the consistency and reasonableness of the adjustments within each report. Other factors to be considered would include the relevance and accuracy of the appraiser's comment and the quality of the report as evidenced by the absence of typos, the completion of all blanks on the form, and the clear presentation of exhibits.

The following comment appeared in an actual appraisal of a two-story residence equipped with an electronic stairlift:

> The house is very well suitable for the handicapped, elderly, or disabled. There is a built-in electric chair which can be used for the elderly or handi-capped [*sic*].

Troubleshooting Appraisals of Complex and Special-Use Properties

Introduction

Occasionally an appraiser is asked to value a complex property that is truly unique. Such an assignment calls for an extra measure of insight and creativity. Complex properties have characteristics that are atypical in their markets and must be valued by appraisers with special qualifications. The determination of complexity is critical, but given the diversity of complex properties and the variety of opinions regarding what constitutes complexity, it is unlikely that a meaningful, universally accepted definition of a complex appraisal assignment will ever be developed. A complex assignment in one market might not be considered a complex assignment in another market.

Properties may be complex because of location, conformity, physical characteristics, or market conditions. In addition, complexity is commonly ascribed to special-use properties and properties with elements of going-concern or business value in addition to real estate value. Such properties are the subject of this chapter.[1]

Most problems with appraisals of complex and special-use properties are due to the appraiser's

- Lack of experience with the property type
- Failure to recognize that the assignment involves elements of going-concern, use, or business value in addition to real estate value

Too often, the appraiser will use the terms *market value, going-concern value,* and *use value* interchangeably, which can confuse the client and mislead him or her into making a bad business decision based on a seriously flawed appraisal analysis.

1. The author gratefully acknowledges the contributions and expertise of the following individuals, who assisted the author in the preparation of this chapter: Harold J. Carlson; Sam Hines, MAI; William H. Reeve III, MAI, SRA; and James K. Tellatin, MAI.

Appraiser Competence

To perform an appraisal, the appraiser should have direct experience with the type and general location of the property. To avoid making a mistake in selecting an appraiser, the client should engage someone with documented experience in the particular property category. The breadth of an appraiser's skills and practice is very important in the selection process. The most qualified appraiser will possess the usual valuation skills plus training and relevant field experience with the specialized type of property to be appraised.

Under the Competency Provision of USPAP, appraisers must determine whether they possess sufficient knowledge and experience to undertake a given appraisal assignment before choosing to accept or reject the assignment. This is particularly important when the assignment involves complex and/or special-purpose real estate. Appraisers who accept assignments for which they do not have sufficient knowledge and experience may be in violation of the Ethics Provision. Although good appraisers are aware that the requirements of the Uniform Standards should be observed in all appraisal assignments, certain aspects of the standards are particularly relevant to complex valuation assignments. The Competency Provision of the Uniform Standards states:

> Prior to accepting an assignment or entering into an agreement to perform any assignment, an appraiser must properly identify the problem to be addressed and have the knowledge and experience to complete the assignment competently; or alternatively:
>
> 1. disclose the lack of knowledge and/or experience to the client before accepting the assignment; and
> 2. take all steps necessary or appropriate to complete the assignment competently; and
> 3. describe the lack of knowledge and/or experience and the steps taken to complete the assignment competently in the report.

Two items in the comment to the Competency Provision are worth noting. First, the provision states, "The Competency Provision requires an appraiser to have both the knowledge and the experience required to perform a specific appraisal service competently." This is especially important in complex valuations because most appraisers do not have sufficient knowledge and experience to handle such assignments and, unfortunately, many do not recognize this fact. Knowledge about appraising complex properties can be obtained by reading books and articles and attending seminars and lectures, but experience can be obtained only by conducting actual field appraisals of complex properties. Knowledge is not enough. The appraiser must have the experience to deal with the situation or risk violating the Competency Provision. Many appraisers have taken the trouble to gain extensive in-depth knowledge about the valuation of certain complex property types. These appraisers are known for their specialized expertise, and they will generally develop valuations and produce reports more competently than others.

The second pertinent comment concerns what an appraiser should do if, during the course of an assignment, it is determined that the assignment is complex. The comment states:

> . . . facts or conditions uncovered during the course of an assignment could cause an appraiser to discover that he or she lacks the required knowledge or experience to complete the assignment competently. At the point of such discovery, the appraiser is obligated to notify the client and comply with items 2 and 3 of the provision.

Often it is only after the appraisal has been started that the complexity is discovered. Some appraisers may be too stubborn or too embarrassed to admit that they did not possess the knowledge and experience required. The resulting appraisal will likely be misleading.

Reviewing Complex and Special-Purpose Property Appraisals

The information provided here is intended to assist in the review of various types of complex and special-purpose property appraisals. Several chapters or even an entire book could be devoted to each of the property types discussed here. This text merely offers general guidelines that the reviewer should be aware of. It is recommended that the reviewer do appropriate research to acquire the specialized knowledge necessary to review complex appraisal reports competently.

The property types highlighted in this chapter are those that present the most problems for appraisers and reviewers. Included are

- regional and superregional shopping centers
- lodging facilities
- health care facilities
- golf properties
- residential subdivisions
- medical office buildings
- bank branch properties
- religious institutions
- restaurants
- monopoly properties

The following discussion offers insights and suggestions about the special features that characterize complex properties and play an important role in their valuation.

Regional and Superregional Shopping Centers

Regional and superregional shopping centers are among the most complex real estate investments that appraisers normally value. Regional centers vary in location, tenant distribution, size, age, design, physical condition, and type of trade area. The dramatic development of these unique retail enterprises, as both a marketing and a cultural phenomenon, has created new and challenging problems for real estate appraisers. Appraisers may be called upon to estimate the values of existing centers, proposed centers, expansions of existing centers, and remerchandising programs. A careful examination and analysis of tenant sale volumes is essential to valuation assignments involving regional shopping centers.

The complexity of shopping centers and malls necessitates careful analysis of the income, cost, and sales comparison approaches to value to ensure that business value is not inadvertently included as part of the value of real property.

Careful analysis of the income and expense statement of a shopping center or mall is a prerequisite for successful valuation. Appraisers must properly recognize the full cost of management, excluding any profits contributed by retail operations, and assign the service profits to the proper entity.

It is generally agreed that a mall has to subsidize the cost of anchor space. Subsidizing the anchor tenant is necessary to ensure the success of all the other tenants. Just as the mall must subsidize the anchor space, certain spaces within the mall will have to help subsidize other spaces.

Mall rents are typically based not on the square footage occupied by a tenant but on the tenant's profit margins and projected sales volume. (In contrast, in-line stores with local retailers are charged rent per square foot.) Mall rents are closely tied to the business success of each tenant and the sales volumes and profit margins earned by merchants selling different types of goods. By charging a percentage of gross sales as rent, the mall owner is able to capture a portion of the business success of mall tenants. Increases in rents are typically based on increases in gross sales, so as the mall tenant's business increases, so does the rent. The appraiser should research rents for specific types of tenants by studying industry-wide sales data as well as the historic sales data from the mall in question. The selection of base rentals should be based on projected gross sales and what a tenant of a particular type can afford to pay in total occupancy costs, including rent. When an occupant of mall space succeeds, rents increase thereby increasing the mall owner's net income and the value of the mall as a going concern. In the long run, the income-producing potential of major retail centers is dependent on the generation of retail sales.

Although the minimum rents, percentage rent clauses, construction allowances, and lease terms in tenant leases vary, many clauses are fairly standard and most mall store leases are greater than triple net. Minimum rents and percentage rent terms are stipulated, operating expenses are paid on a prorated basis, and tenants pay some surcharge (usually 15%) for common area maintenance (CAM). Tenants also agree to follow the mall's rules and regulations in accordance with the Construction, Operation and Reciprocal Easement Agreement (COREA). Typically, the rents negotiated are third-party deals and are considered arm's-length transactions. However, there can be a wide range of rental rates for similar-sized spaces in a mall. In other markets, such as office and industrial markets, it is typical for the rents of similar-sized spaces to reflect a reasonably narrow range, assuming all other terms are comparable. This range becomes what appraiser's term the *market level.* Rents generally vary more in mall properties, particularly rents for smaller stores.

Performance Measures

The following units are commonly used to measure the performance of shopping centers:

- Retail sale volumes. This key measure of the relative performance of individual tenants and major retail properties can be used to assess the reasonableness of rental rates and occupancy costs.
- Annual retail sale volumes per square foot of a store's gross leasable area (GLA) or, for major retail centers with enclosed common areas, per square foot of mall GLA. This measurement usually excludes the annual sales of anchor tenants, freestanding tenants, and some junior department stores or discount stores (usually larger than 10,000 square feet). This provides a relatively direct measure of economic strength that can be used to compare a shopping center with other centers.
- Occupancy cost per GLA—i.e., rent per square foot plus expense recoveries. By comparing the average occupancy cost per square foot with the forecast sales per square foot, the reviewer can quickly discern the reasonableness of income forecasts for an individual tenant or a complex multitenant property with several hundred tenants.
- Price per square foot of mall GLA.

When the existing leases in a major center have been in place for four or five years, overage rent estimates may become increasingly important. The standard leasing practice is to use the overage rent percentage as a means of establishing the "natural" breakpoint at which the tenant will pay overage rent (i.e., the minimum annual rent divided by the percentage rent equals the breakpoint). As sales increase above this breakpoint, overage rent becomes increasingly important as a source of income for the retail center.

The sales of shopping centers and malls often include intangibles in addition to real property. The analysis and adjustment of selling prices must include the elimination of intangibles, fixtures, and business value. A sale price may be overstated unless the appraiser carefully considers what has been paid for the fixtures that will revert at the end of the lease, the value of the management team acquired, if any, and anything paid for retail operations independent of the business of renting space. These specific intangible items may be regarded as business value, but in aggregate they represent only a small portion of a shopping center's total value. As is the case with many income-producing properties, it is difficult to measure and separate tangible and intangible components in terms of their value contributions because the components are all integrated.

The number of regional centers and malls is limited, and transactions are infrequent. Furthermore, due to the relative uniqueness of these properties, comparable sales are unlikely to be found within the local metropolitan area. In the appraisal of regional malls, sale comparables generally must be obtained from the national market in which such properties are bought and sold. The appraiser should investigate the interests conveyed in comparable sales transactions (e.g., leased fee, leasehold). The physical, locational, and income characteristics of the sale comparables must be similar to those of the subject property.

A thorough analysis must be made not only of population data trends but also of the demographics of the trade area. Age-cohort spending patterns vary dramatically and have a strong impact on a property's potential for retail sales, particularly sales of "soft goods" such as apparel, which represent the bulk of a large mall's sales volume. An appropriate tenant mix is vital to the success of any retail center. The key question is: Does the tenant mix match the needs of the market as indicated by its demographics? This issue should be analyzed and discussed in the appraisal.

Competition for sales can be fierce. Consumers can shop at a wide variety of venues—e.g., other large malls, big-box stores, specialty shopping centers, and revitalized central business districts. All these possible competitors must be cataloged as well as any outlet centers within reasonable proximity. Outlet centers such as Gurnee Mills north of Chicago can be a huge sales drain, generating substantial sales dollars that otherwise might be spent closer to home.

Vacancy Factors

The appraiser must consider not only physical vacancy but also the economic vacancies represented by stores that are still operating but not paying full rent or operating charges. To avoid the eyesore of empty storefronts, the management of a center often will permit tenants to remain in the center and pay less or no rent while the leasing department seeks to replace them.

Appraisers must read tenant leases not once, but twice, and develop a spreadsheet analysis listing all key considerations. Renewal provisions should be highlighted and compared to the individual tenant's sales productivity to determine whether it is reasonable to assume the tenant will exercise the option.

Pertinent questions must be asked. Does the lease allow the tenants of local space to terminate their leases if the anchor "goes dark"? How long will it take the center to re-lease a vacant space? What inducements will the lessor offer to obtain a new tenant—delayed rent or tenant allowances? Re-leasing, or "lag vacancy," involves downtime and the expenditure of funds, including appropriate leasing commissions that must be incorporated into the spreadsheet analysis.

Quality of Management

Not all management groups are equal. Those that concentrate their efforts on the shopping center field and know how this form of retailing works will usually perform better than jack-of-all-trades managers. Moreover, more sophisticated management groups have long cultivated good working relationships with the major chains, which can often help accelerate leasing activity.

Appraisers should be aware of the ongoing consolidation of retailers, particularly soft line retailers specializing in men's, women's, and children's apparel. By subscribing to leading trade journals and business-oriented periodicals and reading them carefully, appraisers can keep up with trends in the industry.

Maintenance and Repairs

Appraisers should investigate the potential need for major expenditures to maintain the physical structure (e.g., roofs, HVAC, electrical capacity) as well as the costs to keep the property in step with the times. Many large expenditures cannot be recouped directly from the tenants. Appraisers and reviewers need to be recognize an owner's unwillingness or inability to invest in the physical plant of the center in a timely fashion. The appraiser's analysis must provide for a reasonable annual reserve and periodic major renovation, perhaps expressed as an amount per square foot of public space plus tenant space due to turnover in each year of the projection period. In newer centers, short-term reserve concerns may be handled through contractual outsourcing of services—e.g., roof repair, HVAC, elevators.

Forecast Periods

How long should the financial forecast be for a shopping center? Generally the projection will cover 10 or 12 years, depending on how the lease expirations fall. Analysts should be aware that a major store often owns its own building and pad (the portion of the site directly under the building) and operates under some form of reciprocal easement and agreement. Obviously, these documents must be studied to get a handle on continuous occupancy clauses and co-tenancy agreements, which can be like a house of cards, fragile and capable of collapse. The loss of an anchor is often a traumatic event for everyone involved with a center—owners, tenants, local community governments, and lenders.

Lodging Facilities

Lodging facilities differ significantly from other forms of real estate and, from a valuation perspective, can be far more complex. Several factors distinguish lodging facilities from other property types.

While office buildings, multifamily residential properties, and retail space are typically leased for months or years, hotel rooms must be rented daily so sophisticated, ongoing marketing is required. With rapidly changing supply and demand conditions, hotels are vulnerable to competition and subject to dramatic fluctuations in occupancy. This translates directly into increased risk. Hotels normally command higher rates of return, primarily because of the inherent risks associated with this property type.

As much as 40% of a hotel's operating expenses is devoted to payroll costs and benefits. This level of management intensity is seldom appreciated in the valuation process, yet it can be crucial to the ultimate success or failure of a property.

Affiliation and management are very important in the lodging industry. The public's perception of the brand with which the property is associated can be a primary determinant of success. Some hotels obtain more than half their business (measured in accommodated room nights) through a central reservations system. Thus, the presence or absence of a strong national affiliation and competent management can have a substantial impact on operations and, therefore, on the value of the going concern, which in turn will affect the market value of the real estate component of the property.

Properties that fail to produce sufficient cash flow have severely reduced market values. On average, an occupancy rate of 65% to 70% is required to break even, assuming a typical debt structure. Because of the high fixed costs of a hotel operation, a decrease of 10% to 15% in occupancy can eliminate all net operating income and may even prevent a property from meeting its operating costs. Occupancy declines of this magnitude are not uncommon in light of a hotel's sensitivity to market conditions. In fact, the value of a property can be reduced to a fraction of its cost in a relatively short period of time.

In applying the sales comparison approach, a traditional price-per-room analysis may be inconclusive because many of the adjustments to be made are subjective. For example, two physically identical hotels in similar locations could command vastly different prices per room as a result of differences in affiliation, management, financial performance, and other characteristics. Hotel investors tend to focus on products of a certain type (e.g., full-service versus limited-service), within certain types of markets (e.g., resort versus airport), and located within certain regions of the country (e.g., Sunbelt versus the Northeast). A buyer seldom targets a specific location. Consequently, comparable sales should be similar with respect to product type, market orientation, and region, but need not be located in the same market area. In fact, recent transaction data on properties in different geographic areas are superior to information on dated comparables located in the same market as the property being valued.

Appraisals of lodging facilities require adequate supply and demand analysis, market penetration analysis, and reliable financial projections that are sensitive to the fixed and variable components of each line item of expense. These studies are often overlooked.

In preparing a supply and demand analysis to determine future market conditions, the appraiser should

- Define the current supply of rooms considered to be competitive with the subject property
- Investigate the status of proposed competitive properties and decide which have the highest probability of being constructed
- Analyze the market segments that are demanding rooms at competitive hotels, the rate at which demand is growing, and future sources of room demand

Procedures for analyzing demand growth vary and should be dictated by the nature of the market. In a market dominated by office parks, the future absorption of office space may be a good indicator of commercial demand growth. Traffic volume may be the best indicator in a market where the primary demand for lodging is generated by interstate highway motorists. In an airport market, on the other hand, the appraiser may perform an analysis of historical and projected enplanement activity.

Each line item should be evaluated on the most appropriate basis. For example, rooms department payroll should not be based on a percentage of room sales because increases in average room rate do not result in corresponding increases in payroll. It is much more appropriate to evaluate rooms payroll based on dollars per occupied room. In hotels with large amounts of public space, which may incur significant energy costs regardless of occupancy, energy should be projected on a dollars-per-square-foot basis. In all cases, comparable operating results should be used. The appraiser should obtain and use financial information from comparable, competently managed properties.

The fixed and variable components of each line item should be carefully defined. Because hotels have fluctuating utilization levels, ignoring the fixed and variable nature of expenses can result in a misleading projection.

Expense line items that are frequently overlooked include expenses incurred for special guest services such as limousine service to the airport or a local attraction. Are the vehicles used owned or leased? How are operating expenses handled? Similarly, if the facility has an unusually good collection of art or antiques, the collection may be leased rather than owned and the rental expense incurred should be analyzed. The separation of value components (i.e., real estate, FF&E, business value) is necessary to comply with the requirements of USPAP and FIRREA.

HEALTH CARE FACILITIES

In identifying the interest appraised, the appraiser should disclose not only the real estate interest (e.g., fee simple, leased fee) but also the other assets included in the ownership. These interests may include personal property, licenses, certifications, assembled workforce, patient records, and goodwill. While the real estate component of a health care facility is often owned separately from the operating company that controls the licenses and certifications, the ownership principals are often the same. This exemplifies an ownership situation in which the whole interest is often greater than the sum of the parts.

Failure to analyze salient demographic data on the elderly component of the population, who are the primary users of hospitals and nursing home services, can result in a misleading demand forecast. The relationships between health care demand and population are relatively predictable. Forecast changes in the elderly population have an obvious impact on future demand and revenue.

The appraiser should obtain recent health care facility surveys to determine the extent of any physical or functional deficiencies within the building or operations that must be cured immediately or will cause premature decertification.

Changes in the competitive supply can have a substantial impact on the earnings of existing facilities. Occupancy, outpatient utilization, and quality mix (private pay, private insurance, and Medicare for nursing facilities) often decline in established facilities when additional beds and services are introduced into the competitive market. Net operating income margins are narrow and extremely sensitive to competition. Thus, increased competition can have a significant impact on the future cash flows of a health care facility.

Medicaid reimbursements are cost-driven in most states. When reimbursements are set at facility-specific, cost-driven rates, the appraiser must reconcile the facility's operating expenses with the reimbursement rate. Under most reimbursement systems, previous-period expenses are used to establish the rate for the current period. If, during the interim, there has been a significant change in operating expenses (increase or reduction), the state Medicaid payment system will adjust the reimbursement accordingly. This could potentially produce a significant change in the net operating income of the facility. Capitalizing one-time profits or losses resulting from excessive or deficient facility-specific rates can produce a misleading value indication.

Medicare reimbursements are subject to contractual allowances and final settlement. Like Medicaid, Medicare reimbursements are cost-driven, but Medicare pays an operator an estimated payment or interim rate. After an audit of the facility's cost report is performed, Medicare will adjust the payment made to a nursing facility and to the hospital for outpatient services. These adjustments may result in the operator receiving additional reimbursement or require that the operator return excessive payments, which are referred as *final cost settlements.*

Contractual allowances are deductions from gross revenue that adjust actual payments from third-party payers (insurance, Medicaid, and Medicare). Most hospitals and nursing facilities account for revenues on a gross basis, and each specific service is billed at a "rack" rate. The difference between the rack rate and the rate actually paid is the contractual allowance. This difference is an adjustment to revenue; it is not an expense. Failure to include the contractual allowance will grossly overstate net operating income.

When the net operating incomes of comparable sales are used to derive capitalization rates, the analyst must consider the utilization and reimbursement issues described above. Net operating income calculations should be based on the expected revenues and expenses of the buyer, considering changes in reimbursements, certifications, and services resulting from new ownership as well as changes in census and utilization rates resulting from competitive market conditions.

The appraiser should be consistent in applying management fees and reserves for replacement to both the comparable sales and the subject property. "Do unto your sales as you do unto your subjects," advises James K. Tellatin, MAI, a well-known appraiser of health care facilities.

The sales comparison approach should be independent from the income capitalization approach. Applying an adjustment that compares the per-bed net operating income of the sales to the subject is basically direct capitalization. If the net operating income of the sales or the subject is incorrect, due to rate and reimbursement issues or other faults in the forecast, then neither approach will provide a reliable indication of value. It is better to compare and adjust prices for differences in objective elements that drive the quantity and quality of the earnings, such as payer mixes, occupancy rates, facility ages and conditions, and allowable capital basis or capital improvements. There is often strong market evidence to support price variations for differences in these salient elements of comparison.

The appraiser should investigate the interests that were conveyed in each comparable sale transaction. Did the sale involve only a leased fee or leasehold interest? Were accounts receivable included? Was the sale a stock purchase, and, if so, what were the assets and liabilities of the corporation(s) acquired? Was there any extraordinary motivation to sell or purchase that could have affected the purchase price?

Appraisers and reviewers must beware. Hospitals can have extremely complex business practices that transcend the scope of understanding normally required of real estate appraisers. Separate home health care services, physical therapy, and clinic and physician practices can be wrapped into the traditional hospital operation. Moreover, many hospitals are forming alliances with other health care providers, vertically integrating insurance, health care facilities, medical professionals, and medical product suppliers.

GOLF PROPERTIES

Golf properties are part real estate and part business/management projects, which are highly dependent on maintenance and management expertise. Most appraisal problems arise in the valuation of private golf clubs, but a few deficiencies found in appraisals of public fee facilities are also worth noting.

Public Fee Facilities

- *Rounds.* Round counts should be based on 18-hole equivalents. When course personnel are interviewed and asked for historic round counts, their replies are often based on the number of players listed on their daily tee sheets. The appraiser may take this number and assume that all the customers played 18 holes at the prevailing market rate. Further examination often reveals that all the players did not play or pay for 18 holes. Many played nine-hole rounds or "twilight" rounds at reduced fees (e.g., seasonal or membership rates). Appraisers must ask the right follow-up questions and convert round count into 18-hole equivalents.

- *Cart fees.* Cart fees can also be miscalculated if the appraiser fails to ask the right follow-up questions. Sometimes revenues are overestimated substantially. At many golf courses, the fleet of golf carts is rented.
- *Historic rounds and fees.* One common problem results when "as is" values are developed for developer- or family-owned golf facilities based on an analysis of historical rounds and fees. For example, the appraisal report may state, "This course has averaged 30,000 rounds for four years at $25.00 per round. Therefore, assuming that current maintenance and ownership is maintained, the course will have 30,000 rounds at $25.00 per round, increasing at 3% per year."
- *Inappropriate assumptions.* Highest and best use requires that a property be valued assuming competent management and well-capitalized ownership. Many developers and individual owners do not have the experience, expertise, or motivation to maximize their rounds and fees. They may be more concerned with selling real estate or minimizing taxes for estate purposes. Round counts and fees should be based on market research of comparable properties as well as the actual experience of the subject property.
- *Management fees.* Very few owner-operators, other than corporate multiproperty owners or REITs, charge management fees for the golf course operation on their expense statements. Salaries are generally shown and charged at a reasonable rate, but management fees are not. Again, market value assumes a sale, and management fees must be considered and discussed regardless of the property type.
- *Accounting format.* The appraiser should convert the client's income and expense statements and prepare their pro formas according to "Accounting for Public and Resort Golf Courses - 1990," a publication approved by the National Golf Course Owners Association and prepared by Pannell Kerr Forster, CPAs. This suggested format allows for underwriting analysis and the development of certain ratios, which help financial institutions underwrite loans on golf facilities. Most appraisers tend to use the accounting format utilized by the client.

Private Club Facilities

The biggest problem in the appraisal of private clubs is identifying the rights to be appraised. As memberships are sold in private clubs, certain rights are conveyed by the owner or operator. Some are rights to use and others represent partial ownership in the club. The total membership in an equity club then owns the club, which in turn owns the real estate. When appraising the property, is the total interest to be appraised? Consider, for example, an appraisal for the sale of the club and real estate performed for lending purposes. Do the interests to be appraised consist of only the remaining unsold memberships, or are they the sum of the remaining unsold memberships, the present value of the sold memberships, and the cash flows of the club operations? The documents must be read and the rights identified properly according to the function of the appraisal.

The handling of the reversion in the cash flow model also requires study. If a private club is not an equity club but is operated as a "right-to-use," entrepreneurial-driven, "for-profit" private club, the club owners have conveyed a "right-to-use" similar to a lease but not ownership. Therefore, at reversion the sale price would fit one of three scenarios:

1. Gift to member
2. Sale to anyone based on projected income for Year 11 (10-year cash flow model) and the appropriate capitalization rate
3. Sale to existing members as an equity-owned private club

The accounting format to be used for a private fee club is set forth in the "Uniform System of Accounting for Clubs," promulgated by the Club Manager's Association of America and developed by Pannell Kerr Forster, CPAs.

Generally a golf course property is appraised at its value in use as a golf course. Redevelopment to other, higher density uses is often limited by zoning, restrictive covenants, configuration, and master plans or land use plans that designate the site as recreational or open space land. This is important to recognize when analyzing comparable golf course sales. If a golf course is sold for redevelopment, it is a land sale with a change in use and cannot be used in estimating the value of a golf course. Moreover, golf courses are frequently acquired by government entities to maintain the area as open or green space and prevent redevelopment. In some instances these entities will pay a premium over the golf course value to maintain the open space.

RESIDENTIAL SUBDIVISION ANALYSIS

A thoroughly researched supply and demand study is essential to any residential subdivision appraisal. Most appraisers are not trained as demographers or statistical analysts and are not qualified to perform an independent supply and demand analysis. Some appraisers specialize in valuing residential subdivisions and are well equipped and trained for the task. The vast majority of appraisers, however, are advised to use a professional firm that provides residential market studies. It is important that the reviewer know the qualifications of the firm or individual responsible for developing the supply and demand analysis.

The so-called *aggregate retail value* is the sum of all the retail lot prices, not the value of the subdivision.

The most common problems in appraisals of residential subdivisions relate to the points of value. What are the critical benchmarks for the estimation of value—when the property was purchased as raw land, before permits and approvals, after permits and approvals, with the infrastructure partially complete, with all construction completed, when partially sold, or when model units have been constructed? The appraiser's questions can only be answered through good communication with the client. If the appraisal is for financing purposes, the appraiser needs to know how the loan is structured, when payouts are scheduled, at what point the lender has maximum exposure to risk, and what are the sequence and terms of the principal pay-downs.

In valuing subdivisions the understanding of risk is crucial because risk varies at the different points of value. Basically, there are three types of risk: 1) permitting risk, the risk that results from the approval process; 2) development risk, the risk that occurs after approvals and permits are obtained and during the construction of any off-site improvements and on-site infrastructure improvements; and 3) marketing risk, the risk of selling the lots is a timely and profitable manner.

In reviewing the appraiser's cash flow analysis, the reviewer should be alert for periodic lot pricing increases, if any. Studies have shown that, over the long term, lot prices just barely keep up with inflation. Estimates of price increases should be based on historical and projected trends in prices and supply and demand.

Yield rates used in the cash flow analysis (income capitalization approach) of a residential subdivision can vary widely, more so than with any other property type. It is vital that the reviewer check for the reasonableness of the yield rate by calculating an *IRR* using the periodic net cash flows (gross sales price less expenses) as the yield and the land purchase price as the time-zero investment. Yield rates for subdivision analysis comprise an allocation between the line-item developer's profit and the discount rate. If the appraiser has used a line-item developer's profit as one of the expenses, then the rate used is not a yield rate but simply a discount rate. It is important that the appraiser recognize this distinction. When using a line-item developer's profit, the appraiser should ensure that the comparables used have nearly the same sellout period as the subdivision being appraised.

Interviews with developers are essential in obtaining an estimate of line-item profit. Many developers consider their minimum required return in terms of the line-item profit as a percentage of gross sales. Usually developers do not include the time value of money when quoting their minimum required line-item profit. Therefore, the line-item profit obtained from developers usually has to be adjusted for the discount rate. If not, the combination of the line-item profit and the discount rate will overstate the total developer's profit. The results can be cross-checked by solving for the *IRR* using the cash flow amounts.

Brief Comments on Other Special-Use Properties

Medical Office Buildings

The appraiser must thoroughly understand the many characteristics that make a medical office building unique. There are many significant differences between medical office space and standard office space, which must be considered, researched, and addressed in the appraisal of a medical office building. The appraiser must consider physical, financial, and external influences as well as rental rates, expenses, tenant mix, construction costs, tenant improvement allowances, and building features such as elevators and parking. Data concerning these characteristics must be collected from similar medical office buildings. Using data on standard office space in a medical office building appraisal can undermine the reliability of the appraisal. The building's proximity to a hospital and the financial condition of any adjoining or associated hospital must be examined in detail, as proximity or lack of proximity can be a significant factor. The reviewer should ensure that the appraiser has separately valued personal property, medical equipment, and fixtures.

Branch Bank Properties

The approaches commonly used by appraisers to estimate value often fail to reflect accurately the thought processes of market participants. In the case of branch banks, the market consists of banking executives involved in branch acquisition and development. Real property is of secondary concern to institutions purchasing branches. These operations are acquired primarily to broaden the bank's deposit base or to gain a larger presence within a given market area. The banks seek to achieve economies of scale for marketing efforts as well as greater utilization of management and in-house systems.

In appraising branch banks, appraisers most often rely heavily on the cost and sale comparison approaches. However, market participants generally consider the income capitalization approach to be the most germane because it most clearly reflects the economics of branch operations. When negotiating rent for branch offices, financial institutions usually consider the actual or projected performance (deposit levels) of a facility, which in turn will indicate an affordable rent.

Branch bank operations generally fall into two categories: large, national banks with multistate exposure and local banks with branch operations restricted to a specific one- or two-state area.

Expansion of branch operations in a multistate environment, either through acquisition of existing branches of other institutions or buy/lease/build decisions within the holding company, are more often than not predicated on the concept of a shared expense platform. The holding company or bank considers the total expenses and allocates a pro rata share to a specific branch operation. The lease amount, if the branch is to be leased, is not as important as the capture of market share in the overall decision-making process. A branch occupied by a national, multistate institution may have a lease in place that does not reflect market levels. Again, this lease is considered in the overall income and expense considerations of the entire banking operation and amounts to nothing more than the cost of doing business in that specific area. While deposit levels are a consideration, they are not the only consideration. In the past few years, the institutional lender's service requirements and customer accessibility have been redefined. The service-related income streams of the bank help to maintain the hurdle rate requirements (rates of return on all product lines) of the parent organization. Core deposits, while the basis for lending limits to the institution, now fall behind the income received from customer service-related areas.

In appraisals based on the income approach, the primary considerations should be market acceptability and, more importantly, the magnitude of the institutional operation. The appraiser may find that the end result identified as market value is actually investment value.

The local branch bank scenario differs in that expansion and the sharing of multistate expenses are not considered. Lease terms for outlying branch banks are important for their overall effect on the small bank operation. A tight line is maintained and when expansion is considered, the lease expense is a very important part of the decision-making process. Competition with larger, multistate operations has overshadowed the small, personal banking environment of the past. One of the few situations in which lease amounts are not a consideration is the need of a new operation to establish a corporate headquarters in order to obtain a state charter. Purchases are generally predicated on the desire to obtain the largest building for the least amount of money.

In valuing branch bank operations, particularly using sales comparison, the appraiser must be aware of the current economic trends surrounding the institutional user. Sales must reflect continual institutional use with little consideration for furniture, fixtures, and equipment.

Religious Facilities

The sales comparison approach is generally considered the best indicator of the value of religious facilities. In active markets, sales of similar religious institutions can be compared on a feature-by-feature basis, considering the fixed seating capacity, stained glass, special features (e.g., baptistery, prayer rooms, arks), and other attributes of the facilities. Usually, however, religious facilities cannot be compared directly because they differ widely in their uses, design, and quality.

Relatively consistent prices on a per-seat basis have been found when the properties' support facilities are similar. That is, when the ratios of fixed seating to total building area are similar, per-seat prices for religious facilities can be compared if the properties are of similar quality, size, age, and condition. The vast amount of peripheral space within many facilities makes application of the price-per-seat unit of comparison difficult. Often it is easier to rely on a sale price per square foot. Adjustments for conditions of sale, financing, and market conditions can be based on generally accepted methods. Extracting the land value estimate from each sale is also helpful. This step is needed to calculate depreciation and eliminates the need for land-to-building ratio adjustments and location adjustments (assuming that the differences in site values account for locational characteristics).[2]

Restaurants

In the analysis and appraisal of restaurant properties, many appraisers are inadvertently calling a use value or going-concern value estimate a market value estimate. This error has resulted in lenders unknowingly granting partially unsecured loans at the same terms normally offered for totally secured loans and has caused substantial loan losses when the restaurants failed. It is vital that appraisers differentiate between the market value of the real estate and the going-concern (or use) value of the restaurant to avoid misleading clients.

Restaurant properties have a limited number of potential occupants since only one type of business can occupy them for their original purpose. A potential occupant who wishes to change the use of a special-purpose property would only pay a price for that property equal to the price of comparable space that would accommodate his or her business. The highest price for the resale or lease of a vacant restaurant is usually obtained from a "same-concept"

2. For more information see Martin H. Aaron, MAI, SRA, and John H. Wright, Jr., MAI, *The Appraisal of Religious Facilities* (Chicago: Appraisal Institute, 1997).

Because most properties are replaceable, this assumption is valid for most properties. However, there are some land uses and improvements that cannot be reestablished in their present form or location at any cost. Special applications of the appraisal approaches are required to analyze and reflect the market values of these properties properly. Often monopoly properties are created through restrictive zoning ordinances; they are legally nonconforming or have been grandfathered in after the imposition of downzoning or other land use regulations. Some properties enjoy a special advantage because they predate modern zoning or building codes.

user. However, this scenario represents only a small percentage of vacant restaurant sales since most restaurateurs are reluctant to attempt a venture after another restaurateur has failed.

Estimating the market value of an old restaurant or another successful service business is difficult because it is hard to separate out the history of the operation and the acumen of the owners. If the market value of a property is the present worth of its future benefits, what is the value of such a facility to the owner (value in use) and what is the market value to a third party? The highest and best use of the facility may be its continued use as a service business, but it is likely that a higher net return would be realized by the present owners continuing the operation than by a third party.

Monopoly Properties

The third edition of *The Dictionary of Real Estate Appraisal* defines a *monopoly property* as "A property used by an enterprise that, through franchise, license, zoning, regulation, etc., has the exclusive right to conduct that enterprise." The bulk of appraisal theory is centered on the principle of substitution, and, because most properties are replaceable, this assumption is valid for most properties. However, there are some land uses and improvements that cannot be reestablished in their present form or location at any cost. Special applications of the appraisal approaches are required to analyze and reflect the market values of the properties properly. Often monopoly properties are created through restrictive zoning ordinances; they are legally nonconforming or have been grandfathered in after the imposition of downzoning or other land use regulations. Some properties enjoy a special advantage because they predate modern zoning or building codes.

Nonconforming properties include

- Apartment buildings that exceed current height restrictions or contain more units than are currently allowed.
- Uses that are no longer environmentally permitted such as landfills, junkyards, and a host of industrial uses.
- Oceanfront properties that enjoy views and accessibility to water for uses that are no longer permitted.
- Outdoor advertising signs located in jurisdictions where new signs can no longer be constructed but existing displays are allowed to remain. In this case, the existing displays have monopoly status.

In the valuation of a monopoly property, the appraiser must give careful thought to defining the value to be estimated. The appraisal of such a property should identify and support the conclusion that the property has monopoly property characteristics. Monopoly properties enjoy special advantages but also involve special risks. Both must be considered in the valuation process. In addition to the standard appraisal descriptions and valuation approaches, an appraisal of a monopoly property should

1. Identify the property as having elements of monopoly value and explain how the monopoly value was created, how long it is likely to continue, and what event might cause its termination.

2. Estimate and support the property value as if the property were replaceable. This is a logical starting point and will highlight the significance of the monopoly property features.
3. Use income and value-in-use calculations where possible to demonstrate the property's value as a monopoly property. The appraiser should try to assume the viewpoint of the market or typical user, rather than that of a specific user, which might tend to exaggerate the value. The reviewer should be very cautious if the appraiser seems to be awed by the "cash cow" aura of the monopoly property.
4. Evaluate the risk and degree of transferability that exists for the particular monopoly property.
5. Consider the consequences of replacing the facility and the possible need to consider future costs as an element of its value.

In the majority of cases, the income capitalization approach, using either direct or yield capitalization, will be the most valid and reliable approach for valuing monopoly properties. In some cases application of a gross income multiplier may provide a valid indication of value. As always, the reviewer must be sure that the appraiser's method of valuation reflects the behavior of market participants.

Appraisal of a monopoly property presents a special challenge to an appraiser, who must be prepared to extend the investigation beyond the scope of the sales comparison and cost approaches. These appraisal standbys are often inapplicable or the necessary data simply do not exist. Such difficulties do not justify ignoring the status of a monopoly property or explaining away its special value. A logical and supportable value can be estimated for these properties. When value in use must be substituted for market value, which is legally acceptable under certain conditions, the concluded value should be carefully defined and justified.

Special Problems with Lease-by-Lease/DCF Computer Program Analysis

Introduction

Over the past 15 years, the increased accessibility of personal computers has made discounted cash flow (DCF) analysis the premier tool for valuing multitenant, income-producing, investment-grade real estate. As with any complex and sophisticated technique, misuse and abuse of DCF analysis abounds, due largely to its use by inadequately trained analysts. Users often do not understand the interrelationships among the many variables that can affect a property's worth or recognize the danger of using unsupported data inputs. Appraisers should always critically evaluate the reliability of the methods and data they use to produce a value estimate. When correctly and carefully applied, DCF analysis is a powerful valuation tool.[1]

DCF analysis can provide a more accurate measure of value than direct capitalization because it considers a multitude of variables that affect cash flow and takes into account changes in the value of income over time. DCF analysis is also easier to apply than it once was. Although the computations can be relatively complex, lease-by-lease/DCF (LXL/DCF) programs such as Pro-Ject®, Office2®, Center®, and Argus® reduce the effort needed to perform a DCF analysis. Electronic spreadsheet programs also include net present value functions, which allow a user to create and modify his or her own DCF applications. However, the use of self-constructed electronic spreadsheet DCF programs can be fraught with problems, and the integrity of the outcome can be seriously flawed. Because of these problems, many institutional clients will not accept DCF analyses completed on self-constructed electronic spreadsheets. Instead, they rely only on "black-box" LXL/DCF programs, which have proven integrity and are universally accepted by appraisers and market participants.

1. The author gratefully acknowledges the appraisal review staff of First Chicago-NBD, who provided the author with technical resources and assistance in writing this chapter.

The Need to Forecast

Forecasting is an imprecise art at best. If not carefully prepared, projected cash flows can result in a totally misleading value estimate. Nevertheless, forecasting is integral to the planning of real estate investments and development projects and is, therefore, important to investment value methodology. Forecasting may not answer every questions about the future, but it can at least help investors formulate meaningful judgments about feasibility and value. DCF analysis necessitates forecasts, and in making these forecasts the appraiser should employ the same procedure applied by investors who use DCF in their decision making.

As an expression of the principle of anticipation, forecasting is the essence of valuation. A forecast must be approached in the same way all market data extractions are accomplished—with diligent research and careful verification. Discounted cash flow analysis can only provide accurate results if the forecasts developed are based on accurate, reliable information. Rather than attempt to forecast peaks and troughs over the holding period, a level of precision that is virtually impossible to achieve, appraisers must reflect market expectations as to how the subject property will perform over a reasonably long time frame. Typical forecast categories to be addressed in DCF analysis include

- Current market rental rates and expected rate changes
- Existing base rents and contractual base rent adjustments
- Renewal options
- Existing and anticipated expense recovery (escalation) provisions
- Re-leasing assumptions including new lease terms, vacancy loss and sometimes free rent offered at existing lease expirations, tenant space preparation costs, and leasing commissions
- Tenant turnover
- Operating expenses
- Reversion and any selling or transaction costs
- Changes in inflation (measured by the Consumer Price Index)
- Discount rate(s)
- Business cycle—i.e., the state of the economy and economic trends
- Monetary cycle—i.e., the expansion or contraction of the money supply

Importance of Tenant Schedules

The primary tool for checking outputs and the integrity of the inputs is the single-tenant schedules that are available with most LXL/DCF programs. Single-tenant schedules provide year-by-year outputs for each tenant, including contract rent, expense pass-throughs, market rent, vacancy, tenant improvement costs, and leasing commissions. This schedule allows the reviewer to answer the following questions:

- Are rents growing at the specified step or escalation rate?
- Are start dates and expiration dates correct?

- Are pass-throughs modeled correctly for both the contract term and the renewal or turnover period? Pass-throughs for similar leases should be consistent. When pass-throughs appear to be inconsistent, the reviewer will want to know the reason for the difference. For example, if expense pass-throughs are typically $3.50 per square foot, why does tenant XYZ have a $6.00 per square foot pass-through?
- Are tenant improvement costs and leasing commissions modeled and input correctly? Do the dollar amounts appear reasonable?
- Do contract rents and market rents appear reasonable? Single-tenant schedules allow the reviewer to make a direct, year-by-year comparison for each tenant.

Tests of Reasonableness

There are several tests that may be used to analyze or review the results of a DCF analysis. The tests can also identify risk elements, which can facilitate the selection of a discount rate. The tests of reasonableness presented here include

- Growth rate tests (i.e., comparison of the projected rental rate with the feasibility rental rate and turnover schedule)
- Indicated appreciation over the holding period
- The effect of the holding period on value
- The pro rata contribution from actual and prospective cash flows and reversion
- Operating expense ratios and income multipliers
- The cost of vacancy
- Terminal-year and first-year estimate tests
- The turnover ratio
- Mathematical and discounting tests

These tests are described in the following pages.

Growth Rate Tests

The selection of income and expense growth rates is critical in DCF analysis. Ideally appraisals should include market analyses that project market occupancy. Estimation of an appraised property's competitive position allows occupancy projections to be derived for the subject. In oversupplied markets, rents typically decline until occupancy stabilizes. Rents remain level until market occupancy reaches stabilization, then enhanced demand causes rents to increase faster than inflation until feasibility is achieved. Thus, comparing the annual rental rate to the feasibility rental rate in a DCF analysis is a useful test of reasonableness.

The feasibility rental rate can be extracted from data used in the income and cost approaches. The procedure is demonstrated as follows:

	Estimation of Feasibility Rental Rate
Construction cost of improvements	$100.00
Land (per sq. ft. of net rentable area)	+ 15.00
Total cost	$115.00
Entrepreneurial incentive (7.5%–12.5%, say 10%)	+ 11.50
Total cost and entrepreneurial incentive	$126.50
Overall rate (10%)	× 0.10
Net operating income	$12.65
Expenses (per sq. ft. of net rentable area)	+ 7.50
Effective gross income	$20.15
Vacancy & collection loss (7%)	+ 1.50
Potential gross income	$21.65

The DCF analysis can be tested for the feasibility of both potential gross income and net operating income. The subsequent escalation of costs for inflation allows annual projections of feasibility rents to be developed for each year of the analysis. Comparing the feasibility rent to the rental rate estimated in the DCF analysis and to projected market occupancy provides a test of reasonableness for both the magnitude and timing of the income growth rates employed. Rental rates for existing properties seldom equal or exceed the feasibility rental rate due to physical and functional deficiencies.

Another good cross-checking procedure is comparison of income growth rates with tenant turnover in each year of analysis. Substantial renewals in any year may limit rent increases or result in occupancy attrition as rent-sensitive tenants are displaced to lower-cost alternatives.

When modeling cash flows, appraisers often question when the growth rate should be applied to the market rental rate. For example, if an analysis is being conducted in November or December and the market rental rate is assumed to increase at 3.5% per year, the first rental rate increase would begin one or two months from the start date. To avoid overstating the increase, the appraiser should either hold the growth rate to zero in the first year or model a lower rate of growth for the first year.

Appreciation Over the Holding Period

To perform a fairly simple test of reasonableness, the analyst can use a financial calculator to examine the indicated compound appreciation over the holding period. Comparing the value estimate extracted (present value or *PV*) with the reversion (future value or *FV*) over the holding period (n) and solving for the interest rate (I) results in an estimate of compound annual property appreciation. This rate of appreciation can be compared with the investor criteria gleaned from market research and with projected inflation rates. An implied growth rate greater than market expectations indicates enhanced risk; conversely, a lower growth rate reflects a more conservative projection. This test can also be used to assess the reasonableness of the discount rate via the exponential rate of change formula ($Y_o = R_o + CR$).

Effect of Holding Period

Although most DCF analyses are based on a 10-year holding period, investors in supply-saturated markets sometimes forecast shorter holding periods. The expirations and re-lease potential of significant leases may also affect the selection of a realistic holding period. Sensitivity analyses for various holding periods can provide additional guidance for value maximization. Property income and expenses over shorter holding periods can be estimated with greater reliability, enhancing the dependability of the analysis and replicating the thinking of investors, who often rely on actual income only. However, the analyst must recognize that the shorter the holding period, the greater the reliance on the reversionary portion of the value indication.

Pro Rata Contribution from Cash Flows and Reversion

The risk inherent in a DCF analysis can be identified by examining the contribution of value derived from the cash flows versus the reversion. Examining the contribution from income under existing leases versus income from speculative leases projected by the analyst is another useful test, although difficult to apply. The analyst can also calculate the DCF first with existing leases only and then compare this output with a DCF that models absorption and renewal.

The first test mentioned, examining the contribution from cash flow and from the reversion, is easy to understand and apply. The analyst simply calculates the percentage of total value represented by the present value of the cash flows versus the present value of the reversion. If the cash flow constitutes more value, risk is diminished; conversely, if the reversion makes up the greater percentage of value, risk is enhanced. Similarly, if actual cash flow (i.e., income derived from existing leases) is a substantial portion of value, risk is mitigated; if significant value is derived from speculative leases, risk is increased. These tests assist in the selection of a discount rate. Of the reasonable range of rates indicated, should the analyst choose a rate that is conservative or one that reflects a bit more risk?

Operating Expense Ratios and Income Multipliers

A review of the operating expense ratio and income multipliers for each year in the analysis can also provide insight into the reasonableness of a cash flow statement. The operating expense ratio is defined in *The Dictionary of Real Estate Appraisal* as "the ratio of total operating expenses to effective gross income."

Operating expenses / effective gross income = operating expense ratio

The first-year operating expense ratio should be checked to ensure conformity with market data or to discover the reason for any variance. As properties age, operating expense ratios typically increase and the cash flow projection should reflect this trend. In addition, fluctuations in occupancy affect variable expenses and should be reviewed to ensure consistent estimates.

Gross and effective gross income multipliers can also be examined as a test of reasonableness. Multipliers for the initial years of the analysis should be bracketed using data from the sales comparison approach, with any differences analyzed and discussed. A review of trends in the multipliers over the analysis period may also expose inconsistencies in the analysis.

The Cost of Vacancy

The cost of vacancy is the vacancy rate (i.e., the percentage of units that are vacant) times the rental income for the property. The vacancy rate depends on the typical lease term, vacancy between leases, and the probability of lease renewal. An allowance for credit loss is also considered a part of the overall vacancy rate. The credit loss allowance should reflect the primary creditworthiness of the tenants and whether they are considered by the market to be national, regional, or local credits.

COMPONENTS OF THE VACANCY RATE

1. Typical lease term
2. Lag vacancy
3. Lease renewal probability
4. Allowance for credit loss

The typical lease term is simply what its name implies. For example, if the appraiser determines that the market lease term for typical tenants of the subject property is three to five years, then the typical lease term might be four years. After the primary lease term expires, units often remain vacant for a certain amount of time, depending on property type and market conditions. This vacancy between leases is referred to as *lag vacancy*. The probability of renewal is the chance that an average tenant will renew his or her lease at the end of each lease term. A 100% probability of renewal implies that the tenant will never leave the subject property. A 0% probability of renewal suggests that the tenant will definitely leave after the expiration of one lease term.

Problems arise because of the assumptions included in a typical DCF analysis. Most DCF programs request three or four of the components of vacancy. These figures are used to estimate the cash flow expenses that a property owner will encounter during the normal holding period of a property. These cash flow expenses include leasing commissions for new or renewing tenants, capital costs to refurbish or retrofit a unit after a tenant leaves, and any rental concessions offered as incentives for tenants to renew.

The four variables are mutually dependent, in that setting the values of any three determines the value of the fourth. Because the relationships between the variables are not clearly visible, the problem might be overlooked by the appraiser, the client, or the reviewer. Inconsistency in the application of the four variables can cause serious inaccuracies in the value conclusion. When extracting the components of vacancy from the market, appraisers need to be aware that brokers and property managers may unknowingly offer conflicting responses, which should be checked for consistency.

Another problem for reviewers is that the various vacancy component assumptions may be scattered throughout the report. They might not be stated explicitly anywhere in the report. The more poorly organized the report, the more difficult it will be to find all of the assumptions.

A common vacancy-related error arises in situations where one tenant is vacating a space and another tenant has signed a lease to take over that space. If the appraiser neglects to reflect the expiration of the original tenant at the end of the lease term and provides a speculative renewal assumption, the tenant space will be double-counted throughout the cash flow projection.

Examination of Terminal-Year Estimates

Because terminal-year net operating income is the basis for the reversion estimate, this figure should be reviewed to ensure that an unusual amount of turnover (or fewer-than-typical expirations) has not distorted the net operating income estimate. If the estimate is believed to be distorted, it may be appropriate to review the values indicated by capitalizing income from the preceding or subsequent year (or an average of all three years). The lease expiration schedule should also be reviewed to identify any above- or below-market leases that will expire just after the analysis period ends and thus undermine the reasonableness of the reversion estimate.

The terminal capitalization rate can also be tested against the going-in (or first-year) overall rate. Quarterly investor surveys indicate the difference between these rates as perceived by market participants. The appraiser's analysis should reflect a similar premium or explain why a different relationship is appropriate.

Comparison of First-Year Estimates to Historical Experience

When historical income and expense statements are available for analysis, another good test is to compare these with the first-year estimates used in the DCF analysis to ensure that the cash flow estimates reflect appropriate inflation increases. This can be especially confusing when partial years are involved. Substantial differences should be supported and explained.

Turnover/Retention Ratio

One critical variable that is often overlooked is the turnover ratio, also called the *renewal rate*. Because both tenant improvement allowances and leasing commissions are calculated based on the renewal rate, this rate can have a substantial influence on value. Unfortunately, most appraisals contain little discussion of this variable and provide minimal support for the rate selected.

Because of their importance, renewal rates should be a focus of market research. Examination of renewal rates and rent at the appraised property and sale comparables can provide insights, which should be augmented by interviewing market participants. Over time, this research can be used as a database of renewal rate comparables.

To test tenant improvement costs and leasing commissions, the analyst can compare projected costs with historical costs and look at turnover in relation to tenant improvement and leasing costs.

Mathematical and Discounting Tests

A final, essential test is to check math and discounting calculations manually to catch any errors in the cash flow analysis. This is especially important when custom software and spreadsheets are used. A random check of growth rates, subtraction, percentage calculations, and discounting will enhance confidence in the value conclusion and prevent embarrassing mistakes. The incomes and expenses of several tenants should be reviewed. Rent, expense pass-throughs, tenant improvements, and leasing commissions should be calculated manually and checked against the discounted cash flow. This is especially advisable when substantial property value is created by cash flows derived from a few, large leases. The appraiser should also ensure that the discount rates applied reflect the stated period; this can be a complicated issue if partial years are included.

Other Tests of Reasonableness

The reasonableness of the appraiser's analysis can be further tested by asking the following questions:

- ✓ Is the discount rate reasonable relative to the risk in the cash flows forecast?
- ✓ How reasonable is the terminal overall capitalization rate used to calculate the reversionary value?
- ✓ Do the selling costs represent a reasonable percentage of the reversionary value?
- ✓ Do the discount rate and terminal overall rate reflect a typical or appropriate relationship?
- ✓ What is the implied first-year, going-in, overall capitalization rate, based on the *NOI* for the first stabilized year divided by the value conclusion? Is it greater or less than the terminal overall capitalization rate? Why?
- ✓ What is the final concluded value per square foot of building area? Does this value correlate with the conclusions derived using the other approaches to value?
- ✓ What percentages of total value are derived from the present value of the cash flows and the present value of the reversion? Does the reversion represent more or less than 50% of the final value conclusion?
- ✓ Does the cash flow for the 11th year (or the year used to calculate the reversion) reflect a typical year's income, or is the income greater or less than typical due to lease expirations or other circumstances?
- ✓ Is the calculation of the reversion shown in the report? Did the appraiser "gross up for lag vacancy"?
- ✓ What is the compound rate of growth in the net operating income over the holding period? At what rate are gross income and expenses increasing? How does the current value conclusion compare to the reversionary value?
- ✓ Are the operating expenses greater or less than the expense pass-throughs or recoveries charged to the tenants?
- ✓ If a retail property is being appraised, what are the forecasts of retail sales per square foot? How much of the property's income is dependent on overage payments?
- ✓ If an apartment property is being appraised, is the cash flow based on a forecast of future rents that is in line with past income? What is the expense ratio—i.e., the percentage of total expenses compared to the effective gross income?

✓ Is the vacancy and collection loss estimate reasonable and in line with the market? Has lag vacancy been considered and employed in the cash flow forecast?

✓ Does the subject outperform or underperform the market in terms of occupancy or rental rate? Is its performance likely to continue?

✓ Was a partial year employed for the first year of the cash flow, and if so, are the present value factors correct?

✓ Was a recognized software program (e.g., Pro-Ject®, Argus®) used rather than an in-house, Lotus spreadsheet?

✓ Were line items for reserves, tenant alterations, or leasing commissions included? Do the forecasts appear adequate? If the property has deferred maintenance, was it deducted from the cash flow?

✓ Are there any line items in the pro forma that were not discussed in the report, or were they discussed but omitted from the cash flow? (Such line items might include ground rent, hotel franchise fees, or equipment rental.)

Tests of reasonableness can assist reviewers and analysts who review the output of DCF analyses. Because each property presents unique challenges, common sense and detailed market research are the best tests of reasonableness. Applying the tests described here can, however, provide additional support for the value estimate and assist in the estimation of appropriate discount rates. Reviewers should maintain a database of DCF inputs to help them assess critical variables.

Reviewer Hints

Reviewers are advised to compare the narrative discussion in the report to the printouts of the software assumptions. Where the text and the software input match up, the reviewer can check off the assumption and go on to the next one. Some reviewers color code the assumptions and match the specific tenant assumptions to the general assumptions. Also, the specific tenant inputs should be studied to determine if the current and speculative renewal assumptions are consistent with the discussion provided for each tenant category.

When available, the landlord's rent roll can be compared to the tenant input. In reviewing a regional shopping center or major office building with many tenants, however, it is more efficient (and less time-consuming) to spot-check the specific tenant inputs rather than to verify each. Typically, the appraiser will model various tenant types or categories and set up reference tenants to use as models for each specific tenant in that particular category. If the actual tenants are modeled correctly, it is not always necessary to check all of the assumptions for each tenant in each category. Nevertheless, it is a good practice to check the lease dates and square footage against the rent roll.

Common Problems with Lease-by-Lease/ DCF Models

Reviewers with financial institutions find the following problems or flaws in analyses, assumptions, inputs, and outputs when they review lease-by-lease/DCF programs:

- Failure to consider option rents at re-leasing appropriately or to discuss the implications of the option. For example, some appraisers assume that the lease option will be exercised even though it calls for above-market rent.
- Employing an incorrect market rent for rollover/turnover. There are generally two or more classes of rent, and the appraiser may input the wrong class of rent for a specific tenant space.
- Failure to calculate the renewal cost correctly given the estimated probability of renewal.
- Failure to include a separate lease abstract in addition to the program inputs. The lease abstract is an absolute necessity because it allows the reviewer to cross-check the accuracy of inputs. (Many clients specify in their engagement letters that a lease abstract summary be provided.)
- Improper modeling of pass-through expenses.
- Applying an incorrect growth rate to the market rent.
- Improper inputting of escalations in the contract rent, especially when a Consumer Price Index (CPI) escalator clause is involved.
- "Hard keying" certain inputs for income and expenses and pass-throughs simply because the appraiser does not understand how to model them properly.
- Allowing the program to calculate the value without checking to ensure that it is accurate and reasonable. Also, choosing a reversionary year that does not represent a stabilized year (e.g., using a 10-year projection without considering the effect of rollovers and turnovers).
- Using growth rates that are too aggressive in view of market perceptions.
- Assigning an incorrect market rental rate or expense recovery to a speculative renewal tenant.
- Relying on mechanical procedures without examining risk or applying appraisal judgment to assess the overall effect of the assumptions.
- Modeling the program to the letter of the lease without cross-checking to see if the property is being managed exactly as outlined in the lease. For example, the lease may state that all expenses, capital improvements, and management fees (plus a 15% add-on) are passed through to the tenant, but in a soft market these items may be waived as a tenant concession. In estimating property expenses, the appraiser may fail to ask the key question: Who pays what?
- Failure to consider properly the risk attached to negative cash flows, especially if they occur in the early years of the forecast.
- Capitalizing the income from an atypical year in calculating the reversion. Appraisers often use a 10-year holding period and capitalize the 11th year without analyzing whether or not this year has a typical amount of tenant turnover. Often this can result in an "optimal" value, rather than a typical, "market-oriented" value. A

negative impact on the value conclusion will be produced if there is a great deal of turnover in the 11th year. Pro-Ject® allows the appraiser to compensate for this by "grossing up for lag vacancy," which restores all of the income lost through downtime between leases in the reversionary calculation. However, restoring all of the lost income is probably less market-oriented than simply basing the reversion on a different year.

- Failure to review the cash flow pro forma. Again, an appraiser may use a 10-year holding period without considering whether or not the 10-year period is reasonable. A problem is likely to exist if the total expense recoveries exceed the total amount of operating expenses in a given year or throughout the cash flow analysis period.
- Incorrect inputs in estimating prospective value. To estimate a prospective value using the Pro-Ject® software, the appraiser need only change the starting month if the prospective date of value is in a different month than the "as-is" month of value. However, there is a tendency to change the starting year also, which has the effect of placing today's market assumptions (1998 market rental rates, expenses, etc.) into the future starting year. In other words, if the prospective value is in 2000 and the starting year in Pro-Ject® is changed from 1998 to 2000, then the program assumes that the market rental rates the appraiser estimated for 1998 are also the rates for 2000.
- Using discount rates and capitalization rates that are inconsistent with one another without providing an explanation.
- Placing too much reliance on global assumptions and neglecting to consider specific tenant circumstances. For example, all tenants may be given a renewal/turnover probability of say 60/40, when the report has noted that one tenant is definitely leaving at the end of the lease term while another will most likely not vacate its space.
- Inaccurate estimation of weighted averages for tenant improvements or leasing commissions.

Conclusion

Some appraisers allow the results of the DCF analysis to determine the value conclusion, rather than making the value conclusion the result of the appraiser's own judgment. In other words, the DCF model becomes a substitute for the appraiser's analysis and judgment. Also, when yield capitalization is the method of choice, the cost approach and sales comparison approach conclusions often appear to be "backed-into"—i.e., based on the results of the DCF analysis.

Those lease analysis programs that have universal market acceptance have proven to be accurate and reliable. Their weaknesses are attributable to human error. Thus, the reliability of LXL/DCF programs ultimately depends on the appraiser's analysis of the market data and the appraiser's training in the appropriate use of the programs.

Reviewers' Most Frequently Asked Questions

To conduct a comprehensive review of an appraisal report, the reviewer must proceed methodically through each step of the valuation process. Typically the reviewer considers whether

- ✓ The appraisal is logical and the stated conclusion is appropriate to the purpose and use of the appraisal.
- ✓ The data are accurate, adequate, and properly analyzed.
- ✓ The data have been used in a consistent manner within each approach and are correlated from one approach to another.
- ✓ The calculations are correct.
- ✓ The conclusions are reasonable, based on the data and analysis presented.

To help ensure that the report is a quality product, the reviewer can go over the 70 questions listed below.

Questions Concerning the Cost Approach

1. Did the appraiser actually follow the procedure outlined in the report?
2. Was a map used to locate the land sales and the subject site? (This may or may not be a specification for the report.)
3. Are the land sales truly comparable in shape, size, utility access, and zoning? Are they the most recent sales available?
4. Do the comparable parcels have the same highest and best use as the subject parcel? They should.
5. Do the land sales bracket the per-unit value of the subject site? That is, has the appraiser provided comparable sales that are inferior to the land parcel being

appraised, requiring upward (positive) adjustments, as well as sales that are superior to the subject, requiring downward (negative) adjustments? Bracketing the subject value adds to the reviewer's confidence in the cost approach.

6. What were the subsequent uses of the sites used as comparables? Was the motivation of the buyers and sellers researched by the appraiser?
7. Would a per-unit breakdown of price per allowable square foot of building provide a more meaningful basis for comparison? This unit of comparison is commonly called *price per allowable SF* or *per FAR* (floor area ratio).
8. Are the negative and positive adjustments discussed in the appraiser's narrative consistent and logical? If not, the reviewer should call the appraiser for an explanation.
9. Does the land value conclusion make sense and reflect current land value trends? It should not be just an average or historic mean.
10. Is the source of the cost data identified in the report?
11. Do the appraiser's explanations of items of deterioration and functional and external obsolescence sound logical? This is a very subjective area, and it usually has only minor significance because little reliance is placed on the cost approach. Nevertheless, the appraiser's observations regarding deferred maintenance items and functional and economic obsolescence are very important insofar as these features impact the other two value approaches. (When the cost approach is the primary indicator of value, the appraiser's analysis and estimates of various forms of accrued depreciation should be detailed and substantiated more thoroughly.)
12. Is the effective age of the property consistent with the physical condition reported? Is the same physical condition used as the basis for adjustments to rent comparables, expense comparables, and sales comparables in the income and sales comparison approaches?
13. Are the land value, estimated cost new, and various forms of accrued depreciation reported consistently throughout the report? Has the appraiser considered and properly applied an allocation for entrepreneurial profit? The reviewer should also check all mathematical calculations and compare the summation with the text of the report.
14. Can the cost approach indication be reconciled with the results of the other two approaches? A wide difference could signal a serious problem. The reasons for any significant discrepancy should be explained by the appraiser.

Questions Concerning the Sales Comparison Approach

15. Did the appraiser actually follow the procedure outlined in the report?
16. Are the comparable sales truly comparable in size, use, construction, physical characteristics, and marketability, and are they the most recent available?

17. Were the sales located on a map? Were photos provided? (Photos may or may not be a specification for the report.)
18. Did the appraiser investigate the buyer motivation in each sale and perhaps the subsequent use of the property since the sale? Buyer motivation is often the driving force behind a commercial property sale and a prime determinant of the price paid.
19. Did the appraiser compare owner-user sales with other owner-user sales and investor sales with other investor sales? If not, it could be an "apples and oranges" comparison as owner-users and investors have different property pricing criteria.
20. If the subject property has been sold recently, has the appraiser considered all available information about that transaction?
21. Do the comparable sales bracket the per-unit value of the subject? Is there a representation sample of comparables that are inferior and superior to the property being appraised? An appraiser can inadvertently "steer" a value by selecting comparables that are all inferior or superior to the subject. In such a case, all available comparable sales may not have been fully researched.
22. Have the accuracy and reliability of the sales data been ascertained? What sources were contacted for transactional information? How were the data verified—by the buyer, the seller, an attorney, or a lender? Is the information complete?
23. Were all necessary adjustments made to the sizes of the comparables so that the properties were compared on a common basis? Adjustments are sometimes needed because mezzanine space, basement space, attic area, and wood frame storage additions are normally not included in square foot area computations.
24. Do the negative and positive adjustments discussed in the appraiser's narrative appear reasonable? If not, the reviewer should call the appraiser for an explanation of any apparent inconsistencies. If the comparable is superior to the subject, a downward adjustment must be applied to the price of the comparable; if the comparable is inferior to the subject, the price of the comparable must be adjusted upward to reflect the difference.
25. Does the rationale for the adjustments appear logical from a market standpoint?
26. Does the reconciled value indication appear reasonable and reflect current market trends for the type of property being appraised? It should not be an average or historic mean. In the final step in the sales comparison approach, the reconciliation of the data, the appraiser reviews the reliability, type, and scope of the data available and evaluates the analytical procedures used. The greatest reliance is placed on the comparables that have been sold most recently, are most similar to the subject, and are subject to the fewest adjustments.
27. Has the appraiser used the most comparable, recent, and reliable sales available? The sales comparison approach is often the key determinant of the final value conclusion, so it is doubly important that it be accurate.

28. Is the appraisal report an "off-the-shelf" product? Occasionally a reviewer will encounter a report that is a near copy of a relatively recent appraisal of a similar property located in a similar market, which has been cosmetically altered to pass as a current appraisal work product. Submitting such a report is a total disservice to the client.
29. Does this value concluded by sales comparison reconcile with the value indications derived in the other two approaches?

QUESTIONS CONCERNING THE INCOME CAPITALIZATION APPROACH

30. Did the appraiser actually follow the procedure outlined in the report?
31. Is the appraised property currently subject to an existing lease? If so, was the value determined "subject to the existing lease"? (If the lessee is the prospective purchaser or the lease is to be dissolved as the result of a subsequent transaction, the appraiser may be instructed to ignore impact of the lease on the valuation. In such a case, the instructions should be clearly stated in the letter of transmittal and in the limiting conditions.)
32. Has the appraiser clearly stated whether the property interest being valued is a leased fee, leasehold, or fee simple interest?
33. Are the comparable rentals truly comparable and meaningful? Are they recent enough to reflect the current market accurately? Are they actual rents or asking rents?
34. Does the appraiser make it clear that gross rents are being compared with gross rents and net rents are compared with net rents? Are they all adjusted to a common denominator?
35. Is the vacancy allowance realistic? (Statistical data on vacancy are usually only available for office and apartment buildings.)
36. Do the operating expense estimates appear realistic? Actual operating expenses should provide good guidelines for future expense levels.
37. Are the real estate tax estimates reasonable? Do they correlate with the real estate tax section of the report?
38. Are the real estate taxes in line with comparable properties, and has the appraiser anticipated any increases in the near future? Taxes are usually expressed and compared on a per-square-foot basis.
39. Does the net income estimate appear reasonable? Has it been reconciled with the net operating incomes of the comparables included in the report?
40. Did the appraiser use the appropriate capitalization technique? The choices are direct capitalization and yield capitalization or discounted cash flow analysis. DCF analysis is used primarily for large retail centers, office buildings, and other multitenant properties with varying lease expiration dates and terms. Direct

capitalization is typically used for single-tenant properties such as industrial buildings, neighborhood retail centers, small office buildings, special-use properties, and apartments.

41. What was the source of the discount, capitalization, and inflation rates and the other assumptions used in discounted cash flow analysis?

42. How was the capitalization rate derived for direct capitalization? If mortgage-equity or band-of-investment techniques were used, additional support in the form of published surveys, an analysis of comparables, or an analysis of alternative investments available in the market may be desirable.

43. Does the appraiser treat discount and capitalization rates as equivalent? If so, this could be a red flag indicating that his or her thinking is amiss.

44. Does the reconciled value indication reflect the actual and near-term occupancy status of the property?

45. Are mathematical procedures and assumptions applied consistently? All calculations used in the approach should be checked.

QUESTIONS CONCERNING THE VALUE CONCLUSION

46. Do the value indications derived from the three approaches fall into a reasonable range? An appraisal is more credible if they do. If they do not, did the appraiser explain the rationale for the differences? In reconciliation the appraiser analyzes alternative conclusions to arrive at a final value estimate. The results produced by each of the approaches to value are weighed, and the greatest emphasis is placed on the approach or approaches that are most applicable to the problem and make use of the most reliable, accurate, and representative data. The appraiser's judgment, experience, and proper application of appraisal techniques are critical in final reconciliation.

47. Are the results of all the approaches consistent with the appraiser's determination of highest and best use?

48. Do the indications derived from the approaches applied reflect the same defined value? For example, a value indication derived from income capitalization that is higher than an indication based on the cost approach may or may not include a non-realty or business enterprise value component.

49. Is the appraiser's reconciliation and value conclusion to the point and logical? Reviewers should be extremely wary of appraisers who use phrases like "trust me" and "based on my vast experience and knowledge."

50. Has the appraiser developed a conclusion that reflects the defined value and is subject to the considerations and conditions stated in the front of the report?

51. Do the report and value conclusion comply with the terms of the engagement letter?

52. When applicable, did the appraiser address any improvements and significant capital expenses made by the borrower?

Tests of Reasonableness

53. Did the appraiser break down the value, both of the overall property and its components, into per-unit values to make meaningful comparisons with appraisal data relating to similar properties?
54. How does the report compare with other appraisal reports in the reviewer's files? The quality, location, and physical characteristics of the subject and comparable properties can be compared with the descriptions of comparables in other reports. If several appraisal reports of properties in the same geographic area have been reviewed, some of the comparables will likely appear in several reports. If so, the reviewer can check the property descriptions, prices, and sale dates reported for consistency. For reviewers who deal with a large volume of appraisals, a computerized database system of comparable land and property sales, rates, and rents can greatly facilitate the review process.
55. Does the value conclusion correlate with the market exposure time forecast? A longer or shorter exposure time may be more appropriate to the client's needs. If so, the value will probably need to be adjusted to reflect the atypical market exposure period. (Such contingencies should be agreed on beforehand and spelled out in the engagement letter.)
56. Did the appraiser conduct some independent verification of sales and rental data? The reviewer should check with independent sources. Local business news publications are often good sources for local real estate data on rents and sales. At a minimum, they will provide good leads on active brokers and agents. The published data of local professional real estate associations can also be consulted for verification.
57. Does the value pass the "snicker test"? The reviewer can discuss the appraisal assumptions and conclusions with associates to see if they find them to be plausible.
58. Has the appraiser acknowledged all potential property and market risks and contingencies associated with subject property and the valuation in the report?
59. If the subject property is a new development, do the appraisal conclusions indicate that it will pass the acid test of feasibility? In the final analysis, any real estate development must pass this test, which consists of dividing the capitalized initial stabilized net operating income by total development costs. This procedure should produce a reasonable index of feasibility. Projects should not depend on inflated future growth to achieve a reasonable return. Rather, the current operating figures must indicate a strong likelihood for an attractive return on the investment.

Overall Questions of Concern

60. Do the approaches and methods applied lead to meaningful conclusions that relate to the purpose, use, and scope of the appraisal?
61. Given the definition of value and the assumptions and limiting conditions applied, did the value estimate derived satisfy all of the client's requirements as well as those of professional standards?
62. Did the extent of work carried out in collecting, confirming, and reporting data correspond to the scope of the appraisal as described in the definition of the appraisal problem?
63. Does the appraisal state that it complies fully with FIRREA (if applicable) and conforms to the current edition of the Uniform Standards of Professional Appraisal Practice?
64. Is bonded indebtedness (both existing and proposed) properly analyzed and included in the value conclusion(s)?
65. Are exposure and marketing period point estimates (not ranges) provided for each appraisal premise?

General Questions

66. Does the appraisal report include Federal Emergency Management Agency (FEMA) flood zone information?
67. Does the report provide seismic and/or earthquake zone information?
68. Are wetlands addressed?
69. Is compliance with the Americans with Disabilities Act (ADA) addressed?
70. Does the report contain unreasonable disclaimers purportedly limiting the liability of the appraiser?

Communication with the Appraiser

How Communication Works

Communication is integral to almost everything we do. In fact, it is the most important, complex thing we do. Communication is often difficult because it is an ongoing, constantly changing, ever-building process. When you decide to communicate something to someone, you begin with an idea and visualize an image of what you would like to communicate. Your brain begins to select and sort through words and symbols, all of which have meanings learned from past experience. You then engage in what is called an *encoding* process: you string words and symbols together to create, or encode, a message.

The message you have created travels through some channel to reach the eyes and ears of the receiver, who goes through a similar process to interpret the message. The receiver decodes the message by engaging in his or her own selecting and sorting process, and when all of this is done, you hope that the receiver has reconstructed a semblance of the original idea. The receiver can then provide feedback, which gives you information about how your message was interpreted. During feedback, the roles are reversed: the receiver becomes the sender and begins to engage in the encoding process. Thus, the process of communication is circular and ongoing.

The communication process is complicated because the meaning of words and symbols is derived from each person's past experiences and individual perceptions of the world. Other complicating factors include 1) the situation or context in which the communication takes place; 2) the timing of the message; 3) how each person feels at that particular time; and 4) the degree to which each person is actually attempting to communicate effectively.

Communication style refers to the encoding process. It describes how you say what you say. Style is important because the other person tends to react to the way the message is delivered, rather than the message itself. What you say may be right but the way you say it could be wrong. Quite often, each individual takes a position and tries to defend it to the hilt. Ultimately each ends up digging a hole and the positions get polarized. The discussion gets stuck and further talking gets you nowhere.

To avoid the stalemate of communication gone awry, look for warning signs in a conversation. Are you getting angry? Is the other person speaking louder, repeating himself or herself, or showing other signs of frustration? If so, what is happening is not a miscommunication but a disagreement. No amount of oral volleyball is going to improve the situation. It is important not to let communication break down in this way.

Personal Interaction and Attitude

Most of an appraiser's work is directed toward deriving a supportable opinion of value. To complete the requirements of an appraisal assignment, however, the appraiser's investigation, analysis, and conclusions must be communicated to the client in a convincing manner. In appraisal work, a defined value is usually communicated in a written appraisal report.

If questions arise in reviewing an appraisal report, the review appraiser may communicate his or her concerns to the appraiser who prepared the report. The appraiser should be prepared to defend the method applied, the comparables selected, and the key assumptions made. He or she should also be willing to discuss the report with the client or the review appraiser.

There is a natural tendency for reviewers and writers of appraisal reports to conflict. This conflict may be the result of an "us versus them" attitude, or it may be a natural outcome

DILBERT reprinted by permission of United Feature Syndicate, Inc.

of the friction generated between practitioners of two related disciplines. Some animosity is undoubtedly due to certain reviewers who abuse their role; similarly, certain appraisers may be defensive and "thin-skinned" when their work products are criticized. Most problems, however, are the result of poor communication between the two parties, which makes the review process unnecessarily contentious.

Sometimes the reviewer and appraiser communicate face-to-face across a desk or conference table or via electronic mail, but most often communication takes place over the telephone. This interpersonal contact is critical to the entire appraisal review process, and it does not need to be an egregious experience.

The implicit message of this chapter concerns attitude. Reviewers are encouraged to be empathetic and professional in carrying out their reviewer function. The following discussion will acquaint appraisal reviewers with some interviewing fundamentals and remind them of something we all possess and practice constantly—communication style. Some commonsense recommendations are offered to help reviewers understand their role and accomplish their due diligence function more effectively.

THE REVIEWER'S ROLE

Generally the reviewer's role is to determine if an appraisal report: 1) meets acceptable quality standards and the criteria of the client and users of the report; 2) conforms to the Uniform Standards of Professional Appraisal Practice (USPAP) of The Appraisal Foundation; 3) complies with government regulatory requirements; and 4) most importantly, concludes with a reasonable and reliable market value estimate.

For transactions that trigger an event governed by the Financial Institutions Reform, Recovery and Enforcement Act of 1989 (FIRREA), the appraisal must:

- "be sufficiently descriptive to enable the reader to ascertain the estimated market value and the rationale for the estimate,"
- "provide detail and depth of analysis that reflect the complexity of the real estate appraisal," and
- "contain sufficient supporting documentation with all pertinent information reported so that the appraiser's logic, reasoning, judgment, and analysis in arriving at a conclusion indicate to the reader the reasonableness of the market value reported."[1]

Standards Rule 2-2 (a)(viii) of USPAP states that the appraisal must "describe the information considered, the appraisal procedures followed, and the reasoning that supports the analysis, opinions, and conclusions." Standards Rule 2-2 (a) is a binding USPAP requirement and cannot be departed from within an appraisal report. Further, all reviewers must comply with Standard 3 of USPAP, which governs the review process and states:

---

1. Office of the Comptroller of the Currency, Department of the Treasury. Final rule, 12 CFR, Part 34, Paragraph 34.44, Appraisal Standards, 4 (ii) and (iii), 11. Dated August 20, 1990, effective August 24, 1990. Similar regulations issued by other financial institution regulatory agencies (Board of Governors of the Federal Reserve System, Federal Deposit Insurance Corporation, Office of Thrift Supervision, and National Credit Union Administration) and by the Resolution Trust Corporation.

In reviewing an appraisal and reporting the results of that review, an appraiser must form an opinion as to the adequacy and appropriateness of the report being reviewed and must clearly disclose the nature of the review process undertaken.

Advice for Reviewers

Some general advice for appraisal reviewers follows:

- Get comfortable with the appraisal by reading the report carefully and following the thought process and rationale leading to the concluded value. Ideally the reviewer should be able to confirm that the appraiser's conclusion is reasonable.
- Although some of the noncritical elements of an appraisal may be omitted, may be presented inadequately, or may not conform to stringent format requirements, the appraiser's value conclusion could still be reasonable and reliable.
- The reviewer must have the ability, expertise, experience, and appraisal knowledge and training to understand the appraiser's methods and techniques fully. This is particularly important in reviewing appraisals involving complex property or unusual valuation situations.
- Quite often it is a reviewer's subjective decision that determines what is or is not acceptable. Reviewers should recognize gray areas of interpretation and try to make their decisions as objectively as possible. Their personal preferences should not be seen as doctrine to be imposed on others.
- An appraisal that contains a reasonable value conclusion should not be rejected because of nit-picking by an overzealous or inexperienced reviewer. A report can be acceptable even if it has some typos and minor errors.
- In a marginal case that is subjective in nature, the reviewer should try to give the appraiser the benefit of the doubt. After all, the appraiser has inspected the property and, unless it is a field review, the reviewer probably has not. Also, the appraiser has spent two to six weeks performing the appraisal and is more familiar with the market. In addition, the appraiser was qualified by the reviewer prior to the formal engagement and considered to be competent and knowledgeable. Of course, the reviewer should not hesitate to challenge the appraiser when warranted.
- Both the reviewer and the appraiser can use the review process to understand new techniques and broaden their perspectives.
- If you need to talk with the appraiser, by all means prepare and organize your thoughts in advance. Know precisely what you want to say before you make the initial call to the appraiser. Make sure you have a clear understanding of the issues if you expect to make your reasoning clear to someone else. Conventional wisdom advises, "Seek to understand before seeking to be understood."
- The reviewer should follow up the phone conversation with a written summary of his or her comments and observations regarding the appraisal report and ask the appraiser to provide a written response by a certain date. The reviewer's critique should be objective and concise.

> The reviewer should keep in mind the admonition, "Let him who is without sin cast the first stone."

The following *do*'s and *don't*s may help the reviewer communicate with the appraiser and improve the review process.

Do

- Take the time to engage in some pleasant, courteous dialogue before getting down to business. Establish a positive relationship before discussing the appraisal.
- Be fair and use a little finesse. Always be professional in your conduct and convey your concerns to the appraiser in a positive, constructive manner.
- Be reasonable and listen to the appraiser's explanation. See the problem from the appraiser's point of view. Listening involves patience, openness, and a desire to understand.
- Be receptive to innovative techniques. Do not automatically assume a technique is wrong just because it is different. Consider the appraiser's rationale with an open mind. When markets are difficult to interpret and available market data are minimal or contradictory, new ideas and methods of appraisal may be called for. Listen and read the report carefully. You may learn something new and creative.
- Ask questions that are straightforward, direct, specific, and simple. State the issue as precisely as you can. Ask questions in a nonjudgmental manner. Try not to appear condescending or otherwise insult the intelligence of the appraiser.
- Focus on major problems. Identify key issues and concerns and downplay problems that are not directly pertinent to the value conclusion.
- Be on the alert for incomplete or vague answers or answers that lead to other questions. When you do not understand an answer, ask for a restatement in other words. Ask follow-up questions such as, "What do you mean by that?" Communicate your questions in a neutral, unthreatening manner and resist the desire to be argumentative. The tone in which you ask your questions is of primary importance. Keep your voice controlled and moderate.
- Force yourself to listen and be attentive to what the appraiser is saying.
- Direct your criticism at the report, not the appraiser. This may allay any defensiveness on the part of the appraiser. Always remember that the appraisal report is under review, not the appraiser. Structure your questions and comments from this perspective.
- Discuss the strengths as well as the deficiencies of the appraisal. To encourage a smooth flow of conversation, it is generally a good idea to begin the discussion on a positive note.

- Be certain the value conclusion is consistent with the analysis and the analysis is consistent with the data presented in the report. Keep in mind what effect the deficiencies noted had on the concluded value. If the problem did not have a material effect, then the point should merely be mentioned in the review report. This lets readers of the review report who are not appraisers know what is important and significant to the value conclusion and what is not.
- Provide quality feedback to the appraiser. Many problems are solved just by listening to the appraiser's explanation, which may lead the reviewer to exclaim, "Why didn't you just say that in the report? It's so clear to me now!"
- Anticipate potential problems. Sometimes it is only after the report is delivered that the reviewer finds out that the appraiser assumed an incorrect premise, used the wrong date of appraisal, or was not provided with the latest information concerning the property being appraised.
- Logic and explanation go a long way in making communication effective. The appraiser should be open to the reviewer's questions and not be defensive. Reviewers should establish and maintain an active networking relationship with the appraisers they work with. A mutual desire for good communication, teamwork, and cooperation will help smooth the process. It is fine to ask probing questions, but be sure your wording and manner do not influence the response.
- Use common sense. If you are proved wrong, admit it and back down. If you know you are right, however, defend your position strongly. The proactive approach to a mistake is to acknowledge it instantly, correct it, and learn from it. It is one thing to make a mistake and quite another to refuse to admit it.
- Avoid using absolute or final statements.
- Plan for the interaction to take more time than you think it should.
- Depersonalize any contentious communication before it escalates. When you and the appraiser are at odds, it is a good idea to pause and say, "We disagree about this situation. No one is wrong." When one person is repeating the same point over and over and the other person is not accepting it, that person should say, "Your point is well taken. Let's move on." Such comments will help remove barriers and reopen the channels of communication until a resolution can be reached.
- The reviewer's attitude should be respectful, calm, restrained, and patient. Act as a facilitator and always try to reach a win/win solution.

Don't

- Call the appraiser to criticize a report and to give him or her your own preconceived assumptions and value conclusion.
- Ask general questions and don't accept vague answers. Don't accept "smoke and mirrors" explanations. Let the appraiser know you want specifics.
- Overreact if the report contains minor typos, inconsistent wording, rounding errors, and inconsequential mathematical mistakes. Don't frustrate the appraiser

with unreasonable demands to meet your standard of perfection. Perfection is a worthy goal, but it is often unrealistic and unattainable in the real world.

- Expect the appraiser to write a demonstration-quality appraisal report. This is an unrealistic, unnecessary expectation.
- Jump on the appraiser's responses with an accusative tone. Don't inadvertently provoke the appraiser and put him or her in a reactive, defensive position. This will interfere with addressing the real issues, which are generally technical in nature. Don't lecture the other person or speak in a patronizing voice, which will create hostility and increase interpersonal conflict. Never threaten.
- Ask loaded, leading, confrontational, tricky, or argumentative questions. Avoid double-negative and two-part questions and those that are long and complicated. Present your case intelligently and maintain your professional composure. Don't allow personal appraiser relationships to cloud the objectivity of your review.
- Become enmeshed in a checklist mentality. Checklists are beneficial insofar as they prevent sections of reports from being inadvertently omitted, ensure that the appraisal conforms to the client's requirements, and help verify internal and external consistency. Strict adherence to a checklist can go too far, however. A checklist must not become the ultimate determinant of an appraisal's acceptability; it is merely a tool to help reviewers systemize the process.
- Accept the report unless it satisfactorily answers a few basic questions:
    1. What is the generic profile of a likely tenant for the property?
    2. What is the generic profile of a likely purchaser of the property?
    3. Why would a potential purchaser be motivated to buy the property?
    4. Does the appraiser's analysis emulate the most likely purchaser's value analysis?
    5. Will the property sell for the appraised value within the stated marketing period?

Delivering the Message

When it comes to getting a message through clearly, we can all be verbally challenged. A verbal message is not a neatly wrapped package that will always be received as you intended.

Before you call or write to the appraiser, be prepared with a list of questions to ask. Think through your questions and arrange them in a logical sequence. Ask them systematically so that the discussion flows smoothly. It is usually best to proceed from the general to the specific, from the simplest to the most complex. It is very disconcerting when a reviewer skips aimlessly from one unrelated topic to another with complete disregard for rational interrelationships. Keep your questions on track. A good question is phrased in a neutral manner that does not affect the answer. If you pay attention to what you are asking and how you are asking it, most misunderstandings can be resolved. The essence of miscommunication is, "I know you think you heard what you thought I said, but what I said is not what you heard."

Reviewers must strike a balance with the appraisers they deal with on a day-to-day basis. Trying to be a nice guy will not get the appraisal in on time, nor will it get you the most favorable fee quote or the appraiser's best performance. On the other hand, being obnoxious will not accomplish much either. Try to maintain a delicate balance somewhere between the two extremes.

The job of professional reviewers is to accept, reject, or modify appraisals based on the merits of each appraisal report. They are not expected to educate the public on the basic tenets of real estate valuation. If a minor competency problem is uncovered, the appraiser should be referred to an appropriate course, seminar, text, or other source of information. If the problem is more serious or systematic, the appraiser should probably be removed from the qualified listing of approved appraisers. The reviewer must determine whether the problems are just cosmetic or chronic and acute. There is no need to pamper or nurture inept appraisers. This would be counterproductive to the reviewer's mandated task.

If you also are responsible for hiring appraisers, then it is your responsibility to hire only those who have demonstrated the necessary competence to handle the job properly. Be mindful that you are paying a fair fee in exchange for competent, professional appraisal services.

Speak to your supervisor or manager if a particular appraiser is obnoxious, unresponsive, inept, or incompetent. This feedback will ensure that your institution's approved appraiser panel is limited to those who are most qualified. Consider adapting your communication style as a strategy for dealing with difficult people who create stress and problems in professional relationships. Remember you are the appraiser's client, but this relationship should not be abused.

One good rule is to behave as if it is your own money paying the appraisal fee. Would you accept the appraisal as written? Was it professional, factual, and accurate? Did it provide reliable guidance? Would you spend your own time to educate an incompetent appraiser and patch up an otherwise unacceptable report? Can you comfortably and confidently make a business decision based on this report?

Once an appraiser has been engaged, be certain to check periodically with him or her to monitor the progress of the appraisal process. Be the "squeaky wheel" on the client list. It is vital that delivery date commitments are met. This requirement is second in importance only to an assurance of quality. Taking the initiative does not mean you are pushy, obnoxious, or aggressive. It does mean recognizing your responsibility to get the job done effectively and efficiently.

Conclusion

Good attitudes and communication on the part of both the reviewer and the appraiser will result in an improved report and a better-supported value conclusion. Both should avoid becoming cynical. Oscar Wilde described a cynic as "A man who knows the price of everything and the value of nothing."

Many appraisers embrace the challenge of a thorough review. It gives them information about how their work measures up to that of their peers. If handled correctly and fairly, a good review can produce a better report. After all, a better report serves the best interests of both the client and the appraiser.

In the final analysis, if the appraisal as a whole appears to describe the property adequately, reveal the appraisal valuation process, be written in accordance with applicable standards and regulations, and support the value conclusion in a reasonable manner, it probably should be accepted as satisfactory.

Characteristics of a Quality Report

A quality appraisal, developed and written to serve the business purposes of its intended users, has the characteristics described below.

Current

A quality report is written in real time, with up-to-the-minute financial and market information rather than old, obsolete data and methodology. It contains current property and neighborhood descriptions, current sales and offerings, current capitalization and discount rates, and current information about the state of the market in which the property will be leased or sold.

Complete

All the information needed to identify the subject property and make the appraiser's case are presented. The property description should convey a clear sense of the property's utility and condition. The report should state if the improvements are subject to leases, easements, management agreements, or special financing; whether they need repair or remodeling; or if the management is having trouble with building tenants, neighbors, or inspectors.

An appraisal of an industrial property may require a thorough analysis of the local industrial market. A report on a single-family residence may require only a brief discussion of the condition and reputation of the neighborhood and a statement that the local market is strong or weak. The appraiser's argument should be supported by enough transactional statistics to prove the point. When market value or market rent is at issue, additional concerns may need to be addressed: How long a marketing period is anticipated? How many potential buyers are likely to be interested? What kinds of marketing techniques will be used?

Correct

The appraiser must accurately report and explain the facts and issues relevant to the assignment. There is no excuse for serious errors in property descriptions, tax information, tenant rosters, comparable sales and leases, or other data that significantly affect value.

Cogent

A quality report logically, clearly, and convincingly leads the reader through the steps of the appraiser's argument, taking the shortest path to the correct conclusion. Clients need to evaluate the appraiser's thinking, which means they must be able to follow it. Sloppy organization, poor logic, and imprecise language defeat the legitimate purposes of the report. The appraiser needs to check and recheck the logical flow of the report and the chain of events it describes, scrutinizing everything from data to analysis to conclusion. He or she must make certain the report is clear and can be understood without additional information.

Consistent

An appraisal report must not contain internal discrepancies that might confuse or mislead a reader. If a building needs work, its condition and the cost of the repair work should be noted consistently in the building description, the depreciation estimates, and the capital budgets used in the income approach. If a property fronts on a highway that has both a number and a name, the report should mention both or use either the name or the number consistently when the location of the subject comes up. If a property is initially described as having an area of 20,210 square feet, this figure should not be rounded in later sections of the report. If a property is situated outside the limits of an incorporated municipality, the appraisal should report this fact in describing its location, not just report its postal address.

Convenient

The writer should make it easy for a reader to find the important elements in the report. There is more than one way to do this, and the right way may depend on the purpose of the report or the preferences of the client. The report writer's goal is to make it easy for the reader to get at the essence of the report, test it for quality, and get on with other business.

Concise

A good appraisal wastes neither words nor money. There is no reason to mention the number of flights per day at a nearby airport or the average value of single-family homes in the metropolitan area unless these facts directly affect the value of the property in question. Thus, the appraiser can omit historical information on Jean Baptiste Pointe du Sable's 1781 canoe trip up the Chicago River from an appraisal report on a suburban medical center.

Other Characteristics

A quality appraisal report meets the following objectives:

- Discusses both macro- and micromarket conditions and other factors that impact collateral value.
- Provides the client with an appropriate awareness of all market and property risks pertinent to the property.
- Identifies market trends.
- Complies with USPAP and appropriate regulatory requirements.

- Answers pertinent questions concerning the status of property leasing, the reasonableness of rents and expenses, and the condition of the property in a concise manner.
- Explains and analyzes discount and capitalization rates and provides source data for all rate assumptions.
- Contains well-researched, pertinent market data on land and property sales, rents, expenses, etc.
- Uses charts, illustrations, maps, and photos effectively to help the client visualize the property and its market environment.
- Allows the client to follow the appraiser's rationale and reconcile the value indications derived into a logical, well-supported conclusion.
- Shows an obvious understanding of the client's need for a concise report without excess verbiage or repetition.
- Keeps the focus of analysis on pertinent valuation issues.
- Is written authoritatively with obvious competence.
- Provides the client with a truly useful management tool, which contains relevant data, thorough discussion of the appraiser's logic and rationale, and well-documented conclusion(s).

Key words that describe a good report include: well-written, clear, concise, readable, good logical flow, no extraneous information, factual, business-like, well-organized, thoughtful comments, candid remarks, competent, reliable.

Quality Control = Quality Appraisals

Appraisal review is a key ingredient in an appraisal firm's quality-control program. By signing a report, the lead appraiser accepts full liability for its contents and puts his or her reputation on the line. A careful review by one or more experienced appraisers can provide much insight and strengthen the valuation conclusions contained in the report. Some appraisal companies frequently conduct roundtable reviews and discussions of appraisals, which help management establish a high comfort level with the firm's reports. Regular "lessons learned" sessions and follow-up discussions of transactions resulting from the appraisals are also useful quality-control tools as well as valuable learning experiences. Although small appraisal firms may not have the resources to conduct frequent, in-depth reviews, any additional input may help identify problem areas in appraisal reports.

Another way to implement quality control is to schedule a second or third review before the field appraiser submits the report. The first review can address errors in grammar, math, punctuation, or other mechanics of the report. After putting the report aside for two or three days and then reading it again, the appraiser may find new insights. The appraiser may be more objective about the report after a short break, and he or she may have new analyses or data to add. This is a good quality-control technique for smaller firms that do not have a large staff of appraisers to review reports.

To ensure good quality control, an appraisal firm could take these additional steps:

- Have the lead appraiser inspect the property.
- Invest time and effort in the verification process to increase accuracy.
- Keep good file memoranda.
- Say "no" to an assignment if the delivery date is unrealistic or if the location or property type may present a competency problem.

Using a competent appraiser is the best way to achieve a reliable appraisal developed with sound reasoning and thoughtful analysis.

Communication Is Key

Communicating an appraisal calls for organization, analysis, and writing skill. For appraisers, the actual valuation process begins with the determination of highest and best use, is carried through the application of the three approaches to value, and concludes with the reconciliation and value conclusion.

Appraising is problem solving and the appraisal report follows the problem-solving process of 1) defining the problem, 2) gathering pertinent data, 3) analyzing the data, and 4) forming a conclusion. Like other problem solvers and researchers, many appraisers feel most confident performing the fieldwork, doing the analysis, and arriving at the conclusion. Preparing the report may be anticlimactic, but it is most important. The report is the product

"How do you get a good appraisal here?"

paid for by the client, and clients want their money's worth. A poorly prepared report reflects not only on the individual appraiser and his or her firm but also on the entire real estate appraisal profession.

An appraisal report should allow the reader to follow the data and reasoning presented and accept the conclusion as factual. A good report reflects the skill and judgment of its author, who has communicated the complicated valuation process in a meaningful and interesting way.

WRITING AND SYNTAX ISSUES

The appraiser's goal in writing the appraisal report is to send a clear message. Lack of clarity can result from improper word usage and poor sentence construction. Problems with word selection and composition may indicate the appraiser's failure to think before writing. Leonard F. Read, the late president of the Foundation for Economic Education, once observed, "Whatever cannot be made clear in writing probably is not clear in the mind." A report that contains many redundancies, trite expressions, hedge words, pointless phrases, and false elegance is wordy and imprecise. When an appraiser fails to consider word meaning, the report may be needlessly repetitive.

> I looked up "redundant" in the dictionary. It says, "Characterized by verbosity or unnecessary repetition in expressing ideas; prolix; in excess of requirements; superfluous."
> Is that redundant?

The appraiser must effectively communicate to the reader that his or her judgment is sound. Sometimes the appraiser comes to conclusions that may not be obvious from the data. As soon as the appraiser makes a judgment, appraisal becomes an art, not a science, and he or she must rely on persuasive writing, not just data, to convince the client or reviewer.[1]

IN SEARCH OF PERFECTION

Can perfection be achieved in the performance of an appraisal and the communication of the report? Probably not. Perfection, like beauty, quality, and other such subjective benchmarks, is in the eye of the beholder or, in this case, the reviewer. A high-quality, well-reasoned, thoughtfully analyzed valuation need not be perfect to be accepted as a reliable document. In the final analysis, the reviewer must exercise judgment and an innate sense of reasonableness in critiquing the work of appraisers. Perfection is an elusive goal, but striving to prepare quality reports that meet or exceed market standards is both achievable and required.

THE "HIDDEN VALUE" OF GOOD APPRAISALS

Some clients have the unfortunate attitude that appraisals are a "necessary evil." This probably comes from the fact that appraisals are mandatory for certain transactions that trigger regula-

1. For further guidance on report writing, see *The Appraisal Writing Handbook* by Alan Blankenship, PhD (Chicago: Appraisal Institute, 1998).

tory requirements. In addition, Fannie Mae, Freddie Mac, HUD, FHA , VA, and other governmental and quasi-governmental agencies typically require appraisals for loans to qualify under their programs. Focusing only on these mandatory requirements, clients often lose sight of the important functions appraisals serve and the valuable, objective information and data contained in quality appraisal reports.

The proper estimation of property value and competent analysis of other issues related to real estate contribute to sound judgments about the disposition and use of real estate. Accurate, realistic value estimates help to stabilize real estate loans and investments, which promote socially desirable real estate development. Because decisions about the use and disposition of real estate and the rights inherent in its ownership depend on solid real estate knowledge, appraisers can provide great assistance to those who make such decisions.

In a speech before a national conference of institutional chief appraisers, one banker said:

> I cannot stress enough, we view the appraisal process as an integral part of a sound credit process, appraisal is a key ingredient in the risk management formula. We recognize that the relevance of appraisals to the lending process is being widely contested at this time. But nonetheless, our needs as a lender have not changed. Simply put, to make prudent loans and remain competitive, we need quality, timely and cost-effective appraisals.
>
> Management has to ensure that appraisals are information tools for the line units and add value to the underwriting process. It's now more important than ever that an appraiser employs the appropriate valuation techniques and uses the best available data.
>
> We think that a good appraisal is one that provides the lender with a clear idea of what is happening in the marketplace, and one that identifies market trends. It's also important that the appraisal report focus on the pertinent valuation issues.
>
> Our appraisals are a quality-control function. As such, our appraisers insure that their work is done in accordance with regulations and that their appraisals analyze the true complexity of the property.

Clients want quality appraisals that

- Identify current market trends. The scope and direction of interest, capitalization, and discount rates are of interest to clients as are appreciation rates, rents, leases, land and property sales, expenses, taxes, and absorption trends.
- Clearly describe the property, its condition as of the effective date of the appraisal, and its environment.
- Explain apparent legal obligations that go with the land such as subdivision covenants, easements, and zoning requirements and restrictions.
- Provide detailed sales, rental, and investment information regarding similar properties that are competitive in the market.
- Outline both property and market risk parameters.

- Present valuable macro- and micromarket information.
- Warn the client of potential environmental hazards or other risk factors discovered through casual observation.
- Provide lenders with a clear idea of what is happening in the marketplace.
- Serve as a valuable management tool for portfolio planning and for advising third-party clients. The information contained in an appraisal report can make the investor- or lender-client better informed and more knowledgeable.

Appraisal reports are particularly valuable because they are a totally objective and unbiased source of real estate information. Unlike some other real estate professionals, the appraiser performs a professional service for a fee, not for a commission contingent on the value conclusion or the eventual sale of the property.

Appraisals have a number of uses beyond the presentation of a point estimate or range of value. Other client uses include sensitivity analysis, buy-sell-hold-rent analyses, and market survey data. This list of benefits is by no means complete. As business professionals and the general public expand their understanding of the nature, purposes, and uses of real estate appraisals, they will become increasingly aware of their inherent, or hidden, value.

Open communication between appraisers and clients will optimize the value of the services that appraisers offer. Although many clients use a bidding process to select the appropriate real estate appraiser for a particular assignment, good working relationships can be achieved. The wise appraiser will not attempt to avoid the bidding process, which is a prudent business procedure for the client, but will use it as an opportunity to demonstrate his or her competence and professionalism.

Unfortunately, when it comes to real estate appraisals, many clients have only a vague idea of what they are purchasing. It takes time to learn appraisal terms, techniques, and methodology, and clients can become frustrated with the learning process. There are two ways to avoid potential problems. First, engagement letters can be used to specify what is expected of each party. Second, "A Contract of Understanding" can be drawn up so the appraiser and client agree in advance on the assignment specifications, delivery times, fees, and individual responsibilities. Such contracts are usually updated annually.

An engagement letter can be written by either the appraiser or the client as long as both parties understand and agree to its entire content. In most cases the engagement letter should be drafted after the client and the appraiser have discussed the assignment and have orally agreed to the scope of the assignment, the completion date, the appraisal fee, and other parameters. The engagement letter serves as an affirmation of this conversation. Ideally both parties will sign and date the engagement letter and retain a copy in their files. If it is not possible for both parties to sign and date the letter, each party should document its mutual acceptance. For further information, the reader is advised to consult the Appraisal Institute's Guide Note 11 on the use and applicability of engagement letters.

Avoiding Problems

The appraiser selection process can be the most important step in achieving a reasoned, thoughtful analysis and a reliable appraisal report.

It is critical that the appraiser selected to perform an appraisal assignment have sufficient training, background, and experience relevant to the type of property being appraised. The chance of making a poor selection is reduced by engaging someone with documented experience in a particular property category. Taking the time to identify, qualify, and select the appropriate appraiser for an appraisal assignment will result in fewer review problems. Some general guidelines follow:

- Select only from among competent appraisers.
- Ask for and review each appraiser's qualifications before making a selection.
- If the property to be appraised is considered complex or the valuation is unusual for other reasons, ensure that the appraiser has field experience relevant to the special property type or situation.
- Consider whether the appraiser has demonstrated sufficient knowledge and experience to handle the assignment properly.
- Ask for specific client and assignment references.
- Look for state licensure, professional designation(s), a solid educational and professional background, professional involvement, and comprehensive appraisal experience.
- Ensure that the appraiser has many years of experience, not just one year of experience doing the same work many times.
- If the appraiser is a designated member of a professional appraisal organization with continuing education requirements, make sure that he or she has kept current on those requirements.
- Investigate the satisfaction level of the appraiser's existing clients.
- Ask the appraiser about internal quality control procedures and the background of any field appraiser who will contribute to the final work product.

Appraisers should be provided with all property information that would be available to a prospective purchaser and should have access to those individuals responsible for managing and leasing the property.

Clearly communicating any specific appraisal requirements to the appraiser tends to lessen review problems. Using an engagement letter that clearly outlines the scope of services, delivery date, fee, and other issues unique to the assignment will help prevent misunderstandings when the appraisal is reviewed.

An appraiser should never be selected based solely on price. Given the complexities of real estate appraisal, it isn't surprising that the appraiser who quotes the lowest fee often is selected for the assignment. Comparison by price is easy, quick, and seemingly sensible. However, selecting an appraiser based solely on price can result in an inadequate appraisal. When a purchase, sale, investment, lending, or other real estate-related decision is made based on an unreliable appraisal, the client may discover that taking the lowest price is a costly decision.

Selecting an appraiser who promises the "quickest turnaround" or "24-hour delivery" can result in problems too. If the rushed time frame results in an unacceptable or unreliable appraisal, nothing has been gained. Often a quick turnaround becomes unnecessary because the legal entanglements to be resolved are more complex and time-consuming than the appraisal process. Moreover, an appraisal firm that promises unrealistic turnaround may meet its schedule by performing inadequate research and analysis.

Reviewer Ethics and Professionalism

Introduction

Today the term *professional* is used quite loosely. Some apply the term to those who are not amateurs, who bring a high degree of skill to their work, or who earn money from their occupation—e.g., a "professional athlete." At the other extreme, some individuals reserve the term *professional* for those who pursue fields like law or medicine, which require advanced formal education, a high degree of autonomy, and self-regulation. However, professional identity is not simply a matter of expertise or educational qualifications. The essence of professionalism is ethics. A professional is an individual who is committed to a high standard of conduct on which the public can rely.

Among the many existing definitions of *professional*, those that follow seems to capture the deepest analysis of professional identity. A professional is someone

- Who is paid to provide services based on knowledge or expertise not available to the average lay person
- Whose services are not easily assessed by lay persons but can have a major impact on the client's well being
- Into whose hands the client typically entrusts confidential information or other resources
- Who is trusted to place the client's interests—and, in some cases, the public's interests as well—before his or her own interests
- Who adheres to a code of conduct and belongs to a peer organization that supports and enforces this code

Occupations that are undeniably professions, such as medicine and law, fit this definition well. Most areas of real estate, including appraisal and appraisal reviewing, can also be considered professions. The essence of professionalism is the expectation that one can place one's trust in the integrity and responsibility of the service provider. This expectation is sustained by the provider's adherence to a code of conduct that is publicly recognized and enforced by a peer organization.

If we keep this central attribute of professionalism in mind, we can begin to understand some of the features of appraisal and appraisal review that place stress on professional identity and performance. Of course, occasional episodes of individual misconduct can occur in any field and serve to undermine the image of the profession. Beyond these incidents, however, there are special features of the appraisal field that tend to create dilemmas for the committed professional. Although these features are not absent from other fields, they seem to proliferate in appraisal and appraisal review and can threaten the professional commitment and judgment of even the most dedicated individuals.

The crux of the problem is the deeply uncertain and often subjective nature of valuing real estate. "Under all is the land," says the Preamble to the Realtors® Code of Ethics, but unfortunately the value of that land is notoriously hard to determine. There is no public market for land to supply ready price quotations. It is not uncommon for two appraisal professionals to value the same property and arrive at widely differing estimates of value, both of which are technically correct and comply with accepted professional standards and regulations. This disparity in establishing value provides real estate appraisers and reviewers with an invitation to ethical compromise and makes their personal integrity more important—and more vulnerable to financial pressures and temptations.

The phrase *appraisal professional* is part reality and part aspiration. By identifying and eliminating those aspects of their work that erode professional performance, appraisers can reinforce the public trust that is the ethical and economic strength of the field.

One writer has observed:

> The universal goal of an appraisal is, or ought to be, to provide an accurate estimation of value. There are two broad ways in which appraisal accuracy can be achieved. One is to rely on the individual judgment and experience of an appraiser. A second is to establish scientific procedures that must be followed, which serve to guarantee or at least enhance the objective of accuracy, so that reliance on the subjective expertise and the experience of an individual appraiser is minimized.
>
> Those who emphasize the former tend to think of appraisal as a process akin to art. According to this view, providing an accurate appraisal is not, and can never be, a matter of science; rather, it is more like art, which relies on subjective qualities such as talent, experience, judgment, and in the best cases, the genius of an individual appraiser. At the opposite end of the spectrum is a view of the appraisal process that considers an appraisal to be something more amenable to scientific treatment. Objective standards provide the foundation of the appraisal process, and just as there are accepted and objective standards of scientific procedure, testing, and evaluation, so there are objective standards governing an appraisal's creation, testing, and evaluation.[1]

1. Stephen P. Smalley, PhD, *The Appraisal Journal* (April 1995): 165-171.

The writer goes on to explain that these extreme views both represent "distortions" and "misinterpretations" of the truth. Both elements exist in a good appraisal, and the appraisal process is both a science and an art, relying on objective methodological considerations as well as the subjective judgment and personal experience of the appraiser.

The review process must encompass, and indeed should focus on, the selection, relevance, and interpretation of the data, rather than the appraiser's technical proficiency or ability to manipulate data. A reviewer of appraisals of truly difficult properties, for example, may appear clever, proficient, and objective by focusing on fine technical points in the application of an appropriate method, but such a review rarely gets to the heart of the matter.

Unfortunately, many believe the review process has become trivialized. To appear objective a reviewer is often forced to focus on those elements of appraisal that have been objectified, namely the technicalities of the three traditional approaches to value. Technical proficiency in manipulating data, rather than the selection and analysis of relevant data, has become the measure of a good appraisal.

Reviewers must recognize that certain properties are difficult to appraise, not because appraisers are deficient but because the property and the data are difficult to interpret. Allowances must be made, and the appraiser must sometimes be given license to use his or her learned judgment to practice appraisal more as an art than a science.

One troublesome problem in the review process is the tendency of some reviewers to step over the line of professionalism and impose their own biases and opinions on the appraisal reports they review. Steering an appraiser to a certain value estimate is, by far, the most offensive and unethical act a reviewer can perform. In addition, conscientious appraisers often complain that they are required to "jump through hoops" and complete unnecessary analyses or provide irrelevant data in a report just so the reviewer can mark off an item on the reviewer checklist and avoid having to explain why the analyses or information is not applicable to the valuation problem.

In many instances, such problems are caused by reviewers who do not have sufficient experience in appraisal theory to understand fully the appraisals they review. Reviewers with limited experience tend to rely on a strict, narrow interpretations of textbook ideas, falling back on the recitation of dogma in their critiques. The review process is highly technical and requires a thorough understanding of both valuation theory and practice. Training courses for reviewers are helpful, but they do not adequately address the differences between constructive and destructive reviews and between objective and subjective critiques. Reviewers are not hired by their clients to act as "appraisal police." A broad appraisal background and relevant experience tend to teach reviewers humility and empathy in their dealings with field appraisers.

Ethics refers to standards of conduct, which indicate how one should behave based on moral duties and virtues arising from the principles of right and wrong. To apply this definition to practical decision making, one must specify the nature of the moral obligations considered intrinsic to ethical behavior. These obligations arise from the ethical values of trustworthiness, respect, responsibility, justice, fairness, caring, civic virtue, and citizenship.

There are two aspects of ethics. The first involves the ability to discern right from wrong, good from evil, and propriety from impropriety; the second refers to an individual's commitment to do what is right, good, and proper. Ethics is demonstrated by a person's actions. It is not simply something to think and argue about; it is about conduct and behavior.

An ethical individual has the character and courage to meet the challenge and make the moral decision when doing the right thing will cost more than he or she wants to pay. Today's appraisers and appraisal reviewers may find it hard to define their ethical orientation. They may have difficulty recognizing the long-term benefits of total objectivity. Yet, they must endeavor to develop a sense of responsibility in keeping with their important role in society and the economy. This sense of purpose will protect them from all temptations to be unethical.

Conclusion

Appraisal review is the quality-control function of the appraisal profession. A review appraiser tests the reasonableness of the logic, assumptions, and value conclusion presented in an appraisal report as well as its compliance with professional standards, the client's criteria, and appraisal regulatory requirements.

Most problems with appraisal reports are the result of incompetence, inadequate data research, inadequate support, poor analysis and reasoning, inconsistencies, ineffective quality control, misunderstanding the assignment and its scope, lack of adherence to standards, vagueness, and failure to check for reasonableness before finalizing the appraisal.

The art of appraisal review is constantly developing, just as the technology and methods of appraisal change to reflect the behavior of real estate market participants. However, the ultimate goal of a review appraiser remains the same: to accept an appraisal report in which the data and reasoning presented lead to a valid conclusion.

The real estate appraisal profession experienced a major paradigm shift in the 1990s, causing a powerful change in the supply of and demand for real estate appraisers. The work

"I'm worried about you, Sorenson — you're starting to make sense."

products of appraisers are being more rigorously reviewed and scrutinized by clients. At the same time, greater accountability is expected from other appraisers, users of appraisal services, professional associations, The Appraisal Foundation, state appraisal boards, quasi-public market entities, and federal agencies and regulators. Whether they like it or not, appraisers and their standards are in the spotlight. This prominence requires a heightened level of responsibility and professionalism from both field appraisers and review appraisers. To remain viable, both must perform ethically, conscientiously, and competently. They must endeavor to produce sound, well-supported valuations and other value-related services that serve the needs and best interests of their clients.

Definitions of Key Terms

The sources of many of the following definitions are listed at the end of this appendix. The numbers in brackets at the end of the entries reference this list.

administrative review. A preliminary review of an appraisal to check the calculations and determine whether the appraisal report complies with basic content specifications. The compliance reviewer notes any discrepancies or omissions of items specified in the appraisal contract. Generally performed by a client or user of appraisal services to exercise due diligence in making a business decision (e.g., underwriting, purchase, sale). May be performed by an appraiser to assist a client with these functions. Also known as a *compliance review*.

analysis. The act or process of providing information, recommendations, and/or conclusions on diversified problems in real estate other than estimating value; often used interchangeably with *consulting*. [3]

appraisal. (noun) The act or process of estimating value; an estimate of value. (adjective) 1. Of or pertaining to appraising and related functions, e.g., appraisal practice, appraisal services. [4] 2. An analysis, opinion, or conclusion relating to the nature, quality, value, or utility of specified interests in, or aspects of, identified real estate. [3]

The Appraisal Foundation. A not-for-profit educational foundation organized in 1987 to foster appraisal professionalism through the establishment of uniform standards of appraisal practice and qualifications for the state certification and licensing of appraisers. The Appraisal Foundation has two independent boards, the Appraisal Standards Board (ASB) and the Appraiser Qualifications Board (AQB).

appraisal report. 1. Any communication, written or oral, of an opinion as to the nature, quality, value, or utility of specified interests in or aspects of identified real property. [1] 2. The written or oral communication of an appraisal; the document transmitted to the client upon completion of an appraisal assignment. Reporting requirements are set forth in the Standards Rules relating to Standards 2 and 5 of the Uniform Standards of Professional Appraisal Practice. [3]

Appraisal Standards Board (ASB). An independent board of The Appraisal Foundation charged with promulgating the generally accepted standards of the appraisal profession, the Uniform Standards of Professional Appraisal Practice.

appraiser. One who performs an appraisal. [3]

Appraiser Qualifications Board (AQB). An independent board of The Appraisal Foundation charged with establishing minimum experience, education, and examination criteria for state licensing of appraisers and recommending such criteria for state licensing of appraisers.

assignment. Assignments include appraisal, consulting, and review. [1]

binding requirement. All or part of a Standards Rule of USPAP from which departure is not permitted. [4]

client. Any party for whom an appraiser performs a service. [3] (This definition may vary based on individual state law.)

competence. Having the requisite or adequate ability or qualities to perform the specific assignment. [4]

compliance review. *See* **administrative review.**

consulting. The act or process of providing information, analysis of real estate data, and recommendations or conclusions on diversified problems in real estate, other than estimating value. [4]

critique. A discourse that evaluates or analyzes something; synonyms are *comment, notice,* and *review.*

desk review. An appraisal review that is limited to the data presented in the report which may or may not be independently confirmed. A desk review is generally performed using a customized checklist of items. The reviewer checks the accuracy of the calculations, the reasonableness of the data and the appropriateness of the methodology as well as compliance with client guidelines, regulatory requirements, and professional standards. Also called a *technical review.* [3]

drive-by appraisal. An appraisal service that the appraiser develops without inspecting the interior of the improvements. In most cases the appraiser is not able to identify all the pertinent physical characteristics of the real estate, so there is departure from S.R. 1-2 (a). In a drive-by appraisal, the appraisal process is limited, but any of the reporting formats may be used. This type of appraisal service generally meets the requirements of the federally chartered financial institutions regulatory agencies for an evaluation.

due diligence. 1. A stated or assumed requirement that the party to a contract make a reasonable, good-faith effort to perform his or her obligations under the contract. 2. Refers to a legal obligation, e.g., in connection with the public sale of securities in real estate syndicates or corporations, of the underwriting or selling group to ensure that the offering statement or prospectus does not misstate or omit material information. [3]

evaluation. 1. A study of the nature, quality, or utility of a parcel of real estate or interests in, or aspects of, real property in which a value estimate is not necessarily required; sometimes used to denote consulting. *See also* **analysis.** 2. The Office of the Comptroller of the Currency (OCC) distinguishes between "appraisals" undertaken for any real estate-related financial transaction involving loans of amounts more than the federal de minimus and "evaluations" required for real estate collateral for loans of amounts equal to the federal de minimus or less. The OCC specifies that like appraisals, evaluations are used to validate real estate values that serve as collateral to support a borrower's credit capacity. Further, the OCC states that an evaluation may be required to determine the appropriate carrying value, and probable sales price, for foreclosed properties. (Banking Issuance regarding 12 CFR 34)

evaluator. An individual qualified to perform an evaluation. Qualifications include real estate-related training or experience and knowledge of the market relevant to the subject property. Based on their experience and training, professionals from several fields may be qualified to prepare evaluations of certain types of real estate. Examples include individuals with appraisal experience, real estate lenders, consultants or sales persons, agricultural extension agents, and foresters.

feasibility analysis. A study of the cost-benefit relationship of an economic endeavor. [4]

field review. An appraisal review that includes inspection of the exterior and sometimes the interior of the subject property and possibly inspection of the comparable properties to confirm the data provided in the report. A field review is generally performed using a customized checklist which covers the items examined in a desk review and may also include confirmation of market data, research to gather additional information, and verification of the software used in preparing the report. [3]

Financial Institutions Reform, Recovery and Enforcement Act (FIRREA). Legislation enacted in 1989 to bail out the savings and loan industry; FIRREA created the Office of Thrift Supervision (OTS) under the Treasury Department. The OTS was charged with assuming the functions of the defunct Federal Home Loan Bank Board (FHLBB) and supervising all federal and state savings and loan associations. FIRREA also set up the Resolution Trust Corporation (RTC) to dispose of the assets of insolvent thrift institutions, and the Appraisal Subcommittee to implement Title XI of FIRREA mandating state certification and /or licensing of appraisers who perform assignments for Federal Financial Institutions Regulatory Agencies (FFIRA) as well as all federal and state savings and loan institutions. [3]

FIRREA. *See* **Financial Institutions Reform, Recovery and Enforcement Act.**

file memoranda. Sufficient information to demonstrate substantial compliance with the Standards of Professional Appraisal Practice including in statement, outline or reference form: work sheets, data sheets and related material, [1]

limited assignment. An assignment that calls for something less than, or different from, the work that would otherwise be required. A limited assignment that complies with Uniform Standards of Professional Appraisal Practice rules governing the development of appraisal assignments and meets the Departure Provision is considered a conforming appraisal assignment. [3]

limited report. A report communicating a limited appraisal or consulting assignment. A limited report must comply with the reporting rules set forth in Uniform Standards of Professional Appraisal Practice and the Departure Provision, and contain sufficient information to lead to the appraiser's conclusions. The two types of limited reports most frequently reported are letter reports and form reports. [3]

market analysis. A study of real estate market conditions for a specific type of property. [4]

nitpick. Engage in minute and usually unjustified criticism. [Merriam-Webster Dictionary]

preliminary valuation (also known as a *preliminary value estimate* or *preliminary value analysis*). A limited appraisal performed for a client, which may or may not result in a subsequent assignment to investigate the value of a property further. It is usually reported in a restricted appraisal report.

recertification of value. A limited appraisal performed to confirm whether the completed improvements and the market conditions at the time of completion are consistent with statements made in an earlier, prospective appraisal that was based on plans and specifications for proposed improvements. In other words, a recertification of value tests whether the assumptions made in the earlier appraisal regarding anticipated physical and economic conditions proved to be accurate.

report. Any communication, written or oral, of an appraisal, review, or consulting service that is transmitted to the client upon completion of an assignment. [4]

review. The act or process of critically studying a report prepared by another. [4]

review appraisal report. A supplementary critique intended for use in conjunction with the report under review. An review appraisal report must incorporate all of the items addressed in Standards Rule 3-1.

review appraiser. An appraiser who examines the reports of other appraisers to determine whether their conclusions are consistent with the data reported and with other generally known information. [3]

specific guideline. All or part of a standards rule of USPAP from which departure is permitted under certain limited conditions. [4]

Standards of Professional Appraisal Practice of the Appraisal Institute. This term refers collectively to the Uniform Standards of Professional Appraisal Practice and the Supplemental Standards of Professional Appraisal Practice. [2]

technical review. Performed by an appraiser in accordance with Standard 3 of the Uniform Standards to form an opinion as to whether the analyses, opinions, and conclusions of the report under review are appropriate and reasonable.

Uniform Residential Appraisal Report (URAR). A standardized appraisal form developed jointly by the Federal National Mortgage Association, the Federal Home Loan Mortgage Corporation, the Federal Housing Administration, the Veterans Administration, and the Farmers' Home Administration and used to communicate valuations of one- to four-family residential properties. [3]

Uniform Standards (USPAP). This term refers to the Uniform Standards of Professional Appraisal Practice as promulgated by the Appraisal Standards Board (ASB) of The Appraisal Foundation. [4]

update of an appraisal. An extension of a previous appraisal and report ordered by a client for a prior business decision. The updated appraisal provides a revised value estimate as of a new effective date of value.

USPAP. *See* **Uniform Standards.**

References

1. Code of Professional Ethics of the Appraisal Institute. Chicago: Appraisal Institute. Effective November 9, 1996.
2. Supplemental Standards of Professional Appraisal Practice. Chicago: Appraisal Institute, 1993.
3. *The Dictionary of Real Estate Appraisal,* 3d ed. Chicago: Appraisal Institute, 1993.
4. Uniform Standards of Professional Appraisal Practice. Washington, D.C.: The Appraisal Foundation, 1998 ed.

Data Sources for Reviewers

The following list identifies organizations, publications, and other information sources that can help appraisal reviewers perform more effectively. This list is not all-inclusive, but it can serve as a starting point for reviewers looking for additional reference benchmarking tools. Reviewers can find real estate data in their individual markets by contacting local chapters of the professional organizations listed.

Apartments

Income/Expense Analysis: Apartments, Condominiums & Cooperatives. Institute of Real Estate Management.

Appraisal Courses & Seminars

Appraisal Institute national office. Phone: 312-335-4100.

Appraisal Standards (USPAP)

Uniform Standards of Professional Appraisal Practice. The Appraisal Foundation. Phone: 202-347-7722.

Appraisal Topics

The Appraisal of Real Estate, 11th ed. The Appraisal Institute.

The Appraisal Journal. Quarterly publication. The Appraisal Institute

"Understanding The Appraisal." Brochure. The Appraisal Institute.

Y.T. and Louise Lee Lum Library. The Appraisal Institute. The largest library of appraisal-related literature and resource publications. Fax: 312-335-4486.

Building Cost Information

Boeckh Publications.

F.W. Dodge Corporation.

Marshall Valuation Service. Loose-leaf service. Quarterly supplements. Phone: 213-683-9000.

R.S. Means Co., Inc. Phone: 617-585-7880.

Capitalization & Discount Rates, Investor Preferences

Real Estate Report. Quarterly publication. Real Estate Research Corp. (RERC). Phone: 312-346-5885.

National Investor Report. Quarterly publication. CB Commercial. Phone: 312-861-7828.

Real Estate Outlook. Quarterly publication. Cushman & Wakefield. Phone: 212-841-7500.

Investment Bulletin. Quarterly publication. American Council of Life Insurance. Phone: 202-624-2000.

Real Estate Investor Survey. Quarterly publication. Survey of a cross-section of the major participants in real estate equity markets. Peter Korpacz. Phone: 301-865-5533.

Demographic Reports

CACI. Phone: 800-292-2224

Donnelley Marketing Information. Phone: 203-353-7474.

Information Decision Systems. Demographic reports, market report, employment profile, retail profile, shopping center report. Phone: 800-795-7483.

National Decisions Systems. Phone: 619-942-7000.

The National Planning Data Corporation. Phone: 602-273-8208.

Urban Decisions Systems. Phone: 800-633-9568.

Industrial

Industrial Income and Expense Report. Biannual publication. National Association of Industrial and Office Properties. Phone: 703-904-7100. Fax: 703-904-7942.

Lodging Industry

HOST, Hotel Operating Statistics Annual publication. Smith Travel Research. Phone: 615-824-8664.

Hospitality and Leisure Executive Report. Quarterly publication. Arthur Anderson. Phone: 212-708-4545.

Horwath Hospitality Consulting/Smith Travel Research. Monthly publication.

Office

Downtown and Suburban Office Building Experience Exchange Report. Building Owners and Managers Association International (BOMA).

Real Estate Forecasts

Emerging Trends in Real Estate. Annual publication. Real Estate Research Corp. Phone: 312-346-5885.

Real Estate Market Forecast. Annual publication. Landauer Real Estate Counselors. Phone: 312-899-0100.

Real Estate Source Directory

Korpacz RE Source Directory. The Korpacz Company, Inc. Quarterly newsletter available by subscription. Current source of information about the real estate "information industry." Phone: 310-829-3770.

Retail

Dollars & Cents of Shopping Centers. Includes income and expense data for neighborhood, community, and regional centers as well as statistics for specific tenant types. Urban Land Institute.

Units of Comparison

Units of comparison are the components into which a property may be divided for purposes of comparison. When units of comparison are used to organize the data, comparison of the subject and comparable properties is facilitated. Because only like units can be compared, each sale price is stated in the same units of comparison. The units applied must be appropriate to the appraisal problem. When unit prices relating to size are used, adjustments for differences in size may be unnecessary.

Many properties can be analyzed with several different units of comparison. The appraiser should apply all appropriate units of comparison, compare the results of each application, and examine the reasons for any wide discrepancy.

Naturally, the most persuasive unit of comparison is the one the market uses. The market unit of comparison can be described as the market's basis for purchase and sale decisions, the object of the market's mental comparison, and the unit that produces the most consistent pattern of value in the market analysis.

Some common units of comparison for various property types are listed below.

Apartment buildings

- Per unit
- Per room
- Gross income multiplier* (*GIM*)—i.e., the ratio between the sale price and the annual gross rental income
- Overall cap rate (*OAR*)—i.e., the relationship between the net annual income and the sale price
- Rents expressed in dollars ($) per rentable square foot annually

Condominiums

- Per unit
- Per living area in square feet, usually calculated from interior wall to interior wall

Golf courses

- Per hole
- Per round (annual number of rounds played)

Health and fitness facilities, tennis or racquetball facilities

- Per playing court
- Per square foot
- Per membership

Industrial

- Per square foot (gross)
- Overall cap rate
- Per cubic foot
- Rents expressed in dollars ($) per square foot annually (monthly in some market areas)

Land

- Per square foot
- Per acre (43,560 square feet)
- Per lot or site, if uniform
- Per front foot
- Per floor area ratio (FAR), as permitted by zoning

Lodging facilities

- Per guest room
- Income expressed in "room nights"
- Overall cap rates
- Revpar (revenue per available room)

Marinas

- Per slip

Medical-related and health care facilities

- Income per patient day (PPD)
- Per bed
- Per square foot
- Gross rent multiplier* (*GRM*)

Mobile home parks

- Per parking pad

Office

- Per square foot
- Usually per net rentable square foot for multiple units and per gross square foot for stand-alone units
- Overall cap rate
- Rents expressed in dollars ($) per square foot annually (monthly in some markets)

Religious institutions

- Per square foot

Restaurants, theaters, etc.

- Per seat

Retail

- Per square foot
- Usually per net leaseable square foot for multiple units and per gross square foot for stand-alone units
- Overall cap rate
- Rents expressed in dollars ($) per leaseable square foot annually (monthly in some markets)

Single-family residential

- Gross living area
- Above-grade living area
- Per room or per living unit
- Gross rent multiplier* (*GRM*)—i.e., ratio of selling price to monthly unfurnished rent
- Truck terminals, auto garages, etc.
- Per bay

---

* Three precautions about gross income multipliers must be noted:

1. The reviewer must be aware of the nuances and definitions of the terms *gross rent multiplier, gross income multiplier, potential gross income multiplier,* and *effective gross income multiplier;*
2. Gross income multipliers must be derived from properties that are comparable to the property being appraised and to one another in terms of physical, locational, and investment characteristics; and
3. Gross income multipliers are derived from comparable market data, therefore they must be applied on the same basis as they were derived. The timing of income also must be comparable. If sales were analyzed using next year's income expectation, the multiplier derived must be applied to next year's expected income for the subject property.

Appraisal Development and Reporting Options

An appraisal can be categorized as either a complete appraisal—one without departure—or a limited appraisal—one with departure.

In developing a complete appraisal, the appraiser will use all applicable valuation procedures and the value conclusion will reflect all known information relative to the subject property, market conditions, and available data.

In a limited appraisal, the appraiser and the client agree before the commencement of the assignment that the appraiser will not use all applicable valuation procedures, or that the value conclusion will not reflect all known information about the subject property, market conditions, and available data.

A limited appraisal is not necessarily an easier assignment than a complete appraisal of the same property. For example, if the appraisal is limited because it is prepared without benefit of full information (e.g., the appraiser must rely on a description of the interior because only a drive-by inspection was possible, lease information is missing, or plans for proposed improvements are incomplete), the appraiser will be forced to make assumptions about the missing information. Figure 1 outlines the requirements for the development of an appraisal as set forth in Standard 1.

An appraisal report can be categorized as a self-contained appraisal report, a summary appraisal report, or a restricted appraisal report. When a self-contained appraisal report is prepared, virtually all the information relating to how the appraiser reached the value conclusion is documented in the report. In a summary appraisal report, this information is merely summarized. In a restricted appraisal report, the information is referenced but is not included in the report. Any of these options may be used to report either a complete appraisal or a limited appraisal (see Figure 2).

A self-contained appraisal report contains, to the fullest extent possible and practical, comprehensive explanations of the data, reasoning, and analyses that were used to develop the opinion of value. It also includes thorough descriptions of the subject property, the property's locale, the market for the property type, and the appraiser's opinion of highest and best use. Self-contained appraisal reports are usually written in narrative form.

A summary appraisal report contains summary discussions of the data, reasoning, and analyses that were used to develop the opinion of value. It also includes summary descriptions of the subject property, the property's locale, the market for the property type, and the appraiser's opinion of highest and best use. Any data, reasoning, and analyses not discussed in the summary appraisal report are

FIGURE 1. APPRAISAL DEVELOPMENT REQUIREMENTS

(Reference Guide to Standard 1)

- ♦ Correctly use recognized appraisal methods and techniques.
- ♦ Don't make substantial errors of omission or commission.
- ♦ Don't be careless or negligent; don't make a series of errors that together could result in a misleading appraisal.
- ◊ Identify the real estate, the real property interest, special limiting conditions, and effective date of the appraisal.
- ◊ Consider the appraisal's purpose and intended use and the extent of the data collection process.
- ◊ Define the value.
- ◊ Consider easements, restrictions, encumbrances, leases, reservations, covenants, contracts, declarations, special assessments, ordinances, and other items of a similar nature.
- ◊ Consider whether an appraised fractional interest, physical segment, or partial holding contributes pro rata to the value of the whole.
- ◊ Identify and consider any personal property, trade fixtures, or intangible items that are not real property but are included in the appraisal.
- ◊ Consider the effect of existing land use regulations, reasonably probable modifications of such regulations, economic demand, the physical adaptability of the real estate, neighborhood trends, and the highest and best use of the real estate.
- ◊ Recognize that land is appraised as though vacant and available for development to its highest and best use, and that the appraisal of improvements is based on their actual contribution to the site.
- ◊ Value the site using an appropriate technique.
- ◊ Collect, verify, analyze, and reconcile data to develop the three approaches to value.
- ◊ Support projections of future rent and expenses.
- ◊ Consider lease terms and conditions.
- ◊ Consider and analyze the effect of the assemblage of the various estates or component parts of a property and don't estimate the value of the whole solely by adding together the individual values of the various estates or component parts.
- ◊ Consider and analyze the effect of anticipated public or private improvements, located on or off the site.
- ◊ Identify and consider the appropriate procedures and market information required to perform the appraisal, including all physical, functional, and external market factors as they may affect the appraisal.
- ◊ Appraise proposed improvements only when supplied with appropriate information about the nature of the proposed improvements; probable time of completion; development costs; and anticipated earnings, occupancy projections, and competition at time of completion.
- ◊ Consider all pertinent information above in developing the appraisal.
- ♦ Consider any current sale, option, or listing activity.
- ♦ Consider and analyze any prior sales within the last three years (one year for one- to four-family residential).
- ♦ Consider and reconcile the quality and quantity of data available and analyzed within the approaches used and the applicability or suitability of the approaches used.

Figure 2. Appraisal Product Matrix

The appraisal development process and the reporting process can be combined to allow six different appraisal products. *Complete appraisals* and *limited appraisals* can both be reported in any of the three report types.

Development Process	Report Type
Complete Appraisal	Self-Contained Summary Restricted
Limited Appraisal	Self-Contained Summary Restricted

retained in the appraiser's work file. A summary appraisal report provides the client and intended users of the appraisal with a concise synopsis of how the appraiser arrived at the value conclusion without offering a lot of detail. It may be a short narrative or a form report.

A restricted appraisal report contains statements of the appraiser's findings with virtually no explanation of the data, reasoning, and analyses that were used to develop the opinion of value. All of the data, reasoning, and analyses in support of the appraiser's findings are retained in the appraiser's work file. The restricted appraisal report is the briefest written appraisal report that can be prepared under the standards. One distinguishing feature of a restricted appraisal report is that it provides no information concerning the development of the opinion of value. The key difference between a restricted appraisal report and a summary or self-contained appraisal report is that there can be only one intended user for the restricted appraisal report—the immediate client.

In a self-contained or summary appraisal report, information regarding the development of the opinion of value must be described or summarized; in a restricted report that same information can merely be stated. However, in a restricted appraisal report, the extent of the process of collecting, confirming, and reporting data must be described, not stated, because otherwise it will not be evident to the reader.

As stand-alone products, restricted appraisal reports defy any due diligence (technical) review. They simply do not include enough information for the reviewer to make any judgments about the adequacy of the data, reasoning, and analyses.

The requirements for self-contained, summary, and restricted appraisal reports as set forth in Standard 2 are displayed in Figure 3. Five of the requirements (ii, iii, v, vii, and ix) are the same for all three report options. For the most part, the other requirements differ only in their use of the terms *describe*, *summarize*, and *state*.

- *Describe* means to provide a comprehensive level of detail.
- *Summarize* means to provide a more concise presentation of information.
- *State* means to provide minimal information.

Whether the appraiser produces a self-contained appraisal report, a summary appraisal report, or a restricted appraisal report, he or she must still consider all of the information required to develop the appraisal. Except to the degree that there is departure, all of the pertinent data, reasoning, and analyses must be retained and available for future reference—either in the report or in the appraiser's work file (file memoranda). When more information is contained in the report, less needs to be kept in the work file.

Levels of Reliability

To use the various valuation products correctly, clients must understand the different levels of reliability and business risk associated with them. The level of reliability should also be considered in determining which valuation product is appropriate for a given business decision or situation.

It should be clearly understood that the appraisal development process affects the report's reliability, not the report type. In other words, the fact that an appraiser invokes the Departure Provision and applies fewer approaches to value is what makes a limited appraisal less reliable than a complete appraisal, not the communication of the appraisal in a summary report rather than a self-contained report. The highest level of reliability is associated with a complete appraisal performed without invoking the Departure Provision. Limited appraisals resulting from invoking the Departure Provision have varying levels of reliability.

Users of appraisal services must realize that, as the degree of departure increases, the corresponding level of reliability in the limited appraisal decreases and the client accepts a higher level of risk.

Figure 3. Comparison of Report Types

Self-Contained	Summary	Restricted
i. Identify and describe the real estate being appraised.	i. Identify and describe the real estate being appraised.	i. Identify the real estate being appraised.
ii. State the real property interest being appraised.	ii. State the real property interest being appraised.	ii. State the real property interest being appraised.
iii. State the purpose and intended use of the appraisal.	iii. State the purpose and intended use of the appraisal.	iii. State the purpose and intended use of the appraisal.
iv. Define the value to be estimated.	iv. Define the value to be estimated.	iv. State and reference a definition of the value to be estimated.
v. State the effective date of the appraisal and the date of the report.	v. State the effective date of the appraisal and the date of the report.	v. State the effective date of the appraisal and the date of the report.
vi. State the extent of the process of collecting, confirming, and reporting data.	vi. Summarize the extent of the process of collecting, confirming, and reporting data.	vi. Describe the extent of the process of collecting, confirming, and reporting data.
vii. State all assumptions and limiting conditions that affect the analyses, opinions, and conclusions.	vii. State all assumptions and limiting conditions that affect the analyses, opinions, and conclusions.	vii. State all assumptions and limiting conditions that affect the analyses, opinions, and conclusions.
viii. Describe the information considered, the appraisal procedures followed, and the reasoning that supports the analyses, opinions, and conclusions.	viii. Summarize the information considered, the appraisal procedures followed, and the reasoning that supports the analyses, opinions, and conclusions.	viii. State the appraisal procedures followed; state the value conclusion and reference the existance of specific file information in support of the conclusion.

continued

Self-Contained	Summary	Restricted
ix. Describe the appraiser's opinion of the highest and best use of the real estate, when such an opinion is necessary and appropriate.	ix. Summarize the appraiser's opinion of the highest and best use of the real estate, when such an opinion necessary and appropirate.	ix. State the appraiser's opinion of the highest and best use of the real estate, when such an opinion is necessary and appropriate.
x. Explain and support the exclusion of any of the usual valuation approaches.	x. Explain and support the exclusion of any of the usual valuation approaches.	x. State the exclusion of any of the usual valuation approaches.
xi. Describe any additional information that may be appropriate to show compliance with, or clearly identify and explain permitted departures from, the specific guidelines of Standard 1.	xi. Summarize any additional information that may be appropriate to show compliance with, or clearly identify and explain permitted departures from, the requirements of Standard 1.	xi. Include a prominent use restriction that limits reliance on the report to the client and warns that the report cannot be understood properly without additional information in the work file of the appraiser, and clearly identify and explain any permitted departures from the requirements of Standard 1.
xii. Include a signed certification in accordance with Standards Rule 2-3.	xii. Include a signed certification in accordance with Standards Rule 2-3.	xii. Include a signed certification in accordance with Standards Rule 2-3.

Note: Comment sections are not included in chart.

Federal Agency Appraisal Requirements

Federal regulatory agencies' appraisal regulations include five minimum standards for the preparation of an appraisal for federally related transactions:

1. Conform to USPAP unless principles of safe and sound banking require compliance with stricter standards;
2. Be written and contain sufficient information and analysis to support the institution's decision to engage in the transaction;
3. Analyze and report appropriate deductions and discounts for proposed construction or renovation, partially leased buildings, nonmarket lease terms, and tract developments with unsold units;
4. Be based upon the definition of market value set forth in the regulation; and
5. Be performed by state licensed or certified appraisers in accordance with requirements set forth in the regulation.

What Is an Evaluation?

Federal regulators have ruled that not all transactions require a formal appraisal prepared by a qualified appraiser. Sometimes a less formal, yet appropriate, evaluation by a competent evaluator is sufficient.

According to the Interagency Appraisal and Evaluation Guidelines, the term *evaluation* describes an estimate of value for certain real estate-related transactions that are exempt from the agencies' appraisal requirements.

The federal regulators have ruled that while an appraisal must conform to generally accepted appraisal standards as set forth in USPAP, an evaluation does not need to conform to USPAP. This is an important distinction because appraisers who are bound by USPAP must comply with USPAP whenever they provide an opinion of value.

The agencies' guidelines state that an institution should, at a minimum, require that an evaluation

- Be written;
- Include the preparer's name, address, and signature, and the effective date of the evaluation;
- Describe the real estate collateral, its condition, and its current and projected use;
- Describe the source(s) of information used in the analysis;
- Describe the analysis and supporting information; and
- Provide an estimate of the real estate's market value, with any limiting conditions.

Further, "the documentation in an evaluation report should be sufficient to allow an institution to understand the analysis, assumptions, and conclusions," and the "evaluation should provide an estimate of value to assist the institution in assessing the soundness of the transaction."

Appraisers should be aware that lenders specify different requirements for evaluations based on their interpretations of the agencies' guidelines. The appraiser and the client must have a mutual understanding of the nature and scope of the assignment. By requesting copies of the institution's evaluation requirements, the appraiser can facilitate this mutual understanding.

Under USPAP, an evaluation becomes an appraisal when the evaluation assignment includes a request for an estimate of value. According to the Appraisal Standards Board, a request for an estimate of the value of real property calling for something less than, or different from, the work required by Standards Rules 1-2, 1-3, and 1-4 "can be performed as a limited appraisal when the Departure Provision is properly invoked by the appraiser."

If a client's request for an evaluation does not involve limitations on the appraisal process, the appraiser can accept the assignment and perform a complete appraisal that satisfies USPAP requirements.

If the evaluation request does not require an estimate of the value of a specific property, the appraiser can consider it a real estate or real property consulting service conducted under Standards 4 and 5.[1]

Appropriate Use of the Three Reporting Options

A self-contained appraisal report is appropriate:

- Almost always.
- If the client requests it.
- If the intended use calls for a report that contains full information regarding the data, reasoning, and analyses used to develop the opinion of value.

A summary appraisal report might be appropriate if:

- There are a limited number of intended user(s), and

1. Much of the above material has been adapted from the Appraisal Institute publication *Understanding Limited Appraisals and Appraisal Reporting Options* by Stephanie Coleman, MAI, SRA, and Joseph L. Minnich III, SRPA, SRA.

- The intended user(s) have some knowledge of the real estate and its environment, and
- The intended use does not call for a report that is more detailed than a summary appraisal report.

A summary appraisal report might not be appropriate if:

- There are an unlimited number of intended users, or
- The intended user(s) have limited knowledge of the real estate and its environment, or
- The intended use calls for a report that is more detailed than a summary appraisal report.

A restricted appraisal report might be appropriate if:

- The client is the only intended user, and
- The intended use warrants restricted disclosure of the data, reasoning, and analyses used to develop the opinion of value.

A restricted appraisal report is not appropriate if:

- The client is not the only intended user, or
- The intended use calls for a level of detail that is not provided in a restricted appraisal report.

Calculating Square Footage

One common problem encountered by reviewers of single-family residential appraisals is errors in the calculation of square footage. Appraisers wonder, should rooms below grade, partially finished rooms, or garages be included in the gross living area? Most appraisers rely on standards set by Fannie Mae or Freddie Mac, but there is still a great deal of uncertainty.

Gross Living Area

The most common unit of comparison applied to single-family properties (including units in PUD, condominium, or cooperative projects) is above-grade gross living area. Appraisers must be consistent in calculating and reporting the finished above-grade room count and the square feet of above-grade gross living area. For units in condominium or cooperative projects, the appraiser should use interior perimeter dimensions to calculate the gross living area. In all other instances, the appraiser should use the exterior building dimensions to calculate the above-grade gross living area for each floor of the property. Only finished above-grade areas are included in gross living area; garages and basements (including those that are partially above grade) are not. Generally, any level that is partially below grade, regardless of the quality of its finish or window area, is considered below-grade space. Thus, a walkout basement with finished rooms would not be included in the above-grade room count or area calculation.

Rooms that are not included in the above-grade room count may add substantial value to a property, particularly when the quality of finish is high. The appraiser should report the basement or other partially below-grade areas separately and make appropriate adjustments for them on the "basement and finished areas below-grade" line in the sales comparison adjustment grid. To assure consistency in the sales comparison analysis, the appraiser generally should compare above-grade areas to above-grade areas and below-grade areas to below-grade areas. The appraiser may deviate from this approach if the style of the subject property or any of the comparables does not lend itself to such comparisons. However, the appraiser must explain the reason for any deviation and clearly describe the comparisons that were made.

Areas excluded from gross living area calculations include

- Attic areas
- Porches and breezeways
- Decks and balconies

- Unfinished areas
- Basement areas that are partly below grade
- Garages and outbuildings

When a gray area of interpretation is involved, the appraiser should document and explain the reasoning behind whatever methods he or she applied to resolve the question.

American National Standards Institute

The American National Standards Institute, Inc. (ANSI) recently approved standards for calculating the square footage areas of single-family residences. Before the adoption of the standard (ANSI 2765-1996), no universal standard for measuring the square footage in single-family houses existed in the United States. The standard states in part:

> To be included in finished square footage calculations, finished areas must have a ceiling height of at least 7 feet (2.13 meters) except: under beams, ducts, and other obstructions where the height may be 6 feet 4 inches (1.93 meters); under stairs where there is no specified height requirement; or where the ceiling is sloped. If a room's ceiling is sloped, at least one-half of the finished square footage in that room must have a vertical ceiling height of at least 7 feet (2.13 meters); no portion of the finished area that has a height of less than 5 feet (1.52 meters) may be included in finished square footage.
>
> Garages and unfinished areas cannot be included in the calculation of finished square footage. Chimneys, windows, and other finished areas that protrude beyond the exterior finished surface of the outside walls and do not have a floor on the same level cannot be included in the calculation of square footage.
>
> Calculation of square footage made by using exterior dimensions but without an inspection of the interior spaces is allowed but must be stated as such when reporting the result of the calculation. Calculation of square footage for a proposed house made by using plans must be stated as such when reporting the result of the calculation.[1]

Gross Building Area

Gross building area is the total finished area of the improvements, including any interior common areas, such as stairways and hallways, based on exterior measurements.

1. Excerpted from ANSI 2765-1996, Method of Calculating Square Footage, NAHB Research Center, 400 Prince George's Boulevard, Upper Marlboro, MD 20774-8731.

Sample Performance Rating Form

PERFORMANCE ANALYSIS REPORT

Property ______________________________ File # __________

Property type ______________________________ Property size __________

Appraisal firm ______________________________ Report dated __________

Original report? ❑Y ❑N Update ❑Y ❑N Appraisal fee $ __________

Timeliness

Delivery was ❑ on or before due date __________ days late

Extenuating circumstances ❑ yes ❑ no

Responsiveness

The appraiser's response to questions and problems was:

❑ Excellent ❑ Good ❑ Fair

❑ Unsatisfactory ❑ Not applicable, no problems

Any special problems? ______________________________

Quality Rating

A Excellent: insignificant problems, if any; well written, good logical flow, well supported and reasoned, high confidence level.

B Good: only minor problems, consistent assumptions, well supported and reasoned, strong defensible conclusion.

C Fair: some technical problems, inconsistencies, and/or flawed reasoning, but readily correctable or resolvable; final product was acceptable after problems were resolved; average confidence level.

D Unsatisfactory: serious problems with significant issues; only marginally acceptable after in-house modification.

F Unacceptable: major problems throughout; final report was rejected outright.

Client __________ Reviewer __________ Dated __________

Use of performance report: To be filled out by the reviewer after the review process is completed. At a minimum, the original report must meet USPAP standards, regulatory requirements (if applicable), and the client criteria or specifications outlined in the engagement letter or contract. The rating should consider competency, professional judgment, consistency, adequacy of support, and the reasonableness and soundness of conclusions. The ratings should reflect the review of the appraiser's original work product, not that of the final corrected and approved report.

Sample Review Forms and Reviewer's Certification

On the following pages are examples of a commercial appraisal review format (page 182), a checklist for reviewing narrative appraisal reports (page 189), and the Appraisal Institute's Checklist for Screening Residential Form Reports (page 196). Also included is a sample Reviewer's Certification (page 199). Experience shows that "one form does not fit all." Most financial institutions and independent reviewers prefer to customize the review format to fit their work patterns and staff requirements. The formats presented here are offered merely to indicate the possible content of a review form. They should not be copied and used verbatim, but can be tailored to suit the individual reviewer's style. All of the questions will not be applicable in all cases.

COMMERCIAL APPRAISAL REVIEW

(Not to be used for single-family residential or one- to four-unit properties)

Dated: ____________________

From: ____________________

Title: ____________________

Unit: ____________________

Location: ____________________

Telephone: ____________________

COMPANY LOGO

To: ____________________

Telephone: ____________________

Location: ____________________

Re: ____________________

Assignment # ____________________

Address of property appraised: ____________________

____

____

____

____

Project name/city: ____________________

Interest appraised: ❑ Leasehold ❑ Leased fee ❑ Fee simple ❑ Fee simple, subject to existing lease(s)

Appraisal assignment type, development process: ❑ Complete ❑ Limited

Appraisal report type: ❑ Self-contained ❑ Summary ❑ Restricted

Conclusion:

The identified appraisal report has been reviewed and is found to be: ❑ Satisfactory ❑ Unsatisfactory* ❑ Rejected

*Subject to discussion with appraiser to clarify pertinent questions

Final market value estimate: ____________________

Effective appraisal date: ____________________

Appraisal firm/location: ____________________

Appraisal dated: ____________________

Report signed by: ____________________

Is the principal appraiser appropriately "state certified" for the property type and location of the subject property? ❑ Yes ❑ No

If FIRREA is applicable, was the report addressed to the financial institution as the client? ❑ Yes ❑ No

Special Risks/Extraordinary Assumptions and Limiting Conditions

Does the report note any special or environmental risks associated with the property? ❑ Yes ❑ No

If so, reference the page number(s) and briefly describe: ____________________

____

Did the appraiser state that the property is not in a "special hazardous flood plain"? ❑ Yes ❑ No

Does the appraiser include any extraordinary assumptions or limiting conditions that would detract from the scope of the appraisal, limit the intended use of the appraisal, or limit the liability of the appraiser beyond normal standards? ❑ Yes ❑ No

If so, reference the page number(s) and briefly describe: ____________________

____

Standards Rule 3 Review Appraiser Queries

I. Adequacy and relevance of the data and propriety of adjustments to the data: ❑ Satisfactory ❑ Unsatisfactory

II. Appropriateness of the appraisal methods and techniques used: ❑ Satisfactory ❑ Unsatisfactory

III. Correctness and appropriateness of the analyses, opinions, and/or conclusions: ❑ Satisfactory ❑ Unsatisfactory

IV. Reviewer's reasons for disagreement regarding items I, II, and/or III. ____________________

____

____

Scope of the Appraisal Review Process

❑ Desk review ❑ Field review

Property site inspected by the reviewer ❑ Yes ❑ No

If yes, date of inspection ____________________

Market area inspected by the reviewer ❑ Yes ❑ No

Independent market research conducted by reviewer ❑ Yes ❑ No

Technical report review conducted ❑ Yes ❑ No

Discussed report with appraiser ❑ Yes ❑ No

Provide a brief summary of the discussion and outcome or reasons for no discussion with appraiser: ____________________

____

____

Data Verification

Performed general data verification ❑ Yes ❑ No

Source(s): ❑ Previous reports ❑ Outside appraiser(s)
❑ In-house market data library or files ❑ Other

Error check: Mathematics ❑ Yes ❑ No
Software ❑ Yes ❑ No
Appraiser's disk submitted ❑ Yes ❑ No

Appraisal Checklist

S = Satisfactory U = Unsatisfactory E/O = Error/Omission N/A = Not Applicable

Note: S.R. Citations Refer to Specific USPAP Standards Rules

	S	U	E/O	N/A
1. Correct format/form?	❑	❑	❑	❑

Was the correct appraisal format or form used? Was it appropriate for the property type and size? Does it conform to the specifications of the assignment?

Remarks: ____________________

	S	U	E/O	N/A
2. Report type appropriate?	❑	❑	❑	❑

The appraisal report must be prepared under one of the three options and prominently state which option was used. (S.R. 2-2)

Remarks: ____________________

	S	U	E/O	N/A
3. Identification of interest appraised?	❑	❑	❑	❑

Identify and adequately describe the real estate being appraised. Identify specific realty interest being appraised—i.e., leased fee, leasehold, fee simple. [S.R. 2-2 (a)(i), (b)(i), (c)(i); 2-2 (a)(ii), (b)(ii), (c)(ii)]

Remarks: ____________________

	S	U	E/O	N/A
4. Purpose and scope clearly defined?	❑	❑	❑	❑

Did the appraiser clearly state the correct purpose and describe the scope of the appraisal assignment? [S.R. 2-2 (a)(iii), (b)(iii), (c)(iii); 2-2 (a)(vi), (b)(vi), (c)(vi)]

Remarks: ____________________

	S	U	E/O	N/A
5. Appropriate "as of" value date?	❑	❑	❑	❑

Does the appraisal state the correct effective date and the date of the report, typically "as is," subject to all current market, environmental, and property conditions as of the current date? For "to be built" construction purposes, the critical effective date of valuation is either "as of" (a) construction completion or (b) stabilized operations, that is, fully leased to stabilized occupancy with all tenants paying rent. (FIRREA also requires an "as is" value in either event.) In either case, the projected date of the prospective value should be stated in the appraisal.

Remarks: ____________________

	S	U	E/O	N/A
6. Appropriate market value definition?	❑	❑	❑	❑

Based on the appropriate market value definition requested (if appropriate to the assignment). If the appraisal is subject to FIRREA regulations, the interagency definition of market value must be used. [S.R. 2-2 (a)(iv), (b)(iv), (c)(iv)] Is a reasonable exposure time estimated?

Remarks: ____________________

	S	U	E/O	N/A
7. Prior sales history?	❑	❑	❑	❑

Did the appraiser report and analyze prior sales of the subject property over the past three-year period? [S.R. 1-5 (b)]

Remarks: ____________________

	S	U	E/O	N/A
8. Regional/area overview	❑	❑	❑	❑

Provides relevant information and sufficient analysis.
Addresses emerging trends in land uses and property values.
Information is relevant to specific property valuation.

Remarks: ____________________

	S	U	E/O	N/A
9. Neighborhood overview	❑	❑	❑	❑

Defines boundaries or sphere of influence.
Provides relevant information and sufficient analysis.
Addresses emerging trends in land uses and property values.

Remarks: __________

	S	U	E/O	N/A
10. Market/absorption study?	❑	❑	❑	❑

Market absorption, supply and demand trends, and market competition impact the appraised property and are critical to optimizing its highest and best use. Appropriate market timing is crucial. A thorough analysis of current and future macro- and micro-market trends is an absolute necessity. Projected market (occupancy/vacancy) space trends must be addressed. A supplemental market study should be referenced, if appropriate.

Remarks: __________

	S	U	E/O	N/A
11. Current zoning analysis?	❑	❑	❑	❑

Does the subject property conform to current zoning? Discuss if the zoning is particularly restrictive or legally nonconforming.

Remarks: __________

	S	U	E/O	N/A
12. Taxes and assessments	❑	❑	❑	❑

Includes appropriate tax data.
Describes bonds/special/other assessments.
Describes homeowner's association dues.
Includes tax comparables.
Sufficient analysis.

Remarks: __________

	S	U	E/O	N/A
13. Site description	❑	❑	❑	❑

Describes physical characteristics adequately.
Describes legal characteristics.
Describes sources and availability of utilities.
Includes adequate survey or site plan.
Concludes with a reasonable value.

Remarks: __________

	S	U	E/O	N/A
14. Meaningful highest and best use analysis?	❑	❑	❑	❑

Has the appraiser presented a meaningful HBU analysis? [S.R. 2-2 (a)(ix), (b)(ix), (c)(ix)] Includes analysis of site as though vacant and subject as improved or proposed to be improved.

Remarks: __________

	S	U	E/O	N/A
15. Legal description included?	❑	❑	❑	❑

Typically, the appraiser does not assume any liability for matters that are legal or environmental in nature. The legal description should be obtained from legal documentation such as a title policy, deed, survey plat, or loan documentation provided by the client. The appraiser should verify that the property appraised and the legal description coincide and must not, under any circumstances, "create" the legal description. [S.R. 2-2 (a)(i), (b)(i), (c)(i)]

Remarks: __________

	S	U	E/O	N/A
16. Any excess or expansion land?	❑	❑	❑	❑

If the subject property has any excess or expansion land, was it appropriately identified and its contributory value considered?

Remarks: __________

	S	U	E/O	N/A
17. Improvement description	❑	❑	❑	❑

Describes general construction/physical characteristics and condition.
Includes floor plans/sketch or identifies source of building and floor areas.
Estimates effective age and remaining economic life.
Describe on-site improvements.
Addresses ADA compliance.

Remarks: ________________

18. Investment analysis emphasis? ❑ ❑ ❑ ❑

Since investor motivation essentially evolves from a property's income characteristics, the valuation should place primary emphasis on the investment analysis with the comparative market study providing secondary support. Appraisals of owner-occupied property, including so-called "sweat equity" multitenant property, should generally emphasize the sales comparison approach with secondary support from the income approach.

Remarks: ________________

19. Support and reasoning for key assumptions? ❑ ❑ ❑ ❑

The report should be well documented and contain logical analytical techniques. Rents, expenses, vacancy and occupancy rates, capitalization rates, discount rates, comparable sales, growth (inflation) rates, etc. should be substantiated. The appraisal procedures followed, the data considered, and the reasoning that supports the analyses, opinions, and conclusions should be explained. [S.R. 2-2 (a)(viii), (b)(viii), (c)(viii)]

Remarks: ________________

20. Current operating data? ❑ ❑ ❑ ❑

Did the appraiser analyze and report the current operating experience (revenue, expense, vacancy) of the subject property and reconcile actual operating data with projected amounts?

Remarks: ________________

21. Discounted cash flow analysis or direct capitalization? ❑ ❑ ❑ ❑

For investment-grade properties, a computer-generated discounted cash flow analysis (yield capitalization) is usually the appropriate technique to be applied in the income capitalization approach. The report should include an explanation and a concise summary of critical assumptions used in this technique as well as computer printouts summarizing the current leases in place, lease expiration schedules, revenue and operating expense line items, tenant inducements, lease commissions, capital outlays, and assumed reversionary (residual) value computation.

For direct capitalization using an overall capitalization rate, the appraiser must substantiate the rate used and analyze investor/purchasers' rationale and motivation. Rates derived by use of the mortgage-equity technique or other build-up methods must be supported by comparable data or an analysis of survey data.

Use of either technique must be substantiated as a reflection of the behavior of market participants.

Remarks: ________________

22. Estimate of "lease-up" or "sell-out" discounts and deductions? ❑ ❑ ❑ ❑

The appraiser must analyze and report any deductions relevant to proposed construction, completed properties that are partially leased, or subdivision tract developments with unsold units (or lots). Appropriate deductions and discounts must be made for lease-up and holding costs, marketing costs, real estate taxes, and other expenses likely to be incurred during the estimated lease-up or sell-out period.

Remarks: ________________

	S	U	E/O	N/A
23. Cost, sales comparison, and income capitalization approaches	❑	❑	❑	❑

Discusses relevancy of each approach included.
Adequately describes reasoning and analysis employed.

Remarks: ____________________

	S	U	E/O	N/A
24. Adequate market data and documentation?	❑	❑	❑	❑

The sales comparison approach should document each comparable sale and relate the conditions, features, and characteristics of each sale property to the subject property.

Remarks: ____________________

	S	U	E/O	N/A
25. Exclusion of any approaches?	❑	❑	❑	❑

The appraiser must explain and support the exclusion of any of the usual valuation approaches: cost, sales comparison, and income capitalization. [S.R. 2-2 (a)(x), (b)(x), (c)(x)]

Remarks: ____________________

	S	U	E/O	N/A
26. Reconciliation	❑	❑	❑	❑

Emphasizes approach that best simulates likely purchaser's motives and decision-making criteria.
Reconciles the quality and quantity of available data utilized within each approach.
Refers to estimate of a reasonable exposure time implicit in market value definition.
Concluded value is reasonable.

Remarks: ____________________

	S	U	E/O	N/A
27. Reasonable assumptions and limiting conditions?	❑	❑	❑	❑

Contains reasonable content. The inclusion of limiting conditions and assumptions that effectively remove the appraiser's responsibility are unacceptable. [S.R. 2-1 (c); 2-2 (a)(vii), (b)(vii), (c)(vii)] Report notes appropriate special assumptions including citation of pertinent unavailable information.

Remarks: ____________________

	S	U	E/O	N/A
28. Certification requirement met?	❑	❑	❑	❑

The appraiser's certification must comply with Standards Rule 2-3, plus regulatory and Appraisal Institute requirements, if applicable. [S.R. 2-2 (a)(xii), (b)(xii), (c)(xii); 2-3]

Remarks: ____________________

	S	U	E/O	N/A
29. Conformity with USPAP?	❑	❑	❑	❑

All work must be done in accordance with the Uniform Standards of Professional Appraisal Practice of The Appraisal Foundation. The appraiser must provide any additional information to show compliance with, or clearly identify and explain any permitted departures from, Standards 1 and 2. If the report does not comply, the appraiser must cite the appropriate standards rule section indicating noncompliance. [S.R. 2-2 (a)(xi), (b)(xi), (c)(xi)]

Remarks: ____________________

	S	U	E/O	N/A
30. Conformity with regulatory requirements (if applicable)?	❑	❑	❑	❑

If this appraisal was completed for a "federally related real estate transaction," it is required to comply with all current FIRREA requirements: (a) Conforms to USPAP; (b) Is written and contains sufficient information and analysis; (c) Contains appropriate deductions and discounts (See item #22); (d) Is based on the interagency definition of market value (See item #6); and (e) Is prepared by an appropriate state regulated appraiser. If the response is "U" (unsatisfactory) or "N/A" (not applicable), an explanation is required by the reviewer under "Remarks."

Remarks: ____________________

	S	U	E/O	N/A
31. Personalty separately valued?	❑	❑	❑	❑

If personal property, trade fixtures, intangibles, or other items that are not real property represent a significant part of the overall value, those items must be identified and valued separately. [S.R. 1-2 (e)]

Remarks: ____________________

	S	U	E/O	N/A
32. Appropriate distinction of value in use or going-concern value?	❑	❑	❑	❑

Pertinent to lodging facilities, health care facilities, and many special-use properties. Of particular concern to lenders because without appropriate consideration, the real property may be overvalued.

Remarks: ____________________

	S	U	E/O	N/A
33. Report signed by an approved principal of the firm?	❑	❑	❑	❑

(S.R. 2-5)

Remarks: ____________________

	S	U	E/O	N/A
34. Report written to not be misleading?	❑	❑	❑	❑

The appraisal report should be written in a way that is not misleading. [S.R. 2-1 (a)]

Remarks: ____________________

	S	U	E/O	N/A
35. Are there sufficient data and analysis?	❑	❑	❑	❑

Does the report contain sufficient information and analysis to be clearly understood? [S.R. 2-1 (b)]

Remarks: ____________________

	S	U	E/O	N/A
36. Adequacy and appropriateness of exhibits?	❑	❑	❑	❑

Are the maps, photos, charts, and other exhibits clear and complete? Are the exhibits appropriate in light of the complexity of the assignment?

Remarks: ____________________

37. Summary of specific problem areas/important issues.

(Indicate topic number and standards rule citation.) ____________________

____

____

____

Checklist for Reviewing Narrative Appraisal Reports

Property Address: ____________________

Appraiser/Appraisal Firm: ____________________

Effective Date of Value: ____________________

Value Conclusion: ____________________

Reviewer: ____________________ Dated: ____________________

	Y	N	E/O	N/A
Title Page				
1. Identification as an appraisal?	❑	❑	❑	❑
2. Property type described?	❑	❑	❑	❑
3. Property address and brief description?	❑	❑	❑	❑
4. Name of client?	❑	❑	❑	❑
5. Name and address of person authorizing the assignment?	❑	❑	❑	❑
6. Name and address of the appraiser?	❑	❑	❑	❑
Letter of Transmittal				
7. Date report was prepared?	❑	❑	❑	❑
8. Property identified?	❑	❑	❑	❑
9. Purpose of the appraisal stated?	❑	❑	❑	❑
10. Intended use of the appraisal stated?	❑	❑	❑	❑
11. Appraised value identified and/or defined?	❑	❑	❑	❑
12. The interest of the property being appraised identified?	❑	❑	❑	❑
13. Effective date of value?	❑	❑	❑	❑
14. Value estimate?	❑	❑	❑	❑
15. Extraordinary assumptions and limiting conditions?	❑	❑	❑	❑
16. Appraiser's signature?	❑	❑	❑	❑
17. Appraiser's state license number provided?	❑	❑	❑	❑
Introduction				
18. Table of contents?	❑	❑	❑	❑
19. Certification of value?	❑	❑	❑	❑
20. Summary of important conclusions?	❑	❑	❑	❑
Premises of the Appraisal Report				
21. Identification of type of appraisal and report format, and conformance with request?	❑	❑	❑	❑
22. Purpose and intended use of the appraisal?	❑	❑	❑	❑
23. Assumptions and limiting conditions?	❑	❑	❑	❑
24. Appropriate definition of value and date of value estimate?	❑	❑	❑	❑
25. Property rights appraised?	❑	❑	❑	❑
26. Scope of the appraisal?	❑	❑	❑	❑
Property History				
27. Current agreement of sale, option, or listing discussed?	❑	❑	❑	❑

	Y	N	E/O	N/A
28. Prior sales of subject occurring within preceding 12 months for one- to four-family residential properties and within preceding three years for all other property types?	❑	❑	❑	❑
Presentation of General Data				
29. Complete legal description and recording data?	❑	❑	❑	❑
30. Photographs of subject property?	❑	❑	❑	❑
31. Identification of any personal property or other items that are not real property?	❑	❑	❑	❑
32. Relevant regional and city data (e.g., geographic, legal, social, and economic factors)?	❑	❑	❑	❑
33. Relevant neighborhood data (e.g., boundaries, trends, linkages)?	❑	❑	❑	❑
34. Discussion of adjacent land uses and development trends?	❑	❑	❑	❑
35. Tax and assessment data and analysis?	❑	❑	❑	❑
Presentation of Site Data				
36. Description of size and shape of site?	❑	❑	❑	❑
37. Topographical features?	❑	❑	❑	❑
38. Drainage and floodplain conditions?	❑	❑	❑	❑
39. Soil and subsoil conditions?	❑	❑	❑	❑
40. Zoning restrictions?	❑	❑	❑	❑
41. Other legal restrictions?	❑	❑	❑	❑
42. Ingress and egress?	❑	❑	❑	❑
43. Availability and description of utilities?	❑	❑	❑	❑
44. Easements, rights-of-way, or other encumbrances?	❑	❑	❑	❑
45. Relationship to surrounding properties?	❑	❑	❑	❑
46. Nuisances and hazards?	❑	❑	❑	❑
47. Off-site improvements?	❑	❑	❑	❑
48. Functional adequacy of site?	❑	❑	❑	❑
Presentation of Improvement Data				
49. Physical description of improvements (dimensions and areas)?	❑	❑	❑	❑
50. Adequate photos of improvements?	❑	❑	❑	❑
51. Design and layout?	❑	❑	❑	❑
52. Construction details, including quality of construction?	❑	❑	❑	❑
53. Age and condition of improvements?	❑	❑	❑	❑
54. Equipment, fixtures, etc. described?	❑	❑	❑	❑
55. Current use analysis?	❑	❑	❑	❑
56. Deferred maintenance discussed?	❑	❑	❑	❑
57. Functional utility or inutility discussed?	❑	❑	❑	❑

	Y	N	E/O	N/A
58. Relationship to surrounding area?	❑	❑	❑	❑
59. Site improvements described?	❑	❑	❑	❑
Market/Marketability Analysis				
60. Were the site and improvements' marketability advantages and disadvantages analyzed and compared to the competition?	❑	❑	❑	❑
61. Was the subject location analyzed adequately in regard to items such as linkages to demand, required associated land uses, and the direction and rate of neighborhood and city growth?	❑	❑	❑	❑
62. Was the subject's location compared to the location of the competition?	❑	❑	❑	❑
63. Was the subject's specific submarket identified?	❑	❑	❑	❑
64. Was demand analyzed for the subject's specific submarket?	❑	❑	❑	❑
65. Was the subject's competition identified?	❑	❑	❑	❑
66. Was the subject's future marketability (capture potential) analyzed?	❑	❑	❑	❑
67. Were the character and amount of data presented and the detail of the analysis commensurate with the purpose of the appraisal and complexity of the assignment?	❑	❑	❑	❑
Highest and Best Use Analysis				
68. Highest and best use of the site "as if vacant" analyzed?	❑	❑	❑	❑
69. Highest and best use of the property "as improved" analyzed?	❑	❑	❑	❑
70. Were the character and amount of data presented and analyzed commensurate with the purpose of the appraisal and complexity of the assignment?	❑	❑	❑	❑
71. Legally permitted uses evaluated?	❑	❑	❑	❑
72. Physically possible uses evaluated?	❑	❑	❑	❑
73. Supply and demand factors properly considered?	❑	❑	❑	❑
74. Financially feasible uses evaluated?	❑	❑	❑	❑
75. Conclusion consistent with value reported?	❑	❑	❑	❑
Site Valuation				
76. Comparables used are similar to subject considering zoning, size, location, etc.?	❑	❑	❑	❑
77. Comparable site sales adequately described?	❑	❑	❑	❑
78. Reasonable and proper adjustments made?	❑	❑	❑	❑
79. Site value estimate consistent with the definition of value?	❑	❑	❑	❑
80. Adjustment grid included? (Optional with client requirements.)	❑	❑	❑	❑

	Y	N	E/O	N/A
81. Adustments supported and adequately explained?	❑	❑	❑	❑
82. Adjusted unit value within reasonable range of unadjusted unit values?	❑	❑	❑	❑
83. Land value estimate?	❑	❑	❑	❑
84. Any excess/expansion land was appropriately identified and its contributory value considered? (Excess land must be separately valued.)	❑	❑	❑	❑
Cost Approach				
85. Cost new estimate is supported and reasonable?	❑	❑	❑	❑
86. Source of cost data identified and explained?	❑	❑	❑	❑
87. Entrepreneurial profit identified and explained?	❑	❑	❑	❑
88. Cost to complete, leasing expenses, and/or holding cost during construction considered?	❑	❑	❑	❑
89. Physical deterioration described and deferred maintenance discussed?	❑	❑	❑	❑
90. Functional obsolescence considered?	❑	❑	❑	❑
91. External obsolescence considered?	❑	❑	❑	❑
92. Source and logic of total depreciation estimate explained and/or substantiated with market data?	❑	❑	❑	❑
93. Contributory value of site improvements properly documented?	❑	❑	❑	❑
94. Data considered consistent with those given elsewhere in the report?	❑	❑	❑	❑
95. Value indication consistent with the previously stated definition of value?	❑	❑	❑	❑
Sales Comparison Approach				
96. Adequate description and analysis of comparable sales?	❑	❑	❑	❑
97. Adjustment grid included? (Optional with client requirements.)	❑	❑	❑	❑
98. Significant elements of comparison property considered?	❑	❑	❑	❑
99. Adjustments to sales are supported and adequately explained?	❑	❑	❑	❑
100. Adjusted unit value is within the range of the unadjusted unit values?	❑	❑	❑	❑
101. Reasonable and proper adjustments to comparable sales?	❑	❑	❑	❑
102. Data considered consistent with those given elsewhere in the report?	❑	❑	❑	❑
103. Value indication consistent with the previously stated definition of value?	❑	❑	❑	❑

	Y	N	E/O	N/A
Income Capitalization Approach				
104. Income and expenses for subject property summarized?	❑	❑	❑	❑
105. Existing leases properly analyzed and described?	❑	❑	❑	❑
106. Comparable rentals properly described and compared to the subject property?	❑	❑	❑	❑
107. Reasonable and proper adjustments to comparable rentals?	❑	❑	❑	❑
108. Supportable and reasonable gross income estimate?	❑	❑	❑	❑
109. Supportable and reasonable estimate of rent loss and vacancy?	❑	❑	❑	❑
110. Supportable and reasonable estimate of lease-up absorption?	❑	❑	❑	❑
111. Expenses for subject reasonable and fully explained?	❑	❑	❑	❑
112. Forecast for income and expenses adequately explained and reasonable?	❑	❑	❑	❑
113. Logical selection of capitalization rate(s)?	❑	❑	❑	❑
114. Market support for direct capitalization?	❑	❑	❑	❑
115. Logical selection and market support for discount rate(s)?	❑	❑	❑	❑
116. Stabilized operating statement consistent with historical data for the subject property?	❑	❑	❑	❑
117. All appropriate deductions and discounts accounted for?	❑	❑	❑	❑
118. Thorough analysis and discussion of existing leases?	❑	❑	❑	❑
119. Projected rental income and expenses adequately supported if different from historical trends?	❑	❑	❑	❑
120. Adequate replacement reserves accounted for?	❑	❑	❑	❑
121. Discounted cash flow includes explanation and summary of critical assumptions used and computer printouts summarizing the current leases in place, lease expiration patterns, revenue and operating expense line items, tenant inducements, lease commissions, capital outlays, and assumed reversionary (residual) value computation?	❑	❑	❑	❑
122. Data considered consistent with those given elsewhere in the report?	❑	❑	❑	❑
123. Value indication consistent with the previously stated definition of value?	❑	❑	❑	❑

	Y	N	E/O	N/A
Reconciliation and Final Value Estimate				
124. All three approaches to value utilized or explanation given for exclusion of any value approach?	❑	❑	❑	❑
125. Quantity and quality of data used in the appraisal report properly evaluated?	❑	❑	❑	❑
126. Final value estimate developed through logical reasoning?	❑	❑	❑	❑
127. Consistency among various internal sections of report?	❑	❑	❑	❑
128. Value reasonable based on data presented?	❑	❑	❑	❑
129. Level of detail contained in the appraisal report commensurate with the complexity of the assignment?	❑	❑	❑	❑
Miscellaneous Items				
130. Influence of intangibles (e.g., business value) identified and valued separately?	❑	❑	❑	❑
131. Estimated marketing time consistent with previously stated definition of value?	❑	❑	❑	❑
132. Consistency among three approaches to value with respect to the type of value indicated (e.g., "as is" versus "as of" or "upon stabilization")? In particular, appropriate inclusion/exclusion of entrepreneurial profit and consideration of deferred maintenance within the three approaches to value?	❑	❑	❑	❑
133. Adequate analysis and independent cross-checking to support value indications derived through the use of any DCF software programs in the valuation process?	❑	❑	❑	❑
Residential Subdivision or Multiple-Tract Analysis				
134. Prospective absorption period reasonable and market supported?	❑	❑	❑	❑
135. Projected capital, sales, and holding expenses supported?	❑	❑	❑	❑
136. Developer's profit allowance adequate?	❑	❑	❑	❑
137. Discount rate adequately reflects the associated risk?	❑	❑	❑	❑
138. Report adequately derives the individual retail prices and the market value of the asset in its entirety to a single purchaser?	❑	❑	❑	❑
139. If for lending purposes, do the value and the development completion scenarios match the loan payout provisions (e.g., completion of infrastructure, completion of models, unit-by-unit sales plateaus, etc.)?	❑	❑	❑	❑

Reviewer's Conclusions & Recommendations

Does appraisal conform to:

USPAP requirements?	❑ Yes	❑ No
Regulatory requirements?	❑ Yes	❑ No
Client specifications?	❑ Yes	❑ No

Comments:

Does reviewer concur

S.R. 3-1 (d):	with the adequacy and relevance of the data used?	❑ Yes	❑ No
S.R. 3-1 (d):	with the propriety of any adjustments made?	❑ Yes	❑ No
S.R. 3-1 (e):	with the appropriateness of the appraisal methods and techniques used?	❑ Yes	❑ No
S.R. 3-1 (f):	with the appropriateness of the analysis, opinions, and conclusions?	❑ Yes	❑ No

Conclusion:

❑ Accept appraisal "as is"

❑ Accept appraisal "as revised"

❑ Reject appraisal

❑ Request appraiser make necessary revisions

❑ Request another appraisal

❑ Accept reviewer's revisions with supporting data attached hereto

Reviewer: ______________________ Dated: ______________________

Checklist for Screening Residential Form Reports

NOTE: This form is not intended to be used for Technical Reviews as defined in The Appraisal Foundation's Advisory Opinion AO-6 and as described in Standard 3 of USPAP.

Identification of Report Being Screened:

Address: ____________________

Date of report: ____________ Date of value: _____ Date of screening: _____

Appraiser: ____________ Screener: ____________

	Yes	No	N/A	Rule
General				
Report identified as summary report	❑	❑		S.R. 2-2
Comments: ____________				
Identified as limited, if applicable, and departures noted	❑	❑	❑	S.R. 2-2 (b)(xi)
Comments: ____________				
Summarize extent of process of collecting, confirming, and reporting data	❑	❑		S.R. 2-2 (b)(vi)
Comments: ____________				
Clearly identify date of report and date of value	❑	❑		S.R. 2-2 (b)(v)
Comments: ____________				
Subject				
Property identified adequately	❑	❑		S.R. 2-2 (b)(i)
Comments: ____________				
Summary description of property	❑	❑		S.R. 2-2 (b)(i)
Comments: ____________				
Property rights appraised stated	❑	❑		S.R. 2-2 (b)(ii)
Comments: ____________				
Neighborhood				
Descriptions and classifications section completed	❑	❑		S.R. 2-1 (b)
Comments: ____________				
Describe neighborhood boundaries and characteristics	❑	❑		S.R. 2-1 (b)
Comments: ____________				
Discuss factors that affect marketability	❑	❑		S.R. 2-1 (b)
Comments: ____________				
Discuss market conditions	❑	❑		S.R. 2-1 (b)
Comments: ____________				
PUD (Planned Unit Development)				
Section of the report completed	❑	❑	❑	S.R. 2-1 (b)
Comments: ____________				
Site				
Descriptions and classifications completed	❑	❑		S.R. 2-1 (b)
Comments: ____________				
Highest and best use is "present use," or explained	❑	❑		S.R. 2-2 (b)(ix)
Comments: ____________				
Comments by appraiser	❑	❑	❑	S.R. 2-1 (b)
Comments: ____________				

	Yes	No	N/A	Rule
Description of Improvements				
Complete description, including plat and photo	❑	❑		S.R. 2-2 (b)
Comments: ______				
Identification of personal property included in value	❑	❑	❑	S.R. 1-2 (e)
Comments: ______				
Comments				
Additional features	❑	❑	❑	S.R. 2-2 (b)(i)
Comments: ______				
Condition, depreciation, needed repairs, etc.	❑	❑		S.R. 2-2 (b)(i)
Comments: ______				
Adverse environmental conditions	❑	❑	❑	S.R. 2-2 (b)(i)
Comments: ______				
Cost Approach				
All steps in the approach seem to be reasonable	❑	❑		S.R. 1-1 (a)
Comments: ______				
The calculations appear to be correct	❑	❑		S.R. 1-1 (a)
Comments: ______				
Exclusion of cost approach supported and explained	❑	❑	❑	S.R. 2-2 (b)(x)
Comments: ______				
Sales Comparison Analysis				
Sales appear to be located reasonably near the subject	❑	❑		S.R. 1-1 (a)
Comments: ______				
Sales are dated within a reasonable time period	❑	❑		S.R. 1-1 (a)
Comments: ______				
Adjustments agree with appropriate descriptions, and are in the proper direction	❑	❑		S.R. 1-1 (a)
Comments: ______				
Extraordinarily large adjustments are explained	❑	❑		S.R. 1-1 (a)
Comments: ______				
Income				
If income approach is used, are income and *GRM* supported in the addendum?	❑	❑	❑	S.R. 2-2 (b)(viii)
Comments: ______				
Final Reconciliation				
Appraisal supports final value estimate reasonably	❑	❑		S.R. 1-1 (a)
Comments: ______				
If estimate is based on future work or bad conditions, are they clearly explained and supported?	❑	❑	❑	S.R. 2-2 (b)(viii)
Comments: ______				

	Yes	No	N/A	Rule
Attachments				
Complete certification included	❑	❑		S.R. 2-3
Comments: ______				
Certification is signed	❑	❑		S.R. 2-2 (b)(xi)
Comments: ______				
Certification includes name(s) of person(s) providing significant professional assistance	❑	❑	❑	S.R. 2-3
Comments: ______				
Comments regarding contributions of named person(s): ______				
Market value is defined	❑	❑		S.R. 2-2 (b)(iv)
Comments: ______				
Statement of assumptions and limiting conditions	❑	❑		S.R. 2-2 (b)(vii)
Comments: ______				
Investigation of property history:				
if no current item or recent sale -	❑	❑		S.R. 1-5 (a), (b)
Comments: ______				
and				S.R. 2-2 (b)(xi)
if current item or recent sale	❑	❑		S.R. 2-2 (b)(viii)
Comments: ______				
Statement to show that data were verified	❑	❑		S.R. 1-4 (b)
Comments: ______				
State purpose and intended use of report	❑	❑		S.R. 2-2 (b)(iii)
Comments: ______				
Signature and license/certification number (if any) of appraiser included on report	❑	❑		(Not USPAP)
Comments: ______				

Screener's Analysis

❑ Report accepted "as is"

❑ Report accepted, but minor violations noted

❑ Report rejected

Comments: ______

(Screener's signature)

Sample Reviewer Certification Format

Reviewer Certification

I certify that, to the best of my knowledge and belief:

- The facts and data reported by the review appraiser and used in the review process are factual and accurate.
- The analyses, opinions, and conclusions in this review report are limited only by the assumptions and limiting conditions stated in this review report, and are my personal, unbiased professional analyses, opinions, and conclusions.
- There is no present or prospective interest in the property that is the subject of this review report, and there is no personal interest or bias with respect to the parties involved.
- The compensation for this assignment is not contingent on an action or event resulting from the analyses, opinions, or conclusions in, or the use of, this review report.
- The subject property of the report under review was not inspected by the reviewer, xxxxx x. xxxxxxxxx, MAI.
- The appraisal analysis and opinions were developed, and this appraisal review has been prepared in conformance with, and the use of this review is subject to, the requirements of the Uniform Standards of Professional Appraisal Practice (USPAP) of The Appraisal Foundation.
- No one, other than xxxxx x. xxxxxxxxx, provided significant professional assistance in the review process.
- This review satisfies the requirements of USPAP Standard 3 and includes only those items as listed in this report. Research has not been verified by the reviewer. Reliance has been placed upon the qualifications of the appraiser to provide accurate, comprehensive information regarding the subject property and the primary and secondary data as shown in this report.
- The reported analyses, opinions, and conclusions were developed, and this report has been prepared, in conformity with the requirements of the Code of Professional Ethics and the Standards of Professional Appraisal Practice of the Appraisal Institute.
- The use of this report is subject to the requirements of the Appraisal Institute relating to review by its duly authorized representatives.*
- As of the date of this review report, xxxxx x. xxxxxxxxx, MAI, has completed the requirements of the continuing education program of the Appraisal Institute.*

______________________________ (Signature)

xxxxx x. xxxxxxxxx, MAI

xxxxxxxxx State Certified Real Estate Appraiser # xxx-0000000

* The last two bulleted items apply only to Appraisal Institute members.

Eleven Quick Steps for an Appraisal Review

But I only have one hour to review this appraisal!

The following 11 steps can be used by an administrative or compliance reviewer who has only a limited time to conduct a review:

1. First, check out the **location maps and photos** to help you envision where the property is located and what it looks like.
2. Read the **letter of transmittal.** Are the facts right (e.g., property address, ownership interest, square foot area)? Was the assignment completed as agreed? Are any mysterious "subject to" conditions mentioned? Are there any hedge words or warning signals in the appraiser's verbiage?
3. Review the **summary of important conclusions (executive summary).** Convert taxes, gross and net income amounts, appraisal indications, and the value conclusion into convenient units of comparison. Make quick mental checks for reasonableness. Make a copy of this section and use it to check consistency as you review the remainder of the report.
4. Scan the report for any **special or extraordinary property or market risks.** Risk may be addressed in several sections of the report. In the property description, check for building code violations, features of extreme obsolescence, and ADA compliance. In the environmental section, look for potential problems with hazardous waste or materials and the presence of wetlands.
5. Look at the **property history** section. Is a sale pending? Has there been any activity during the past 36 months? How do past sales or listing prices compare with the current value? If a wide discrepancy is evident, does the appraiser offer analysis and an explanation?
6. Read the **assumptions and limiting conditions** carefully. Look for unusual assumptions and unreasonable limiting conditions that could limit the effectiveness and reliability of the value conclusion and the usefulness of the report.
7. Study the **approaches to value applied.**

Income capitalization approach (for an income-producing property). Consider:

- The rent estimate. Are there any gaps between actual and forecast amounts?
- Operating statement. Compare it with an actual statement and analyze it using ratios and units of comparison.
- Net operating income (*NOI*). Apply units of comparison.
- Cap rate. Check for reasonableness. If mortgage and equity cap rates are derived, check the financing assumptions against market reality.

Sales comparison approach. If this approach is primary, check the comparables for reasonableness. Are they recent and truly similar? Does analysis using units of comparison bracket the concluded value?

8. Review the **reconciliation.** Does it flow logically to a reasonable value conclusion? Does it ramble or consist largely of boilerplate? Do the cost, sales, and income value indications fall within a reasonable range? If not, does the appraiser explain any apparent discrepancies?
9. Do a **reality check.** If the property is new or nearly new, check the appraised value against the owner's land and building construction costs. Do they reconcile? There are few "bargains" in real estate except for sales transacted under duress and dispositions. Generally, a seller is not going to give a property away for anything less than its market value.
10. Test for **reasonableness.** Cross-check value conclusions with estimates derived in previous assignments and recognized sources of market information.
11. **Follow up** with the Appraisal Standards Requirements and Regulatory Compliance Checklist on page 202.

APPRAISAL STANDARDS REQUIREMENTS AND REGULATORY COMPLIANCE CHECKLIST

	Yes	No	N/A
1. The appraiser must be engaged directly by _____ Bank (or another financial institution) and must not have any direct or indirect interest, financial or otherwise, in the transaction or the property.	❑	❑	❑
2. Conforms to the Uniform Standards of Professional Appraisal Practice (USPAP) of the Appraisal Standards Board of The Appraisal Foundation.	❑	❑	❑
3. Appraisal was performed by a state licensed appraiser.	❑	❑	❑
4. The appraiser has disclosed the steps taken to comply with the Competency Provision of USPAP, if applicable.	❑	❑	❑
5. Appraisal development option and report type stated.	❑ Complete/self-contained ❑ Complete/summary ❑ Limited/self-contained ❑ Limited/summary		
6. Written and presented in narrative form, containing sufficient detail.	❑	❑	❑
7. Market value is based on the definition set forth in 12CFR, paragraph 34.42 (f).	❑	❑	❑
8. Considered and analyzed any current agreement of sale, option, or listing of the property being appraised.	❑	❑	❑
9. Analyzed and reported, with reasonable detail, sales of the property occurring during the previous three years.	❑	❑	❑
10. For income-producing property, analyzed and reported data on current revenues, expenses, and vacancies.	❑	❑	❑
11. Analyzed and reported on current market conditions.	❑	❑	❑
12. Analyzed and reported appropriate deductions and discounts for proposed construction or renovation, partially leased buildings, nonmarket lease terms, and tract developments with unsold units.	❑	❑	❑
13. Includes USPAP certification and statement that the assignment was not contingent on a specific value or loan amount.	❑	❑	❑
14. Contains sufficient supporting documentation to indicate reasonableness of conclusions.	❑	❑	❑
15. Includes legal description.	❑	❑	❑
16. Separately values personal property, equipment, or fixtures.	❑	❑	❑
17. Uses applicable value approaches, explains any approaches omitted, uses appropriate techniques, and shows reasonable rationale for reconciliation of approaches.	❑	❑	❑
18. Reported and discussed the reasonable marketing time for the subject property.	❑	❑	❑

Comments: ____

____

____

Bibliography

Books

Appraisal Institute. *The Appraisal of Real Estate.* 11th ed. Chicago: Appraisal Institute, 1996.

______. *Appraising Residential Properties.* 2d ed. Chicago: Appraisal Institute, 1994.

______. *Dictionary of Real Estate Appraisal.* 3d ed. Chicago: Appraisal Institute, 1993.

Coleman, Stephanie, MAI, SRA, and Joseph L. Minnich III, SRPA, SRA. *Understanding Limited Appraisals and Appraisal Reporting Options.* Chicago: Appraisal Institute, 1996.

Simpson, John A., MAI. *Property Inspection: An Appraiser's Guide.* Chicago: Appraisal Institute, 1997.

White, John Robert. *The Office Building: From Concept to Investment Reality.* Chicago: Counselors of Real Estate, Appraisal Institute, and the Society of Industrial and Office Realtors Educational Fund, 1992.

Seminar

Wiley, Robert C. Loss Prevention Program for Real Estate Appraisers. Santa Barbara, Calif.: Liability Insurance Administrators, 1997.

Reports

American National Standards Institute, Inc. *American National Standard for Single-Family Residential Buildings-Square Footage—Method for Calculating.* 1996 ed. Upper Marlboro, Md.: NAHB Research Center, Inc., 1996.

Appraisal Standards Board. *Uniform Standards of Professional Appraisal Practice.* 1996 ed. Washington, D.C.: The Appraisal Foundation, 1996.

Fannie Mae. *Property and Appraisal Analysis.* 1994 ed. Washington, D.C.: Fannie Mae, 1994.

Articles

Aaron, Martin H., SRA, and John H. Wright, Jr., MAI. "The Appraisal of Churches and Religious Facilities." *The Appraisal Journal* (January 1992): 99-106.

Accetta, Gregory J., MAI. "Testing the Reasonableness of Discounted Cash Flow Analysis." *The Appraisal Journal* (January 1998): 62-67.

Anglyn, William Ted, MAI, and John A. Robinson, MAI. "Scope of the Appraisal—A Practical Analysis." *The Appraisal Journal* (January 1992): 74-78.

Bell, Randall, MAI. "Medical Office Building Appraisal." *The Appraisal Journal* (April 1995): 186-194

Bottum, MacKenzie S., MAI. "Discounted Cash Flow Analyses: Tests of Reasonableness." *The Appraisal Journal* (January 1993): 138-143.

Boykin, James H., MAI, SRA, Ph D. "Seeking the Elusive Discount Rate." *The Appraisal Journal* (July 1990): 328-333.

______. "Impropriety of Using Dissimilar-Size Comparable Land Sales." *The Appraisal Journal* (July 1996): 310-318.

Bruckner, Kevin L., MAI. "Mid-Year Versus Year-End Present Worth Factors in DCF Analysis." *The Appraisal Journal* (January 1991): 126-130.

Carneghi, Chris, MAI. "Determining Ground-Lease Rental Rates." *The Appraisal Journal* (April 1994): 256-263.

Ditchkus, Larry, MAI, and Sally Bladasz. "Rethinking Speculative Subdivision Valuation for Loan Purposes." *The Appraisal Journal* (July 1996): 263-272.

Fisher, Christine A., MAI, and John H. Wright, Jr., MAI. "A Review Appraiser's Perspective." *The Appraisal Journal* (April 1992): 178-183.

Francis, John M., MAI. "The Elusive Definitions of *NOI* and *OAR*." *The Appraisal Journal* (January 1998): 56-61.

Gehrlein, David P. "Appraisers Should Exercise Caution When Using the Property Observation Checklist." *The Appraisal Journal* (April 1997): 186-187.

Gragg, Steven R., MAI, SRA. "Appraisals and Evaluations—Matching Valuation Products to Credit Risk." *The Appraisal Journal* (October 1996): 356-362.

Granger, Joseph H., SRA. "Writing Comparative Analyses and Correlation." *The Appraisal Journal* (July 1996): 252-262.

Hanford, Lloyd D., Jr., MAI. "The Reviewer Is Always Right?" *The Appraisal Journal* (July 1994): 358-362.

Hartmann, Robert W. "Valuation for Loans on Restaurants." *The Appraisal Journal* (October 1996): 406-415.

Hirsh, Lawrence A., MAI. "Golf Courses—Valuation and Evaluation." *The Appraisal Journal* (January 1991): 38-47.

Hughes, Stephen R., MAI, and Kevin K. Nunnick, MAI. "Appraising Golf Courses for Ad Valorem Tax Purposes." *The Appraisal Journal* (October 1993): 611-616.

Karvel, George R., and Peter J. Patchin, MAI. "The Business Value of Super-Regional Shopping Centers and Malls." *The Appraisal Journal* (October 1992): 453-462.

Keating, David Michael, MAI, and Gary L. Brace. "Appraising Continuing Care Retirement Centers: The Income Approach." *The Appraisal Journal* (October 1994): 546-552.

Kenney, Mark T., MAI. "Does Shopping Mall Development Create Business Value?" *The Appraisal Journal* (July 1991): 303-313.

Klaasen, Romain L. "The Long and Short of It." *The Appraisal Journal* (July 1993): 431-436.

Lovell, Douglas D., MAI. "Improve Your Appraisals by Avoiding Forecasting Errors." *The Appraisal Journal* (April 1994): 222-228.

Lynch, Gregory F., MAI. "User-Friendly Appraisal Reports." *The Appraisal Journal* (October 1992): 500-509.

Martin, Robert S., MAI, and Scott D. Nafe, MAI. "Segregating Real Estate Value from Nonrealty Value in Shopping Centers." *The Appraisal Journal* (January 1996): 1-13.

Martin, W.B., Ph D. "Direct Capitalization or Discounted Cash Flow Analysis?" *The Appraisal Journal* (July 1993): 390-393.

Mathieson, Kieran, Ph D, and Brent J. Dreyer, MAI. "Improving the Effectiveness and Efficiency of Appraisal Reviews: An Information Systems Approach." *The Appraisal Journal* (July 1993): 414-418.

May, Frank O. "Valuation, Full Disclosure, and Discrimination." *The Appraisal Journal* (October 1995): 465-468.

Meacham, Allen, MAI. "The Role of a Quality Control Checklist in Avoiding Appraisal Report Errors." *The Appraisal Journal* (April 1993): 261-266.

Mitchell, Phillip S., Ph D, and Joseph A. Cuffaro, Jr., SRA. "Due Diligence in the Single-Family Residential Review Process." *The Appraisal Journal* (July 1997): 286-290.

Owens, Robert W., MAI. "Increased Accountability in the Appraisal Profession." *The Appraisal Journal* (July 1990): 347-352.

Pardue, William P., Jr., MAI. "Writing Effective Appraisal Reports." *The Appraisal Journal* (January 1990): 16-22.

Planner, Robert, Ph D. "Income Capitalization Problems." *The Appraisal Journal* (October 1992): 549-555.

Ramsey, Ranney, MAI. "Retail Sale Data and the Evaluation of Major Retail Centers." *The Appraisal Journal* (October 1994): 497-506.

Rattermann, Mark, MAI, SRA. "Consistency Problems in Residential Appraisals." *The Appraisal Journal* (October 1994): 518-534.

Rex, Charles W., III, MAI, and Susan Motycka Rex. "Market Analysis in Appraisal Reports: Vitalizing Key Data Sections." *Valuation Insights & Perspectives* (Fall 1996): 8-10.

Roberts, Joe R., MAI, and Eric Roberts, MAI. "The Myth About Appraisals." *The Appraisal Journal* (April 1991): 212-220.

Rushmore, Stephen, MAI. "Ethics in Hotel Appraising." *The Appraisal Journal* (July 1993): 357-363.

Schafer, Scott M., MAI. "Bank Branch Valuation: An Empirical Approach." *The Appraisal Journal* (April 1994): 171-180.

Shlaes, Jared, MAI. "The Quality Appraisal Report." *The Appraisal Journal* (October 1993): 483-488.

Simpson, John A., MAI. "How to Review a Nursing Home Appraisal." *The Appraisal Journal* (October 1994): 542-545.

______. "Limiting an Appraisal Firm's Liability and Exposure." *The Appraisal Journal* (January 1994): 94-97.

Skolnik, Martin A., MAI. "Comments on Discounted Cash Flow Analysis." *The Appraisal Journal* (July 1993): 394-398.

Skolnik, Martin A., MAI, and M. Carla Domingo. "Supply and Demand Considerations in Residential Subdivision Analysis." *The Appraisal Journal* (January 1994): 57-63.

Slay, Kelley D. "The Capitalization Rate, the Discount Rate, and Projected Growth in Value." *The Appraisal Journal* (July 1990): 324-327.

Smolen, Gerald E., Ph D, and Donald Casey Hambleton, MAI. "Appraisal Company Status and Direction for Survival." *The Appraisal Journal* (July 1997): 156-164.

Sorenson, Richard C., MAI. "Appraising the Appraisal: Advice for Underwriters." *The Journal of Commercial Bank Lending*, Robert Morris Associates (December 1991): 33-43.

______. "Let's Communicate." *The Appraisal Journal* (April 1994): 197-202.

______. "The Art of Reviewing Appraisals." *The Appraisal Journal* (July 1991): 353-369.

Walsh, Charles B., MAI, and Henry B. Staley, Jr. "Considerations in the Valuation of Hotels." *The Appraisal Journal* (July 1993): 348-356.

Williams, Scott R., MAI, SRA. "Disclosing an Appraisal's Limitations: An Update." *The Appraisal Journal* (July 1993): 364-372.